BYRON
AND THE NEED OF FATALITY

Charles du Bos

BYRON

AND THE NEED OF FATALITY

Translated by
ETHEL COLBURN MAYNE

HASKELL HOUSE PUBLISHERS Lᴛᴅ.
Publishers of Scarce Scholarly Books
NEW YORK, N. Y. 10012
1970

First Published 1932

HASKELL HOUSE PUBLISHERS Ltd.
Publishers of Scarce Scholarly Books
280 LAFAYETTE STREET
NEW YORK. N. Y. 10012

Library of Congress Catalog Card Number: 78-95423

Standard Book Number 8383-0971-2

INTRODUCTION

WRITTEN FOR THE ENGLISH EDITION

Habent sua fata libelli. . . . When I wrote this study of Byron
as the man of fatality, I never dreamt that, among its *fata,*
might be included the perilous honour of appearing before
the English public. As I do not share Byron's love of fatality
as such, I am quite conscious that the honour is a heavy
weight for the book to bear. Yet there was no resisting the
kind proposal of the publisher, since he made it through the
only translator who was sure to disarm my reluctance. I am,
in this very field, too much the debtor of Ethel Colburn
Mayne not to give in to her flattering wishes, even if for once
her judgment seems to me at fault.

To make use of the serviceable title under which Henry
James grouped some of his essays, the book is a *partial portrait.* Indeed it is partial in all possible meanings of the term.
The Preface (hereafter reproduced) defines and limits my
purpose. It is the man whom I study, not the work. On the
work—on the poetry of Byron in so far as it possesses a worth
of its own and, in that measure, independent of its author—I
do not deem myself qualified to speak: I remain convinced
that, on the aesthetic plane, no criticism can be of value that
does not originate in and proceed from a fund of admiration
that I am here unable to contribute. I have therefore considered the work only in the degree in which it sheds light
upon the man. And the man himself is not followed through
the whole of his career : I have concentrated my attention on
the period of four years that begins with the publication of
the first two Cantos of *Childe Harold* (March 10, 1812) and
ends with the departure from England (April 25, 1816) and,

even during this period, the man is not examined under all his aspects: he is focussed strictly from one point of view, focussed as the man of fatality: it is self-evident that if I did not believe that both the period and the point of view were central, the book would never have been written.

But, grounded on lectures in 1925-1926, it was written at the end of 1928, and it appeared at the beginning of June, 1929. Since that date, important events have taken place on what might be called the Byronic battlefield, and the object of this Introduction is to define the position I have adopted towards them.

*   *   *

'How much it were to be wished that a Life of Lady Byron should be written, and that it should be entrusted to some one possessing, I do not say, of course, the genius, but certain of the qualities of George Eliot, to some one capable, among other things, of sympathizing fully with the character of Catherine Arrowpoint in *Daniel Deronda*, which offers more than one affinity with that of Annabella—and if the task were undertaken by Ethel Colburn Mayne (here the most desirable of biographers) what a fine diptych it would make with her *Byron!* If for such a prospect Mary, Countess of Lovelace, should authorize the publication of the indispensable documents, there are many who would feel towards her a respectful and lively gratitude.' Such was the wish that I had ventured upon—and, a fortnight after the appearance of my book, it so happened that the wish was fulfilled. The *Life of Lady Byron* (Constable, 1929) by Ethel Colburn Mayne not only has what was here the first and fundamental merit of being 'authoritative', it is instinct with that rarer and subtler authority which springs from talent, psychological insight, and a perfect balance of mind. The model has at last come to life, and, thanks to the most dexterous handling, the picture is securely framed. With the exception of *Astarte*, in my characterization of Lady Byron I had to rely entirely upon what may be termed intuitive guess-work; the scarcity of

vi

documents preventing individualization proper, what I tried to bring to life was the individualization of *a moral nature as such*—the type of nature which to-day is the most utterly misunderstood, one might say ignored, and of which Lady Byron is the incarnation at least as much as Byron is the incarnation of the man of fatality. I even went a step further. Because, at the side of the 'thing of dark imaginings' (to use Byron's expression in *Lara*), at last a light was present, I assumed that for once we had to deal with *un être irréprochable*, and that no better opportunity could be offered to probe that hatred of perfection which lies so curiously ingrained in the depths of humanity: I must here run the risk of courting ridicule by frankly avowing that I tried my hand at a portrait of virtue. But the model has come to life, and on the guess-work of intuition *that* process has almost always an effect which is both disturbing and sobering. From the marriage onwards, I do not think that this coming to life puts my interpretation anywhere in the wrong, but now we are informed of all that preceded: we know that when Byron's first proposal was made through Lady Melbourne, even if one takes into account that the indirect mode of approach is always liable to disappoint and to hurt, in her answer Miss Milbanke, otherwise truthfulness itself, departed from the truth: she wrote to her aunt that she did not and thought that she never could love Byron,[1] when already she loved him and foresaw that she never could love anybody else. Having entered on that course, she was obliged, on opening a direct correspondence with him, to accentuate her departure from truth, to assert that her heart was hopelessly engaged, and Byron believed her. For each the white lie had far-reaching consequences. It turned against Miss Milbanke when, for motives that were both interested and disinterested (but she has here to bear the charge, so unlike her, of the mixed motive), she

[1]'I should be totally unworthy of Lord Byron's esteem if I were not to speak the truth without equivocation. Believing that he will never be the object of that strong affection which would make me happy in domestic life...' (*Life of Lady Byron*, p. 49).

wished to retrieve the truth: she retrieved it, but, in so doing, there can no longer remain any doubt that she did all she could to bring about Byron's second proposal; so that what she gains in humanness, she must of course lose in irreproachability. After the publication of the *Life of Lady Byron,* I was therefore in duty bound to re-write parts of my last chapter in accordance with the new data: this I have done—so that this edition has at least the small merit of novelty. But except for this, and for the correlative addition of the implied shades and correctives, I have let my portrait of Annabella stand. Of the two sculptors working at the temple, Victor Hugo wrote:

L'un sculptait l'idéal et l'autre le réel.

Having tried my hand at a portrait of virtue, I was committed to the ideal; but it does not much matter, since Ethel Colburn Mayne has given us the real.

★   ★   ★

Eight months after my partial portrait, appeared the full-length portrait of Byron by my friend André Maurois. It is needless to say that I read it with the interest and the appreciation that his writings always awaken in me; yet, in the common ground that we cover—essentially the relations with Mrs. Leigh, the marriage and the separation—on no matter of importance did I feel prompted to modify my opinion. Both before and after the publication of our books, Maurois and I had often compared notes on the subject of Byron: we knew where we agreed, we knew where we disagreed, and we even know one another too well not to understand why it should be so.

But I have trespassed enough on the patience of the reader —and even on my own, for by now, as far as the Byron case is concerned, I am wholly in the mood of the closing line of *Lycidas:*

To-morrow to fresh Woods, and Pastures new.

VERSAILLES, *October 6,* 1931.   C. D. B.

ANDRÉ GIDE

DEAR FRIEND,

You have been kind enough to accept the dedication of this book, which appears on the same day as my *Dialogue* with you. Though I do not remember that Byron's name ever came up between us—except when you so gracefully offered me (having found it on the Quays one day on your way to Ile Saint-Louis) a translation of Medwin's book, and added: 'This belongs to you by right'—these pages may possibly furnish us with an opportunity, in the Park which has already been propitious to our talks, of repairing that omission. In that event they will have doubly fulfilled their purpose, by procuring me a pleasure which you know how dearly I value, and by permitting me to witness thus to our unfailing affection.

C. D. B.

VERSAILLES, *December* 27, 1928.

NOTE

In giving permission for the use of extracts from Byron's letters, Lt.-Col. John Murray and the other controller of the copyright, to whose attention this book has been called, wish to dissociate themselves from some conclusions reached in the book.

They regret that, after the lapse of more than a century, the memory of one who had very great qualities, (as well as admittedly bad ones) and who gave his life in the cause of freedom, should still be pursued by scandals of which there is no positive evidence and the very nature of which makes proof impossible.

They also regret that this uncharitable pursuit should be renewed in association with such distinguished literary names as the author and translator of this book.

"Poetry is the lava of the imagination
whose eruption prevents an earthquake"

Byron to Miss Milbanke
November 29, 1813

PREFACE

THE six chapters of which this book consists, formed part of my fourth year's series of lectures. They were originally delivered, at less length, between December 1925 and January 1926, at the house of my friends, Comte and Comtesse Guy de Pourtalès; afterwards resumed in May and June 1926 at the house of other friends, M. and Mme Jacques-Emile Blanche, in the more extended form which, with some additions, they now present.

They are in no sense a biography. That task has been achieved, and with a master-hand, in England by Ethel Colburn Mayne; and I have no doubt that the book announced as coming from André Maurois will give us in France a perfect solution of the problem. Still less do these chapters aim at being a study of Byron's works in themselves, regarded as separable or detached from their author, or at formulating in his respect a considered judgment on the aesthetic plane. Their aim is exclusively psychological—it might even be more precisely described as zoological ; for what solicits me here is not the *psyche*, but the *species*. Byron, in my view, is predominantly a human animal of the higher species—a type which, in the literary sphere, finds its *expression* very much less frequently than is assumed, which fascinates me whenever I encounter it, and for which I must indeed confess that I have a somewhat culpable weakness. I cared little for Byron, of whom all I knew was his poetry, when twenty years ago my very dear friend B. Berenson, with that infallible perception of his, applied to him in my presence the words of Napoleon to Goethe: 'M. Goethe, you are a man'. This led me to read those *Letters and Journals* in which the Byronic faculty so sovereignly asserts itself, and, generally speaking, to impregnate myself with what pertains to the man. Whence these six chapters which, under the necessary limitations of a course of lectures, I grouped around the one theme regarded by me here as central: the theme of fatality.

C. D. B.

September 17, 1928.

BYRON
AND THE NEED OF FATALITY

CHAPTER I

'He was in turn dominated by frenzy and master of his frenzy, able to
direct it to a purpose. He had a fancy for some Oriental legends of pre-
existence, and in his conversation and poetry took up the part of a fallen
or exiled being, expelled from heaven, or sentenced to a new Avatar on
earth for some crime, existing under a curse, predoomed to a fate really
fixed by himself in his own mind, but which he seemed determined to
fulfil. At times this dramatic imagination resembled a delusion; he would
play at being mad, and gradually get more and more serious, as if he
believed himself to be destined to wreck his own life and that of everyone
near him.'

THIS observation—and for my part I know of none more
penetrating, or more nearly approaching the very core of
Byron's nature—is to be found in *Astarte*, that authoritative
work which takes its title from the heroine of Byron's *Manfred*, and which (in 1905) was published in a limited edition
for approved purchasers only. Byron's grandson Ralph Milbanke, Earl of Lovelace, there gave us the truth about the
central mystery in Byron's life, his purpose being to defend
his grandmother, Lady Byron, against unjustified attacks.[1]
It is a document in which there is not a word but must rivet
the psychologist's attention, and which we shall have to keep
incessantly in mind ; but the first and most important point
—and this is why I have chosen to begin with it—is that
Astarte brings home with a maximum of insight and precision what was in Byron a primal and a permanent sense—
and more, a *need*: namely, the sense and the need of fatality.
Unless we clearly perceive that fatality was for him the one
necessary condition, that his whole life was wrought upon by
this idea, that he declared himself, believed himself, wished
himself to bè, and in fact prodigiously *was*, the fatal being,

[1]The second edition, published in the usual way in 1921 (after Lord
Lovelace's death) by his widow, Mary, Countess of Lovelace, contains a
preface by her and numerous valuable additions. My quotations are taken
from this edition. That above is on p. 117.

we shall never understand the problem, or better to express it, the case of Byron. For Byron is a case rather than a problem, the latter always implying some insoluble elements which I do not believe to be present here—a case, and, as the experts say, a very fine one.

Of this fatality it will be well immediately to define the nature. It is in no sense external, it in no way partakes of that antique fatality which he on whom it falls repulses with horror, from which to escape were his dearest desire; and neither is it a purely internal fatality such as is known, and possibly known only, to either wholly angelic natures or great adventurers of the spirit—a Shelley, a Hölderlin, a Nietzsche. The sense of fatality peculiar to Byron is a compound: exterior in so far as it is written in his heredity, in all the humours of the bile and blood, the accidents of physical form and social rank, and not less in a very few momentous acts, regarded by him as such—for perhaps no one has in the same degree as Byron held that the whole of life is governed by a minimum of acts which it is futile to think one can ever retrieve. Interior, on the other hand, and instantly made so, by reason of the impassioned, impressive, grandiose closeness with which Byron adheres to his first bases, identifies himself, insists on identifying himself, with them; and the result is that the Byronic reaction, both the spontaneous and the symbolic, appears as the antipodes of that of Nessus—Byron never feels wholly himself until the poisoned shirt enwraps him. Baudelaire's line, describing those whom he calls 'the real travellers', applies to Byron in a quite otherwise extensive and profound sense:

De leur fatalité jamais ils ne s'écartent.

This notion of the fatal being, in treating of Byron, its supreme incarnation, I want to strip, to purge for our vision, of the innumerable and ridiculous counterfeits which were the outcome of the mimicry that abounded at a time when (as certain English critics have well expressed it) the whole of Europe had gone mad about Byron; counterfeits which ulti-

mately obscured the original, and robbed it of that immobile
—if you will, that monotonous—greatness which undeniably
belongs to it. To detract from the Byronic personages, it has
been repeated *ad nauseam* that every one of them was simply
the author in disguise, got-up as he thought most becoming
to him at the given moment. Nothing could be truer than
this, but nothing falser than the consequences that are usually
drawn from it; for Byron—who, as we shall see, never wrote
but as a means of relief—was always intent, in his work, on
the expression of himself. This self-expression has in our
time become, and perhaps tends increasingly to become, the
ideal of some of the best among us; Byron, in his day, practised it radically, heroically—whether in a poem, an intimate
letter, or the Journals, it never fails to burst forth, always
bearing to the utmost the stamp of the inevitable, and always
invested (even when questionable) with a character of final
authority. That is Byron's excellence; Swinburne was thinking of that when he said that the power of his personality lay
in 'the splendid and imperishable excellence which covers
all his offences and outweighs all his defects: the excellence of
sincerity and strength'. Strength is the essential Byronic
attribute; and sincerity no less, if on the one hand we are
careful to distinguish, as we should, between sincerity and an
exact, detailed self-knowledge[1]; and if on the other we admit
(and Byron is the most convincing of examples) that there can

[1]In maintaining this distinction, I do not think I am contravening the
view—so profound, and moreover fully consonant with my own—of
Ethel Colburn Mayne in her Introduction: 'Humour we like to term our
lesser form of self-consciousness; but Byron's self-consciousness was
supreme, and towered high above the subterfuge of humour. Through its
excess, it became its own antithesis—it became unconscious. He "did not
know when he was doing it". Each time we use that pedestrian saying, we
define the last triumph of expression' (p. xv.). When the genius of expression reaches the degree it did in Byron—and in this respect a Rivarol,
a Joseph de Maistre, a Barbey d'Aurevilly are of the same family—not
only sincerity but self-consciousness are inevitable, and inevitable to the
point where, as Ethel Colburn Mayne consummately puts it, 'they become
unconscious'. Hence writers of this family will be infallible psychologists,
and even introspectives, in the precise measure—but in that measure only
—in which psychology and introspection are served by the *immediate*

be, even in their extremest puerilities, poses which are sincere, poses which are so much the appurtenances of the essential being that there is a sense in which his very sincerity itself demands their presence. Yes, Byron is authentic; and he is what it has become so difficult for us to conceive of, and what we must conceive of, else we shall misunderstand him —he is the *authentic fatal being*.

An inherent prestige, and perhaps the most intrinsic, the most inalienable of all, attaches to the authentic fatal being; the case of Byron is that which enables us most closely to examine both this notion of prestige and the value of the notion of prestige in general. But let me at once point out what is one of the sources and one of the explanations of that prestige—the fact that a being of this sort is always not only *like* himself, but *equal* to himself; by which I mean that take Byron where we will, how we will, by surprise or otherwise— in a word, a gesture, an act which is to him significant, or on the contrary in those which are essentially quite the reverse— always he gives us himself with the same volume and even, one might say, with the same calibre. And this, at bottom, in the significant moment not less involuntarily (whatever he thinks) than in the insignificant. That the content should turn out to be quite negligible in regard to the effect produced: there lies the very core of personal prestige, and in this respect Byron is unsurpassable. His nature—Ethel Colburn Mayne has said nothing which better defines him—was an 'immovable nature', a nature that nothing could move out of itself, could cause to depart from itself. At the climax of frenzy he never escapes from himself; his frenzy leaves him where it finds him, his sallies and explosions infallibly come home to roost. This is why, writing solely for relief, though

intervention of the genius of expression. But in psychology, and still more in introspection, the ocean-depths will yield their treasure only as the result of a process of dragging which will sometimes be greatly prolonged, and for which, on the contrary, a too immediate intervention of the genius of expression is the least serviceable of all things. The introspective genius of Benjamin Constant took twenty years to attain the flawless statement of *Adolphe*.

finding that outlet essential to him—for the act of writing more than once in his life represented the only antidote against the temptation of suicide—his sense of relief does not last, does not heal, above all does not liberate ; never with Byron is the work liberating, and had it been possible for his nature thus to liberate itself, we feel that he would never have wished it to do so. As Paul Bourget has observed with a masterly sureness of touch, Byron is the prototype of 'those who write for the one purpose of keeping their wounds alive'.

Intrinsic, inalienable, the prestige of the fatal being sheds, in addition, a prodigious glow of light—sheds it because it is what it is in despite of the man himself, even before the moment when he feels the desire to exercise it. By merely existing, he creates in others fatalities subject to his own, which then gravitate round his star like 'those piteous satellites' of which Mauriac speaks in *Le Désert de l'Amour*. The power of seduction possessed by the authentic fatal being is doubtless the greatest here below; but it belongs to a wholly different order from that of deliberate seduction, and—as the instance of Byron attests in more than one document, uncommonly difficult to refute—there is no more delicate task than to distinguish in such a case between the zones of responsibility and irresponsibility. It is evident that in the current acceptation of the term there was in Byron, at certain moments, something of the seducer; that there was also something, and perhaps more, of the martyr of women is not less evident in him who wrote by way of jest, but at bottom seriously: 'They accuse me of treating women harshly: it may be so, but I have been their martyr. . . . I have been more ravished myself than anybody since the Trojan war'.[1] We shall

[1] And (leaving aside the secondary and wholly transient affairs, and the kind of debauch in which there is no question of seduction) Byron was never really the seducer of anyone but Augusta; there, as he acknowledges and indeed insists, he was the responsible agent; but this was in a zone so irresistible for him that in itself it constitutes a species of irresponsibility. As to Lady Frances Webster, I shall show that Byron was at heart by no means the *deliberate* seducer, but on the contrary the seducer *in spite of himself*.

return to this; but for the moment my point is that the Byronic fatality creates other fatalities. The most typical and tragic example of this is the unfortunate Lady Caroline Lamb who, on the evening that she first saw Byron, wrote in her diary: 'Mad, bad, and dangerous to know'; but in the same diary wrote a few days afterwards: 'That beautiful pale face is my fate'. This is what gives to Byron's relations with women so inevitable a character, predictable as are the great phenomena of nature, so devastating and yet so poetical—the image of the star and its satellites is precisely the right one here. It is, so to speak, action at a distance, by no means an exchange, and still less a veritable union; the prestige of the fatal being fascinates, subjugates, draws destinies into its orbit; and thus the fatal being himself, solitary by nature, and as it were chained to self, he too in his own way a slave but so panoplied that he always stands out as the master, is dispossessed of his very solitude by the victims to whom he cannot give himself, and who are all eventually shattered on his invincible attraction.

'Whole as the marble, founded as the rock'.

This line from *Macbeth*, which Byron was fond of quoting in his Journal, is wonderfully applicable to him. Byron is all of a piece; and his personality is the most important thing about him—that personality which was such an absorbing mystery to his contemporaries, and still solicits us to-day. Yet this mystery is perhaps less inscrutable than certain others of by no means so obvious a kind. At any rate, my sole object in these chapters will be to try to decipher it; I shall use Byron's works for one purpose only, that of casting light upon his being, and we shall lose nothing thereby, but very much the contrary; for Byron's masterpiece—a masterpiece which, despite the assertions of some, is much more spontaneous than 'worked-up'—is indubitably Byron himself.

*　　　*　　　*

George Gordon Byron, who in his tenth year was to succeed as sixth lord to the title of Baron Byron, was born on January 22, 1788, in London, at 16 Holles Street—a house since destroyed. He was the only son of Captain John Byron, and Catherine, born a Gordon of Gight. His ancestors on both sides are all described as beings of unbridled passions and defiant self-will, professing an arrogant contempt for the accepted order of things, and endowed, every one of them, with unusual energy. Byron's grandfather, Admiral John Byron, had been nicknamed in the service 'Foul-weather Jack', because he never could make a voyage without encountering a hurricane. According to Mrs. Piozzi, Jack's temperament was likewise a conductor of domestic hurricanes, for of Byron's grandmother she writes: 'She is wife to the Admiral, *pour ses péchés*'. In obedience to a tradition prevalent among Byron's ancestors—that of inbreeding—one of his grandparent's daughters, Juliana, had married her cousin-german, the son of William, fifth lord, known as the Wicked Lord. This tradition was for our Byron a subject almost of obsession, which literally fascinated him, on which he perpetually brooded, gloating on it with morbid and proud delight, and which had a strong influence on his life. The Wicked Lord, already nearly insane at the time of his son's marriage—and to that extent, as Ethel Colburn Mayne remarks, justified of his wrath against the consanguineous Byronic unions—was so infuriated by this one that he resolved to avenge himself by a proceeding no less Byronic, that of handing his son a purposely ruined heritage. He was frustrated in this, for his son died before he did; and it was our Byron who eventually came in for the devastated property, by that time so impoverished that it suited ill with title and rank—and our man was certainly not the man to restore the family-fortunes. In fact, they never were restored in his lifetime.

To this tendency towards inbreeding was added, in Byron's ancestry, a peculiarity which impressed him not less forcibly —in both his mother's and father's families there had been a succession of only children. In his *Detached Thoughts*—the title he gave to the 120 fragments forming the diary kept between October 15, 1821, and May 18, 1822, at the close of the Ravenna, and at the beginning of the Pisa, sojourns—this is what he says in Fragment 119: 'I have been thinking of an odd circumstance. My daughter, wife, half-sister, mother, sister's mother, natural daughter, and myself, are or were all *only children*. My sister's mother (Lady Conyers) had only my half-*sister* by her second marriage (and she herself was an only child); my father, by his second marriage with my mother (also an only child) had only me. Such a complication of *only children*, all tending to *one family*, is singular enough, and looks like fatality almost. But the fiercest animals have the fewest numbers in their litters—Lions, tigers and even Elephants, which are mild in comparison'.[1] With the exception of an error which Ethel Colburn Mayne points out in a note—for Byron's half-sister, that Augusta of whom there will be so much to say, was not an only child; she had had a brother and sister, who, it is true, died before she was born—how right the same writer is in saying that 'not many passages of Byron's characteristic prose are more characteristic than this one'; and the comment it suggests to her is both so apt and so amusing that I transcribe it here: 'He would be exceptional at any cost; thus horses (the one-litter animal *par excellence*) are omitted from a list in which 'Lions, tigers and even Elephants, which are mild in comparison' are eagerly displayed. Horses, though spirited, are not fierce—and horses are ignored'.[2]

But what is essential in this passage is that here Byron him-

[1] *Letters and Journals*, v. 467. Not only every word, but every detail of this passage is so revealing that I have copied the italics and capitals from the original. I call attention to the italics in the word 'sister', which, considering the incest, should be of interest to a psycho-analyst. In the brief (too brief, as a remark of Ethel Colburn Mayne's will show us) zoological list, Lions are honoured with a capital letter, to the detriment of tigers; for this, the reason is self-evident; as to the Elephants getting a capital too, I suppose their dignity was held to make up for their 'mildness'.

[2] *Byron*, Ethel Colburn Mayne, p. 5 (edition 1924).

self uses the word 'fatality'; that in the unparalleled intimacy of a Journal (and, with peculiarities to be noted, Byron was a master of the *journal intime*) he reveals himself to us as brooding—and with what concentration!—on the theme which always obsessed him, that of his family-history; and we see plainly that, though he does not go so far as to say so, he represents that family to himself, and delights in thus representing it, as a latter-day brood of the Atrides.

Byron's father, John Byron, who died when his son was three years old, was an officer in the Guards, and had served in America. He is described to us as a spendthrift, gambler, and libertine, very properly cast off by his father—fathers who produce hurricanes being prone to prefer that their sons should preserve what is so well called a dead calm. In 1778 he ran away with, and next year married, the Marchioness of Carmarthen, wife to that Francis Carmarthen who afterwards became the fifth Duke of Leeds, herself born Amelia d'Arcy, only daughter (of course) of the last Earl of Holderness, and Baroness Conyers in her own right. The couple lived in Paris and had three children, of whom the first two died, the third being the renowned Augusta, born in 1784, half-sister to our Byron. She married (again of course) her cousin-german, Colonel George Leigh. In 1784 Lady Conyers died, and Captain Byron returned to England, over head-and-ears in debt, and on the look-out for an heiress.

Now in the county of Aberdeen a rhyming saw was current:

'When the heron leaves the tree
The laird of Gight shall landless be';

and tradition has it that on the wedding-day of Catherine Gordon of Gight, our Byron's mother, and John Byron (called in that neighbourhood Mad Byron), the heronry of Gight flew over to Haddo, the estate of the Earl of Aberdeen. Upon which his lordship calmly remarked that the lands would follow; and so it came to pass. Mrs. Byron-Gordon (for her husband and she, for once in agreement, chose to assume the double name, imbued as both were with a sense of privilege in bearing their respective patronymics) remained for some months at Gight; then, the ever-increasing debts rendering this position untenable, Lord Aberdeen's prophecy came true—Gight was sold. Nevertheless, at the end of eighteen months, Catherine Gordon, accustomed to opulence, was reduced almost to penury—a penury which she always endured with dignity and courage, though it had its effect in developing her native pride of birth, and the insane arrogance she showed in all things pertaining to rank and title. After the sale of Gight she went to France with her husband, and did not return to England until just before our Byron's birth. Then she settled for eight years in Aberdeen, Captain Byron—who, as we shall see, thought his wife a very amiable person provided one could admire her from a distance—staying in France, and dying at Valenciennes in 1791. We have a few letters from Byron's father, but only one makes any allusion to his son—and this is significant enough for me to quote a fragment. It belongs to the year of his death, is dated from Valenciennes on February 16, 1791, and is addressed to his sister Mrs. Charles Leigh: 'I am glad you hear from Mrs. Byron. She is very amiable at a distance, but I defy you and all the apostles to live with her two months, for if anyone could live with her, it was me. *Mais jeu de Mains, jeu de Vilains*. I am glad to hear my son is well; but as to his walking, it is impossible, for he has a club-foot'.[1] I have called this letter significant, because in tone and accent it is so like Byron's that it might be mistaken for one of his. It has that curtness in the enunciation of facts which is characteristic of one who is sure of what he sets forth, and—to go deeper into the matter—equally sure of thinking what he thinks. This is the Byronic trait *par excellence*. A Byron either holds his tongue, resorts sullenly to a scornful silence, sometimes insulting, always morose; or else he expresses himself on the spot, without any kind of groping, with a perfect pre-

[1] *Letters and Journals*, I. ix.

cision. His position has been adopted, and adopted once for all, before he opens his lips; and the stated fact is followed by no commentary. Nothing less contaminated by second thoughts, restrictions, fumblings, can be conceived than the Byronic *It is so*; and when formulated by the son's genius, as in the Letters and Journals, it has the noble brevity of an epitaph. Byron's father had made up his mind that since the child had a club-foot—we shall return to this important question of Byron's lameness—he could not walk; that was enough; if the child did walk, the child was in the wrong. I purposely insist on this, because such details help us to perceive what lies at the heart of that mysterious attribute, no less mysterious than prestige, and no less sovereignly displayed by Byron—the attribute we call authority. He who possesses it need not at all be right; sometimes it seems that he never is more invested with it than when in fact he is wrong. Intrinsic, inalienable to the same degree as prestige, authority is one of the human faculties which most defies analysis; its despotism casts a spell. Those who in the course of their lives have encountered, or better still been subjected to, some impressive and formidable instance of authority are best able to understand its effect when coupled with the genius of a Byron.

As I have indicated, Byron scarcely knew his father, whom he lost when he was only three years old. But there were rumours that Jack Byron's wife, Lady Conyers, had died of grief caused by his vices and brutalities. These rumours were mentioned in the *Essai sur le génie et le caractère de Lord Byron*, by Pichot, which prefaced the first translation of Byron's works; and Byron was told of it by one of his Swiss admirers, J. J. Coulmann. In a letter to Coulmann of July 10, 1823, he protests against these allegations. The letter is interesting as a proof of how Byron—at bottom somewhat indifferent to, and sometimes even complacently vain of, the accusations made against himself—was always stirred to defend his family; I quote some passages:

'I have nothing to object to it, with regard to what concerns myself personally, though naturally there are some of the facts in it discoloured, and several errors into which the author has been led by the accounts of others. I allude to facts and not criticisms. But the same author has cruelly calumniated my father and my grand-uncle, but more especially the former. So far from being 'brutal', he was, according to the testimony of all those who knew him, of an extremely amiable and (*enjoué*) joyous character, but careless (*insouciant*) and dissipated. He had, consequently, the reputation of a good officer, and showed himself such in the Guards, in America. The facts themselves refute the assertion. It is not by 'brutality' that a young officer in the Guards seduces and carries off a Marchioness, and marries two heiresses. It is true that he was a very handsome man, which goes a long way. His first wife (Lady Conyers and Marchioness of Carmarthen) did not die of grief, but of a malady which she caught by having imprudently insisted upon accompanying my father to a hunt before she was completely recovered from the accouchement which gave birth to my sister Augusta. His second wife, my respected mother, had I assure you too proud a spirit to bear the ill-usage of any man, no matter who he might be; and this she would have soon proved. I should add that he lived a long time in Paris, and was in habits of intimacy with the old Marshal Biron, Commandant of the French Guards; who from the similitude of names, and Norman origin of our family, supposed that there was some distant relationship between us. He died some years before the age of forty, and whatever may have been his faults they were certainly not those of harshness and grossness (*dureté et grossièreté*). If the notice should reach England, I am certain that the passage relative to my father will give much more pain to my sister (the wife of Colonel Leigh, attached to the Court of the late Queen, *not* Caroline, but Charlotte, wife of

George III) even than to me; and this she does not deserve, for there is not a more angelic being on earth. Augusta and I have always loved the memory of our father as much as we loved each other, and this at least forms a presumption that the stain of harshness was not applicable to it. If he dissipated his fortune, that concerns us alone, for we are his heirs; and till we reproach him with it, I know no one else who has a right to do so.' [1]

In this defence of his father, there is a point at which Byron seems for him—and for once—naïve. It is when he says: 'It is not by brutality that a young Officer of the Guards seduces and carries off a Marchioness, and marries two heiresses'. Certainly, he immediately adds the indispensable qualification: 'It is true that he was a very handsome man, which goes a long way'. But I should like to be sure that he would so rigorously have denied the seductive force of 'brutality' if a Marchioness had not been in question. Here there is a touch—not precisely of snobbery, but of that haughtiness in which Lady Blessington, with admirable penetration, perceived the mark of the *parvenu*, quite out of place in Byron, and yet discernible. We shall encounter it again when we consider his views on the question of social rank.

To return to Byron's mother. Here too heredity has much to tell us. Catherine Gordon of Gight was a direct descendant of the Royal House of Scotland, for Annabella Stewart, daughter of James I of Scotland, had married the second Earl of Huntly, and their third son became Sir William Gordon of Gight. The lairds of Gight are depicted as 'a hotheaded, hasty-handed race, sufficiently notable to be commemorated by Thomas the Rhymer'. Catherine's father, George, was the fifth to bear the two names which his grandson was to make immortal. She lost both her parents while she was still very young, and was brought up by her grandmother, a Mrs. Duff, who was commonly called Lady Gight. This Mrs. Duff, miserly and illiterate, nevertheless gave her

[1] *Letters and Journals*, vi. 231-233.

grand-daughter a fairly good education. Mrs. Byron loved reading, and could tell good literature from bad. When she died in 1811, Byron had published only those poems anterior to *Childe Harold*, which we think almost negligible to-day; but we possess some shrewd comments of Catherine's on her son's early verses and the adverse criticisms of them then published. But she never lost the provinciality, the uncouthness of the atmosphere of her childhood; and above all she was endowed from birth with an uncontrollable temper which expressed itself not only in speech, but in immediate action. We have not forgotten her husband's saying: '*Jeu de Mains, jeu de Vilains*', and his use of the proverb was undoubtedly inspired by his conjugal experiences. When she had exhausted invective on the victims of her wrath, they would sometimes find plates flying at their heads. And in this undisciplined personality, coarse, gross in more than one sense, pride of birth (in which she was overweening) had a ludicrous and surprising effect. This is how the editor of *Letters and Journals* (Lord Ernle) presents her: 'Miss Catherine Gordon had her full share of feminine vanity. At the age of thirty-five she was a stout, dumpy, coarse-looking woman, awkward in her movements, provincial in her accent and manner. But as her son was vain of his personal appearance, and especially of his hands, neck, and ears, so she, when other charms had vanished, clung to her pride in her arms and hands. She exhausted the patience of Stewardson the artist, who in 1806, after forty sittings, painted her portrait, by her anxiety to have a particular turn in her elbow exhibited in the most pleasing light. Of her ancestry she was, to use her son's expression, as "proud as Lucifer," looked down upon the Byron family, and regarded the Duke of Gordon as an inferior member of her clan. In later life, at any rate, her temper was ungovernable; her language, when excited, unrestrained; her love of gossip insatiable. Capricious in her moods, she flew from one extreme to the other, passing, for the slightest cause, from passionate affection to equally passionate resentment.'[1] Catherine Gordon was twenty years old when she met and married John Byron. She met and married him at Bath, where a few years earlier her father had drowned himself; and superstitious though she was—and as if by this defiance of destiny uniting in herself the Byron and Gight propensities—it was at Bath that she chose to be married, and that on the 13th of May.

* * *

But I must defer to my next chapter the account of Byron's childhood and youth, as well as that of his relations with his mother. Here I want to give you the extraordinary testimony of Dr. John Galt, who met Byron at Gibraltar in 1809, afterwards crossing with him to Malta—the Byron of twenty-one, already in possession of his genius, though no one knew it. Nothing else that has been written better enables us to imagine the intrinsic Byronic prestige, that which was anterior to his resounding fame. 'If my remembrance is not treacherous, he only spent one evening in the cabin with us . . . for, when the lights were placed, he made himself a man forbid, took his station on the railing . . . and there, for hours, sat in silence, enamoured, it may be, of the moon. All these peculiarities, with his caprices, and something inexplicable in the cast of his metaphysics, while they seemed to awaken interest, contributed little to conciliate esteem. He was often strangely rapt—it may have been from his genius; and had its grandeur and darkness been then divulged, susceptible of explanation; but, at the time, it threw around him, as it were, the sackcloth of penitence. Sitting amidst the shrouds and railings, in the tranquillity of the moonlight, churming an inarticulate melody, he seemed almost apparitional, suggesting dim reminiscences of him who shot the albatross. *He was as a mystery in a winding-sheet, crowned with a halo.*' [2] It is this mystery, at once fatal and prestigious, which still so solicits and absorbs us.

---

[1] *Letters and Journals*, i. p. 2.

[2] *Byron*, Ethel Colburn Mayne, p. 109 (2nd edition revised, 1924).

CHAPTER II

But I have lived, and have not lived in vain:
My mind may lose its force, my blood its fire,
And my frame perish even in conquering pain;
But there is that within me which shall tire
Torture and Time, and breathe when I expire.

THERE is, in these lines from Harold's apostrophe to the Colosseum (*Childe Harold*, Canto IV), a sublimity of accent which was fully justified in Byron's case; for here, more perhaps than in any other instance, force of personality is everything, and as he rightly divined, his was proof against wear and tear. In Byron the rallying-point and connecting-link of all that he was is strength in the most elementary, I might almost say the crudest, sense of the word. It is by virtue of this that Byron, as I have said, is all of a piece; and that, nevertheless, his whole attitude, his whole nature, exhibit those mixed elements which we have seen to be present even in his most essential need—the need of fatality. Equally dependent on external and internal conditions, caught, as it were wedged, between the two, he incessantly expends his inmost energies upon the transformation of events into omens, injunctions from destiny. All of a piece and yet a compound: in the co-existence of these contradictories lies his most marked characteristic, his limitations as compared with both greater and purer natures, but also his composite value as a human being. For Byron's greatness cohabits with innumerable pettinesses; he signally brings off the combination— seldom found in men of genius, when both attributes are authentic—of pride and vanity; a massive pride, and a vanity so puerile, so transparent, as to be disarming. He is at once the most rebellious and the most social of men, in his relations with others alternately restive, morose, and supremely companionable. Impossible to be more contemptuous of public opinion than he was, in attitude—or more precisely in his way of affronting it (Byron is, for that matter, always affronting something); yet in reality always taking it into consideration, even his bravadoes are conditioned by that which he claimed to over-ride; in a word, he was the most conventional of convention's intractable foes. Ethel Colburn Mayne has well perceived and analysed this in one of the most important passages of her book:

'Childe Harold was called, in the MS. of the first canto, Childe Burun, which was the old Norman rendering of Byron; yet after the poem was published with the altered name, his creator was strenuous to deny any identity. As Dallas told him, however, "the not identifying yourself with the travelling Childe is a wish not possible to realise". And, paradoxical as it may sound, the fact that Harold is not an accurate portrait of Byron merely makes the resemblance more complete. One of his most characteristic sequences was the perpetual revelation to the world of his idea of himself, and the annoyance which he never failed to express (and to feel) at that world's credulity—for the idea was of course devoutly hailed as the reality. This sequence grew out of the uncertainty of touch to which I have already alluded. The ambition and the pusillanimity of his vanity were for ever at war with each other—the one driving him, in fancy, to flagrant revolt against convention; the other bending him, in actual life, meekly before it. There is something tragic in his perpetual battle with this duality, which is the real problem, as I think, of his character'.[1]

It could not be better expressed; and as one studies his life in full detail, it is this duality which opens the door to the comic spirit even when we are confronted with some of the forms that greatness in him assumes, while on the other hand his pettinesses shine with a reflected light of prestige; so that,

[1] *Byron*, Ethel Colburn Mayne, p. 102 (Edition 1924).

to sum up, at every point we are presented with something which wins upon and instructs us.

*   *   *

As was the case with another force, but how much more significant and important—that of Browning—the earliest manifestation of the Byronic individuality was, appropriately, a destructive one. But while the baby-Browning, having thrown a piece of his mother's lace into the fire, clapped his hands at the spectacle and joyously exclaimed: 'A pitty baze, mamma!', the baby-Byron, scolded for having soiled a new frock in which he had just been dressed, seized it in both hands and tore it from top to bottom. True, we are told that he had often seen his mother do the same with her gowns and caps; but what he had not seen her do—and here' the originality of his destructive impulse asserts itself—was to bite a large piece out of a china saucer. That saucer has, of course, been preserved in Aberdeen as a precious relic; Thomas Moore, Byron's first biographer, was in 1830 proudly shown the marks of the infant-teeth. 'One of my silent rages', wrote the mature Byron in his diary, recalling the incident. Silent rage—a cardinal trait of Byron's, never shed, and in him representing the climax of that moroseness which was so prominent a temperamental feature that it almost seems his very nature. Byron is the grand, the sovereign example of moroseness; a moroseness in his case strongly tinctured with race, and quite inexplicably invested with some abrupt majesty, as of a beetling rock. All his life Byron was what he threw off in a rapid phrase belonging to the Ravenna diary: 'Not quarrelsome if not spoken to'.[1]

---

[1]*Letters and Journals*, v. 156. I must point out that in my use of this text I have taken a liberty purely psychological in intention. Byron is here describing the effects on himself of wine and alcohol. I give the passage as it stands: 'But wine and spirits make me sullen and savage to ferocity—silent, however, and retiring, and not quarrelsome if not spoken to'. Moroseness, unfortunately, is liable to accompany even a state of perfect sobriety; I am convinced that Byron was temperamentally morose, and I believe the text to be descriptive of the state of moroseness as such.

Laconic enough, but no one has more profoundly stated the mood peculiar to the morose—that mood which, without being Byron, we all have known in our bad hours. Now, imagine this silent rage confronted by a loquacious rage—the most loquacious conceivable—and at once you have both a vivid picture of Byron's relation with his mother, and the clue to their perpetual and quite inevitable dissensions. Moroseness and choler probably, indeed certainly, derive from the same disease, but the disease is one which affects its victims in such totally different ways that they cannot but hate one another, and when confronted, severally behave with the complex but deep-rooted hostility of two animal species which feel the more alien because they are in fact closely akin. Mrs. Byron would break out, and what with her vulgar and corpulent coarseness—and her pride of birth—the sight must have been afflicting. Her son's concentrated exasperation would take the form of sardonic silence, which we may be sure that he knew how to make insulting: strictly speaking, he looked on, and afterwards, the ruthless precision of his observation found expression in letters to his sister Augusta—the first in date of his masterpieces, which reveal him at sixteen in full possession of his powers in that line, and above all of that gift of *statement*, of bare, incisive enunciation, which is the Byronic gift *par excellence*.

'The more I see of her, the more my dislike augments: nor can I so entirely conquer the appearance of it, as to prevent her from perceiving my opinion; this, so far from calming the Gale, blows it into a *hurricane* which threatens to destroy everything, till exhausted by its own violence, it is lulled into a sullen torpor, which, after a short period, is again roused into fresh and revived phrenzy, to me most terrible and to every other Spectator astonishing. She then declares that she plainly sees I hate her, that I am leagued with her bitter enemies, viz. Yourself, Ld. C(arlisle) and Mr. H(anson), and as I never Dissemble or contradict her we are all *honoured* with a multiplicity of epithets, too *numerous*, and some of

c   33

them too *gross*, to be repeated.' (August 18, 1804).[1] ' She flies
into a fit of phrenzy, upbraids me as if I was the most un-
dutiful wretch in existence, rakes up the ashes of my *father*,
abuses him, says I shall be a true Byrrone, which is the
worst epithet she can invent. Am I to call this woman
mother? Because by nature's law she has authority over me,
am I to be trampled upon in this manner? . . . goaded with
insult . . . loaded with obloquy, and suffer my feelings to be
outraged on the most trivial occasions? I owe her respect as
a Son, but I renounce her as a Friend. What an example does
she shew me! I hope in God I shall never follow it. I have not
told you all, nor can I: I respect you as a female, nor, although
I ought to confide in you as a Sister, will I shock you with the
repetition of Scenes, which you may judge of by the Sample
I have given you, and which to all but you are buried in
oblivion. Would they were so in my mind! I am afraid they
never will'. (November 11, 1804).[2]

Buried in oblivion they never were—they could not have
been; in a Byron there was no such thing as forgetting, and
this incapacity constitutes both the adamantine basis of his
genius, and the morbid delectation of his inmost self. All his
life he was the man of that rending phrase from Tasso which
he chose as motto for *The Corsair*: '*I suoi pensieri in lui dormir
non ponno*'. ('His inmost thoughts could never slumber').
How often does he not represent himself as the sleepless
being, the being condemned to eternal vigil; and what in
another might seem an affectation, in Byron answers to the
most profound stratum of sincerity—by which I do not
mean to say that he is unconscious of the beauty in the attitude, but it is only as a side-issue, and there is nothing, even
to that very touch of conscious posing, which is not here
sincere. In the opening of *Manfred*: that is to say, in the
hour when the great secret of his life—that of his incestuous
love for his half-sister Augusta—is about to escape him at

[1] *Letters and Journals*, i. pp. 30-31.
[2] *Letters and Journals*, i. pp. 46-47.

last . . . a secret far from being buried in oblivion, but on the
contrary, in Homer's phrase for his heroes, ceaselessly re-
volved in his heart, never allowed to fade from memory—
here is how, amid the rich impressive gloom of the opening
lines, he depicts himself:

> The lamp must be replenished, but even then
> It will not burn so long as I must watch:
> My slumbers—if I slumber—are not sleep,
> But a continuance of enduring thought,
> Which then I can resist not; in my heart
> There is a vigil, and these eyes but close
> To look within; and yet I live, and bear
> The aspect and the form of breathing men.

'In my heart there is a vigil'; and though that vigil did not
assume all its tragic intensity until after the intercourse with
Augusta, I think there can be no doubt that the terrible
scenes with his mother, in his childhood, were what sowed
the first seeds of it.

But Mrs. Byron's loquacity had other disadvantages, in
Byron's eyes not less objectionable. He wrote to Augusta in
the same letter of November 11, 1804:

'A talkative woman is like an Adder's tongue, so says one
of the prophets, but which I can't tell, and very likely you
don't wish to know, but he was a true one whoever he was.'

More than once he refers to his mother's love of scandal-
mongering and still more of tittle-tattle, her insatiable and
interminable delight in talking, always censoriously, about
the weaknesses and oddities of her acquaintances. Now,
calumny, disparagement, tittle-tattle cannot but arouse the
most impatient aversion in those who have some greatness in
their composition, and on the other hand are versed from
infancy in the dictum of Ecclesiastes, that all is vanity and
emptiness. Byron was a stern, even a rigorous judge of
character; but his judgments were always of that penetrating
general nature which embodies, without revealing or ex-
pounding the personal sources, one's experience of a being

as a whole. He never comes down to details, which are always something of a degradation—he scorns to display them; with one exception—indubitably a very serious one, but to this day not completely cleared-up: his strangely ambiguous attitude towards a calumny about Shelley—Byron appears to me as the judge, but never as the exhibitor, of others.

Let me add that Mrs. Byron's furies would sometimes, as a climax of misfortune, alternate with attacks of sentimentality—not unlike the maudlin stage of drunkenness; and that Byron, like a good Englishman, detested all manifestations of sentiment, and all the more of this kind. When Mrs. Byron was in this mood, she would overwhelm her son with compliments on the beauty of his eyes; and appreciative of personal flattery though Byron was throughout his life, he preferred that it should not come from his mother. I have said enough, I think, to show that the incompatibility of these two was radical; and so, when on his majority Byron became independent, though materially speaking he did his duty by his mother, he saw her as seldom as possible, and sailed on his first Eastern trip—which lasted two years—without having said farewell except in a letter which deeply wounded Mrs. Byron by the very politeness of its frigid conventionality. On his return from his voyage, business in London delayed his departure for Newstead, where during his absence he had installed his mother. It delayed him so long that he arrived too late to see her alive.

'On the first day of August she died. In the beginning her indisposition had seemed a trifling one, so he had not been summoned; but excessive corpulency rendered her a dangerous subject for illness, and just as this one took a critical turn, the upholsterers' bills came in, so infuriating her by their amount that she was seized by one of her unhappy rages, and never recovered from its effects. . . . Always superstitious, she had had a haunting fancy, when he left England in 1809, that she should never see him again. The farewell letter had

36

doubtless heightened this imagining, and the more because their last parting had been the scene of one of her most terrible outbursts. He had returned safe and well; yet when he wrote to tell her so and promise that he would soon be with her, she had said to her maid: "If I should be dead before Byron comes down, what a strange thing it would be!".

'He came down, and she was dead. On the night after his arrival, the maid was passing the room where her former mistress lay, when she heard a heavy sigh from within. She entered. The room was in darkness, but she could distinguish the young lord's figure by the bed. She tried to utter some words of comfort: "he must not give way to grief". But his tears came irresistibly; she stood beside, embarrassed and distressed, till at last she heard him articulate amid the sobs, "I had but one friend in the world, and she is gone" ... Such a sudden experience had been this woman's ; and it must have been with amazement that, on the day of the funeral, she not only saw him refuse to follow the procession to the churchyard and stand watching it from the Abbey door till it was out of sight, but then turn to one of the inferior men-servants and desire him to fetch the sparring-gloves, that they might have their usual morning exercise. He was silent and abstracted all the time; the man thought his blows were more violent than usual—then, suddenly flinging the gloves away, he left the hall and was unseen for many hours. "Not Shakespeare", said the *Quarterly* in 1831, reviewing Moore, "could have conceived such a scene." ' And Ethel Colburn Mayne adds this comment, which I here reproduce because it seems to me to be the last word concerning Byron's relation with his mother: 'We may not too closely analyse his emotion. When he wrote, on his way to the Abbey after hearing the news, to his old friend John Pigot of Southwell —who alone among his present acquaintance had known Mrs. Byron—and quoted Gray's "We can only have one mother", a deeper than the obvious meaning may well have pierced his consciousness. The mother *he* had had—

37

what mingled wretchedness and anger she had stirred in him! And all had been reciprocal; what she had called forth from him, he had called forth from her. . . . Such sorrow is the more poignant for its ambiguity. Which, in truth, was he mourning—her death or her life?' [1]

But Byron's childhood was shadowed by another circumstance which, almost as much as his relation with his mother, influenced his whole life—to wit, his infirmity. You remember Captain Byron's peremptory assertion: 'As to my son's being able to walk, it is impossible, for he has a club-foot'. The child did succeed in walking; but was he really club-footed? Strange as it may seem, we cannot even now be certain, and the testimonies are so discrepant that we actually do not know which foot was affected—some, for instance Stendhal and Trelawney, saying the right one, while Mrs. Leigh Hunt and Thorwaldsen say the left. Anyhow, the trouble was the outcome of infantile paralysis, and the view generally accepted to-day is that the foot was not a club-foot, but that there was a contraction of the Achilles tendon. If Byron could come back to us, only this connection with the hero of the *Iliad*—and indeed he resembles Achilles in more than one respect—could console him for having to give up his club-foot. He was very fond of it; for, as Ethel Colburn Mayne remarks, with her usual and amused justness of perception, once there was a question of infirmity, nothing would satisfy Byron but 'the big word'. He always maintained that he had a club-foot, never suffered anyone to maintain otherwise. Perhaps the trait is susceptible of a more subterranean and more complex interpretation—one which would have a more general bearing on the Byronic nature—even than that suggested by Ethel Colburn Mayne. For on the one hand, Byron extended this need of the maximum (or, more precisely, the need that each thing should abound in its

[1] *Byron*, Ethel Colburn Mayne, pp. 129-130.

own sense) to everything; not only to things which, strictly speaking, concerned his person, not only to casual events which, happening around him, were at once tyrannically enthralled to *his* destiny, made inseparable from him; but even to other human beings—as for instance those Venetian women of the people, Marianna Segati and Margarita Cogni, who roamed his palace like bright wild beasts half-tamed, and whose domestication had gorgeous relapses, which indeed made the greater part of their attraction for him. He liked nothing better in women, and said so more than once, than the alternation of leaping and lying low in those whom he called 'these splendid animals'; in every sphere he was satisfied with, fascinated by, what a zoologist would call plenitude of type. And besides (and this is why it had to be the club-foot or nothing) he wanted everything that concerned himself to be stamped on the imagination, and that in the largest letters—those capitals of which at all times he was so fond. Byron's faculty for creating the personal myth amounted to genius—I say to genius, for with him we always assist at the fabrication of the myth, which yet in the end infallibly imposes itself—with the result that it becomes identified with the prestige-value of which I have spoken.[1]

Many are the anecdotes relating to Byron's lameness; here I can give no more than two. One is sinister, and casts a pain-

[1]During the useless and often unnecessarily cruel tortures inflicted on him for the cure of his lameness, I must add that in childhood Byron showed the courage and self-control which, in physical suffering, distinguished him all his life. 'Since he had become Lord Byron, his mother was less patient than ever at the sight of his lameness. She had been recommended to try a Nottingham quack named Lavender, and had entrusted the ailing lad to his care. Lavender was a brute. His treatment consisted solely of forcibly twisting the child's hapless foot, and screwing it tightly in some wooden contrivance. Byron was then taking Latin lessons from an American, Mr. Dummer Rogers; and this worthy man was pained by the sight of the agonised expression on his pupil's little face as they read their Virgil and Cicero together. It was caused by Lavender's instruments of torture. "It makes me uncomfortable, my lord, to see you sitting there in such pain as I *know* you must be suffering".—"Never mind, Mr. Rogers", said the boy, "you shall not see any signs of it in *me*".' (Maurois, *Byron*, English edition, p. 44).

ful light on the underlying causes of his relation with his mother. In one of her attacks of fury, she called him a lame brat. The child answered: 'I was born so, mother.' . . . The second anecdote belongs to the latter years of Byron's life, and has a pleasant touch of quiet humour. In 1821 he was walking in his garden at Genoa with Hobhouse, and suddenly turning on him said: 'Now I know you're looking at my foot'. Hobhouse, who for twenty years had known how to manage His Lordship's little tempers, suavely retorted: 'My dear Byron, no one ever thinks of or looks at anything but your head'.

But very probably it is to his lameness and his constant preoccupation with it that we must attribute what in a very felicitous phrase, almost untranslatable into French, Ethel Colburn Mayne calls Byron's 'uncertainty of touch'—that comparative lack of ease in the social sphere, that sense of being, in all surroundings, slightly out of place. This man, who in his writings is so sure of himself, so well in the saddle, was in his relations with human beings—and very especially with the world to which he belonged by right of birth—by no means inwardly assured or securely balanced; and would either keep his distance with exceeding haughtiness, or else accentuate, underline his 'conceit of rank' by a painful insistence on little matters of etiquette—the very matters which the English aristocrat is so careful to sink and to ignore. And here we join hands with Lady Blessington's acute remark, which this time I must quote in full: 'His conceit of his rank was abnormal. It resembled more the pride of a parvenu than the calm dignity of an ancient aristocrat'. Nothing could be truer, and be it said in passing that nothing gives us a clearer idea—and this before he became notorious, before there was any talk of incest—of the apparently impassable gulf between Byron and the English society of his time, and (in so far as the true aristocrat still survives in England), perhaps I ought to say of all time. For if there are probably no inward vanity and pride comparable to those of the English-

man, and, in the second degree, to those of the English aristocrat—and Byron was very English in his combination of
these two things—there is nevertheless nothing which the
English aristocrat holds to be in such bad taste as any showing
through of either, not only for reasons of general 'good form',
but (to go deeper) because he is always afraid that vanity and
pride may lose weight if they show through, and that is what
he will avoid at any cost. Yes, there was a touch of the parvenu in Byron; it is certain that he never could quite assimilate the fact that he *was* Lord Byron—I mean, assimilate it so
thoroughly as never to remember it. This resulted partly from
his lameness and the insecurity it caused him to feel; partly
too from the provincial atmosphere of his neglected and even
abandoned childhood.

For he was provincial, shy and—in view of the future,
shocking to relate!—fat and almost plain, this adolescent of
sixteen who in the drawing-rooms of provincial little Southwell gave Elizabeth Pigot such trouble before she could win a
smile from him—she who was to be for her hour the Egeria
to whom he confided his earliest verses, so frigid and so tame.
This was the Elizabeth Pigot who worshipped him in
memory, and who when Moore came to interview her many
years after Byron's death, would not admit that he had a
single fault, no matter how trifling. A constancy the more
admirable because, once Byron had the drawing-rooms and
belles of London at his disposal, he showed her very plainly
in a letter that he no longer took any interest either in Southwell news or her own—displaying there, as he did more than
once with women, that brutal want of tact which one would
like to attribute to his lack of early training, but which unfortunately seems to derive from a much more serious strain
of the parvenu in him, disagreeably perceptible at certain
periods of his life—I mean the parvenu in affairs of the
heart.

Elizabeth Pigot was perhaps unconsciously the inspirer,
later to be disdained, of the great Thinning Campaign which

Byron kept up with such stoical obstinacy to the day of his death—there, little as he would have liked to think so, joining hands with women, and more womanish than any of them. A campaign in which his lameness made it peculiarly difficult for him to be successful, since he was confined to exercises that do nothing for slenderness, and was thus obliged to resort to abstinence, which he very drastically did. Of the many anecdotes about these thinning precautions, I give that relating to his first dinner with the poet Samuel Rogers.

'Early in November 1811 the famous dinner took place. Rogers had never seen Byron before; neither had Moore, nor Thomas Campbell (already past his zenith, though but thirty-five), who was the only other guest. Rogers arranged with them that he should be alone in the drawing-room when the stranger arrived—a trait of delicate consideration for his lameness. Shortly afterwards the other two returned, and Moore saw Byron for the first time. He was in mourning for his mother, and the "pure, spiritual paleness of his features", enhanced by the dark dress and the "curling picturesque hair", made the usual indelible impression. The beautiful voice added its spell to the rest; and so, among the three small men, one with his keen spectral face, the other two with their round and lively countenances, Byron, Adonis of the Ages, sat down to dinner.

'Rogers asked him if he would take soup.

' "No; I never take soup".

' "Some fish?" as the soup vanished.

' "No; I never take fish".

'Presently the mutton arrived. The same question; the same answer.

'Our perfect host bore up. "A glass of wine?"

' "No; I never taste wine".

' "It was now necessary", says Rogers in his account of this far from perfect guest, "to ask what he *did* eat and drink; and the answer was, "Nothing but hard biscuits and soda-water".

42

'Unfortunately, neither hard biscuits nor soda-water were at hand; and he dined then upon potatoes bruised down upon his plate and drenched with vinegar. . . . Some days after, meeting Hobhouse, I said to him, "How long will Lord Byron persevere in his present diet?"

'He replied, "Just as long as you continue to notice it".

'Rogers adds that he came to know as a fact that Byron, after leaving his house very late, went to a club in St. James's Street and ate a hearty meat-supper. That may be true, but it seems unlikely. He was sincere in his austerities, for (as we have seen) the best of reasons.' [1]

Certain details here prove that Byron had not only gained the Promised Land of slenderness, but at the same time (and in his case, the two facts seem to have been simultaneous) had developed the really extraordinary beauty by virtue of which for once—and only for once—the horrible *cliché:* 'fatal beauty' is re-invested with freshness and prestige. Whether they come from friends or foes, from women or (still more significant) men, all contemporary witnesses are in agreement. 'The pure, spiritual paleness of his features', says one; and Miss Jane Porter, who saw him only once and of course never forgot him, wrote: 'The complexion . . . a sort of moonlight paleness. It was so pale, yet with all so softly brilliant'. 'Like an alabaster vase, lighted up from within', observes some one else; and here is the most wonderfully-phrased description of all, that of Coleridge on April 10, 1816: 'If you had seen Lord Byron, you could scarcely disbelieve him—so beautiful a countenance I scarcely ever saw. His eyes the open portals of the sun—things of light and for light'.[2] If to this we add the charm of a voice about which the witnesses are equally unanimous—the sweetest, most beautifully modulated of voices—there is nothing surprising in Byron's having been irresistible. 'That beautiful pale face is my fate': you

[1]*Byron,* Ethel Colburn Mayne, p. 137.

[2]Gilman, *Life of Coleridge* (Pickering, 1838, p. 236. Quoted in *Astarte,* pp. 14-15.)

43

remember poor Caroline Lamb's second thought, her pre-
sageful sigh—and in presence of Byron, without his being in
the least aware of it, how many another woman must have
murmured the same words to herself before she silently made
Gautier's poignant line come true: '*Un regret, ramier qu'on
étouffe*'.

* * *

But women began by winning some victories over the boy
and the adolescent; and it was perhaps the remembrance of
these which made the man (who, as we have seen, was incapable of forgetting) so harsh in his reprisals. On one of these
we need not dwell, for the heroine of it died at fifteen, two
years after meeting Byron, who was then only twelve. It concerns—there is certainly some monotony in this aspect of the
Byron doom—his cousin-german, Margaret Parker, of whom
he wrote in 1821 in the Ravenna journal: 'She looked as if she
had been made of a rainbow, all beauty and peace'. For the
rest it seems that here the feeling was reciprocal; for shortly
before the girl's death, when Augusta happened to mention
Byron's name, Margaret blushed exquisitely 'to her very
eyelids'; and doubtless it was this blush, as Ethel Colburn
Mayne remarks, which made her memory live for him. But
even this young love had been preceded by another, notably
more serious—that which Byron felt at nine, for yet another
cousin (but not a cousin-german this time), Mary Duff, and
which is of importance to us because it inspired a very
characteristic passage in his diary for November 26, 1813:

'I have been thinking a good deal lately of Mary Duff.
How very odd that I should have been so utterly, devotedly
fond of that girl, at an age when I could neither feel passion,
nor know the meaning of the word. And the effect! My
mother used always to rally me about this childish amour;
and at last, many years after, when I was sixteen, she told me
one day, "Oh, Byron, I have had a letter from Edinburgh,
from Miss Abercromby, and your old sweetheart Mary Duff
is married to a Mr. C(ockburn)". And what was my answer?

I really cannot explain or account for my feelings at that moment; but they threw me nearly into convulsions, and alarmed my mother so much, that after I grew better, she generally avoided the subject—to *me*—and contented herself with telling it to all her acquaintances. Now, what could this be? I had never seen her since her mother's *faux pas* at Aberdeen had been the cause of her removal to her grandmother's at Banff; we were both the merest children. I had and have been attached fifty times since that period; yet I recollect all we said to each other, all our caresses, her features, my restlessness, sleeplessness, my tormenting my mother's maid to write for me to her, which she at last did, to quiet me. Poor Nancy thought I was wild, and as I could not write for myself, became my secretary. I remember too our walks, and the happiness of sitting by Mary, in the children's apartment, at their house not far from the Plainstanes at Aberdeen, while her lesser sister Helen played with the doll, and we sat gravely making love, in our way.

'How the deuce did all this occur so early? where could it originate? I certainly had no sexual ideas for years afterwards; and yet my misery, my love for that girl were so violent that I sometimes doubt if I have been ever really attached since. Be that as it may, hearing of her marriage several years after was like a thunder-stroke—it nearly choked me—to the horror of my mother and the astonishment and almost incredulity of everybody. And it is a phenomenon in my existence (for I was not eight years old) which has puzzled, and will puzzle me to the latest hour of it; and lately, I know not why, the *recollection* (*not* the attachment) has recurred as forcibly as ever. I wonder if she can have the least remembrance of it or me? or remember pitying her sister Helen for not having an admirer too? How very pretty is the perfect image of her in my memory—her brown, dark hair, and hazel eyes; her very dress! I should be quite grieved to see *her now*; the reality, however beautiful, would destroy, or at least confuse, the features of the lovely Peri which then existed in her, and still lives in my imagination, at the distance of more than sixteen years. I am now twenty-five and odd months. . . .' [1]

Because it was his, such precocity in love had to be an inexplicable maximum. In sober fact, precocity in love is by no means uncommon even in ordinary mortals; Ethel Colburn Mayne cogently reminds us that Alfieri—who considered it an unerring sign of the artistic soul, but this may have been because Alfieri himself fell in love at nine years old—remarks that it is frequent enough in men of genius. Dante and Heine are in this respect at least as conspicuous instances as Byron. Doubtless Ethel Colburn Mayne's interpretation of the Mary Duff episode is the true one—that the Byronic convulsions were due not so much to genuine amorous despair as to the unpardonable circumstance that he could be forgotten to the point of the lady's marrying some one else—a circumstance, as it happened, the more unpardonable because he heard of Mary Duff's marriage at the very time when his love of the moment, Mary Chaworth, had shown a

[1]*Letters and Journals*, ii. pp. 347-348. Mary Duff married Mr. Robert Cockburn; she and her husband appear in Ruskin's reminiscences of childhood, and are thus described: 'In the first chapter of the Antiquary, the landlord at Queen's Ferry sets down to his esteemed guest a bottle of Robert Cockburn's best port; with which Robert Cockburn duly supplied Sir Walter himself, being at that time, if not the largest, the leading importer of the finest Portugal wine, as my father of Spanish. But Mr. Cockburn was primarily an old Edinburgh gentleman, and only by condescension a wine-merchant; a man of great power and pleasant sarcastic wit, moving in the first circles of Edinburgh; attached to my father by many links of association with the "auld toun" and sincerely respecting him. He was much the stateliest and truest piece of character who ever sate at our merchant feasts.—Mrs. Cockburn was even a little higher—as representative of the Scottish lady of the old school—indulgent yet to the new. She had been Lord Byron's first of first loves ; she was the Mary Duff of Lachin-y-Gair. When I first remember her, still extremely beautiful in middle age, full of sense; and, though with some mixture of proud severity, extremely kind' (*Praeterita*, chap. v. p. 143).

Regarding the Mary Duff episode, a hitherto unpublished note of Hobhouse's reads: 'With respect to the early development of these propensities in Byron, I am acquainted with a regular fact scarcely fit for narration, but much less romantic and more satisfactory than the amour with Mary Duff' (André Maurois, *Byron*, English edition, p. 442).

like oblivion of him by becoming engaged to John Musters. To receive two simultaneous proofs that he could be forgotten, clinched by the cold fact of marriage (and this was where the blow came home), was certainly enough to convulse a Byron.

But though the influence of Mary Chaworth on Byron's life has been grossly exaggerated,[1] it is none the less true that the affair with her is much the most illuminating of any which preceded his relation with his half-sister; and so it must detain us for a while. Byron was fifteen when he first met Mary Chaworth, who was two years older; she was the great-niece of the Mr. Chaworth whom the fifth Lord Byron had killed in a duel, brought about by a quarrel over the amount of game preserved in their adjoining estates. They fought with swords in the empty room of a tavern, and so irregular were the proceedings that Lord Byron was tried by his peers at Westminster Hall, and acquitted only by favour of one of those archaic English statutes which can always be revived in embarrassing cases. This caused enmity between the families, an enmity which had only just died out at the time of Byron's adolescence, and was doubtless in his eyes a considerable attraction, savouring of Romeo and Juliet. Or rather he chose to regard it in that light, for the families had recently agreed to bury the hatchet. Byron himself recounts the situation, when alluding towards the end of his life to the summer in which his passion flamed highest.

'*My* M. A. C., my Mary Annesley Chaworth' (Miss Chaworth was the heiress of Annesley Hall, neighbouring estate to Newstead Abbey, and it was there that Byron made love to her) 'was there. Alas, why do I say *My*? Our union would have healed feuds, in which blood had been shed by our fathers; it would have joined lands, broad and rich; it would have joined at least *one* heart and two persons not ill-matched in years (she is two years my elder) and—and—and—what

---

[1] Mr. Richard Edgcumbe's book represents a final and entirely unavailing attempt to refute, in Mary's favour, the central reality of Byron's existence—the reality of the incest.

has been the result? She has married a man older than herself, been wretched and separated. I have married, and am separated; and yet *We* are *not* united.'[1]

We have no very clear idea of Mary Chaworth at eighteen —conscious of her dawning powers, vivacious, volatile; while the Byron of fifteen was serious. She was a brunette with masses of dense black hair and very dark eyes. We must remember that Byron, at fifteen, was still fat and in no way physically attractive; besides, he was lame and the girl adored dancing. At their respective ages, and especially when the boy is the younger, there is perhaps nothing more certain to keep apart. Did Mary do anything more than let herself be loved? Most likely not; but when a woman lets herself be loved and multiplies opportunities for proving it to her, that fifteen should not suppose some reciprocity of feeling, should be capable of believing itself quite unloved, is rather too much to ask of it. Moreover, she had given Byron her picture (which in those days meant something); she is even said to have given him a ring, but it seems that she gave it only to receive one herself from somebody else, for immediately afterwards her engagement to John Musters was announced. Here is the story of the ring, and how it obliged Mary to reveal the real state of her feelings:

'The story goes that Mr. John Musters—a fox-hunting squire of the neighbourhood—was bathing with Byron in the river which ran through his estate of Colwick Hall, and suddenly perceived among the boy's clothes, scattered on the bank, a ring which he recognised as Mary's. He at once took possession; Byron claimed it, but Musters refused to restore. They contended hotly, and soon Musters mounted his horse and galloped to Annesley Hall, there to confront the girl with the disputed token. She confessed that Byron wore it as her gift—but she solaced the rival by promising to declare without delay her engagement to himself.' [2]

[1] *Letters and Journals*, v. p. 441.
[2] *Byron*, Ethel Colburn Mayne, pp. 38-39.

48

But as she did not marry Musters until the August of 1805, the engagement left her free to keep Byron dangling at her side, and suffering incessant torture at the balls where she danced from beginning to end, and he looked on, a love-sick spectator who could not join in the exercise. She excelled in it, and—a pioneer of modern custom—would accept total strangers as partners. This caused Byron his most poignant pangs—yet no! for the worst of all was that of which Moore tells us, on the authority of the Memoirs that were so unfortunately destroyed. Byron was either told of, or overheard, Miss Chaworth saying to her maid: 'Do you think I could care anything for that lame boy?' This speech was like a shot through the heart. Though it was late at night when he heard it, he instantly darted out of the house, and scarcely knowing whither he ran, never stopped until he found himself at Newstead—three miles away. That this did not put an end to the affair, that on the contrary he was more devoted than ever during the ensuing months, is the proof that this was a serious infatuation, assuredly the most serious he ever felt before the Augusta-days.

But it is the speech itself that here arrests us, for it is a typical instance of the sayings which colour all the future, all the life, of those beings (and Byron supremely belongs to that class) whom Mérimée has once for all set before us in the person of his Saint-Clair in *Le Vase Etrusque*—those who care as children care for opinion. Yes; but if they so care, it is just because some speech overheard—and nearly always in their childhood—has roughly revealed to them what that opinion really is, and because it has proved to be in complete contradiction with the appearance shown to them. Thenceforth their motto is: 'Never give yourself away'; most comprehensible but most perilous of mottoes, in that it may sterilize some of the deepest sources of feeling. And that they may never give themselves away, they must above all be the dupe of no one. *Memnas' apistein* (*Remember to distrust*)— that was Mérimée's motto, for Saint-Clair is evidently a self-portrait; and we know that that distrust was born of what he heard his mother say, when after having been gravely scolded for some misdemeanour and taking the scolding in earnest, he caught, as the door was shutting on him, her words to a third person: 'Poor child, he really believes that we are very angry'. From that day Mérimée never believed in anything, and was utterly incapable of taking anything in earnest, or ever being quite in earnest himself—thus tracing for us the limited circle in which his talent and even his nature were to move. Tolstoy underwent a similar conflict with his youthful bent, which was exactly the same—a childish fear of opinion. We do not yet know whether it originated in a speech of this kind; and as Tolstoy soars high above either Byron or Mérimée, it did not so much matter, being submerged in the irresistibly flowing tide of his genius. But Byron, Mérimée and Tolstoy are, in my view, the supreme examples of the way in which a human being, who was perhaps not innately susceptible to opinion, is led by opinion itself to assign to it a momentous and excessive importance.

In process of time Byron characteristically exaggerated the Mary Chaworth episode, and (as was his way) quite sincerely both in mind and imagination. As regards the mind, we have seen the fragment of diary; and the imagination played its part in 1816 at the Villa Diodati on the borders of the Lake of Geneva—that crowded period which gave us *Manfred* and the Journal kept during his expedition to the Bernese Alps. Then the memory of Mary Chaworth came over him, and (since he must always find an outlet) inspired him with the poem called *The Dream*, written in a few nights. It is the Mary Chaworth theme at its full value for the Byronic myth; he poured into *The Dream* all he had elected that it should mean for him, recklessly and perhaps without any real remembrance of the true facts. The poem is not without beauty; but though written in the same mythical strain, it fades into utter insignificance when compared with Byron's mythical masterpiece—when compared with *Manfred*. And that alone is enough to define the distance, in the region of intimate feeling, between a Mary Chaworth and her who, taking everything together, represents both the essential event of Byron's life and the central factor in his mythical vision of himself—his half-sister Augusta.

CHAPTER III

XVII

In him inexplicably mixed appeared
Much to be loved and hated, sought and feared;
Opinion varying o'er his hidden lot,
In praise or railing ne'er his name forgot:
His silence formed a theme for others' prate—
They guessed—they gazed—they fain would know his fate,
What had he been? what was he, thus unknown,
Who walked their world, his lineage only known?
A hater of his kind? yet some would say,
With them he could seem gay amidst the gay;
But owned that smile, if oft observed and near,
Waned in its mirth, and withered to a sneer;
That smile might reach his lip, but passed not by,
Nor e'er could trace its laughter to his eye:
Yet there was softness too in his regard,
At times, a heart as not by nature hard,
But once perceived, his Spirit seemed to chide
Such weakness, as unworthy of its pride,
And steeled itself, as scorning to redeem
One doubt from others' half withheld esteem;
In self-inflicted penance of a breast
Which Tenderness might once have wrung from Rest;
In vigilance of Grief that would compel
The soul to hate for having loved too well.

XVIII

There was in him a vital scorn of all:
As if the worst had fallen which could befall,
He stood a stranger in this breathing world,
An erring Spirit from another hurled;
A thing of dark imaginings, that shaped
By choice the perils he by chance escaped;
But 'scaped in vain, for in their memory yet
His mind would half exult and half regret:
With more capacity for love than Earth
Bestows on most of mortal mould and birth,
His early dreams of good outstripped the truth,
And troubled Manhood followed baffled Youth;
With thought of years in phantom chase misspent,
And wasted powers for better purpose lent;
And fiery passions that had poured their wrath
In hurried desolation o'er his path,

And left the better feelings all at strife
In wild reflection o'er his stormy life;
But haughty still, and loth himself to blame,
He called on Nature's self to share the shame,
And charged all faults upon the fleshly form
She gave to clog the soul, and feast the worm;
Till he at last confounded good and ill,
And half mistook for fate the acts of will:
Too high for common selfishness, he could
At times resign his own for others' good,
But not in pity—not because he ought,
But in some strange perversity of thought,
That swayed him onward with a secret pride
To do what few or none would do beside;
And this same impulse would, in tempting time,
Mislead his spirit equally to crime;
So much he soared beyond, or sunk beneath,
The men with whom he felt condemned to breathe,
And longed by good or ill to separate
Himself from all who shared his mortal state;
His mind abhorring this had fixed her throne
Far from the world, in regions of her own:
Thus coldly passing all that passed below,
His blood in temperate seeming now would flow;
Ah! happier if it ne'er with guilt had glowed,
But ever in that icy smoothness flowed!
'Tis true, with other men their path he walked,
And like the rest in seeming did and talked,
Nor outraged Reason's rules by flaw nor start,
His Madness was not of the head, but heart;
And rarely wandered in his speech, or drew
His thoughts so forth as to offend the view.

XIX

With all that chilling mystery of mien,
And seeming gladness to remain unseen,
He had (if 'twere not nature's boon) an art
Of fixing memory on another's heart:
It was not love perchance—nor hate—nor aught
That words can image to express the thought;
But they who saw him did not see in vain,
And once beheld—would ask of him again:
And those to whom he spoke remembered well,
And on the words, however light, would dwell:
None knew, nor how, nor why, but he entwined
Himself perforce around the hearer's mind;
There he was stamped, in liking, or in hate,
If greeted once; however brief the date
That friendship, pity, or aversion knew,
Still there within the inmost thought he grew.

You could not penetrate his soul, but found,
Despite your wonder, to your own he wound;
His presence haunted still; and from the breast
He forced on all unwilling interest:
Vain was the struggle in that mental net—
His Spirit seemed to dare you to forget!

THESE three stanzas from Canto I of *Lara*[1] belong, in my opinion, to a very rare order of achievement—that of a *full-length portrait of a human being's subterranean self*; a subject-picture with a background as tempestuous, as fuliginous as some of Tintoret's, treated with the imperturbable ease of a Velasquez. The three stanzas of *Lara* are the very triumph of *beat*: in each line, the Byronic statement falls with the curt cadence of a straight, infallible hammer-stroke; and the beat here is applied to the most complex subject-matter which, by

[1]It is worth recording that only stanza XVII appears in the first version; stanza XVIII was written on a separate sheet belonging to the Murray MS; stanza XIX also on a separate sheet, but this was inserted in the original MS. As E. H. Coleridge observes in his definitive edition of the Poems, stanzas XVIII and XIX were probably composed after finishing the first version. Interesting, even important for the Byronic psychology as *Lara* is (though like all the rest secondary in this respect to the incomparable *Manfred*), these stanzas so pre-eminently stand out that there is a satisfaction for the mind in the knowledge that two of them came to Byron 'of themselves', were dictated to him after the event by an impulse of that genius for auto-expression which we admire so much in him. Moreover, Byron afterwards knew what he had done—afterwards, as is the way with all such feats of auto-expression, and only afterwards; for if there is any intention *beforehand*, or even any consciousness *at the time*, these things are apt to turn out not feats but failures. In one of Lady Byron's Narratives of which *Astarte* gives us the essential passages, the Narrative of March 1817, this is how Byron speaks of *Lara*: 'One of the conversations he then held with me turned upon the subject of his poems, and—tacitly between us—of their allusions to himself. He said of *Lara*: "There's more in that than any of them", shuddering and avoiding my eye. I said it had a stronger mysterious effect than any of them, and was like the darkness in which one fears to behold spectres. The remark struck him as accidentally more characteristic than he thought I could know it to be—at least I presume so from his singular commendation of it with the usual mysterious manner. He often said that *Lara* was the most metaphysical of his works' (*Astarte*, 20-21). If we except *Manfred* (which had not then been written) the saying is profoundly true. *Lara* is pervaded through and through by that metaphysical atmosphere for which there is no better definition than the *metaphysic of the sub-soil*, where we come upon the roots, the 'Mothers' of the inmost self.

54

its certainty of stroke, it liberates. Here Byron has said the final word about himself; and though these *Lara* stanzas splendidly give the lie to the distinction I drew on an earlier page between the genius for expression and the introspective genius, I am too deeply indebted to them not to rejoice in being thus confuted. Still, even here I am inclined to attribute the feat less to introspective genius, properly so called, than to the most magnificent eruption that ever burst from the heart of the Byronic volcano. I remember that on the day when very tardily (it was in April, 1924) I discovered them, I was torn between two extremely discrepant feelings—that of the futility of taking Byron as a theme when he had done so himself, and that of the impossibility of getting away from him, precisely because he *had*.

*　　*　　*

At the point we have reached, it is necessary to isolate the line:

'His Madness was not of the head, but heart'. [1]

For the moment has come when we must face and examine that disjunction of head and heart which in Byron played so essential a part. And let us make no mistake—the head in this case is the sanest, the soundest of heads: its lucidity, indeed its equilibrium, of judgment was never impaired, not even amid the cloud-wrack that Byron conjured, piled up, insistently wrapped round himself. Meredith says of one of his heroines: 'She could make for herself a quiet centre in the heart of the whirlwind, but the whirlwind was required'. For Byron too the whirlwind was required; but perhaps chiefly because in him there always was at its core, invulnerable, a centre which I do not call 'quiet' but immovable—a centre which was lucid, too lucid, that of the unperturbed intellect,

---

[1] At the post-mortem examination it was found that the sutures were completely obliterated—a condition usually associated with old age. There were also observable (though the official document is silent on the subject) some symptoms of ossification of the heart—'the madness of the heart', Lady Byron comments in one of her memoranda (*Astarte*, p. 19).

for ever probing deep, if I may so express it, into the bowels of nothingness. And it is with intention that I venture on this apparently contradictory metaphor; for when Byron probes them, expresses them, it seems that negatives themselves take on a positive quality.[1] Byron is the most positive of human beings, and this quality in his nature has a very strangely contagious effect. Whatever he touches, happens to touch—for in him there is no deliberate design whatever, but on the contrary a lordly negligence—at once exists for us, and inexplicably matters to us. That is the clue to the prestige of his private journals, which are almost entirely concerned with facts, most of them in themselves trivial; but they have been touched by the wand of a species of Midas whose peculiar privilege it is to endow all things with import, with significance. And that is why B. Berenson was so right in applying to Byron Napoleon's words to Goethe: 'M. Goethe, you are a man'. Words which in Goethe's case do not by any means satisfy me; for after all, though Goethe *was* a man, he was a great many other things as well; but for Byron I think the phrase covers the ground. For Byron was that, and possibly no more than that; and he was that in precisely the way that a beech-tree is a beech-tree—self-sufficing, deeply-rooted, standing erect, unshaken; like the tree, he leaves nothing to be desired, seems by his presence to fill, and more than fill, the given measure of his species.

Head sane and sound, yes; heart mad—so Byron tells us. But to begin with, *was* there a heart? Perhaps the Byron case

[1]This is my third encounter with this idea of the positiveness of negatives; but in the two earlier instances, those of Flaubert and Hardy, the question was essentially of negative states as disintegrated, as liquid as can be, reaching a positive crystallization through their intensity alone. With Byron, on the contrary, it is always with facts that one has to deal, everything, in him, is of its nature positive, including the states themselves and not excepting those which in others unmake the individual man. Every Byronic state is put before us with the density, mass, and volume of an object.

offers no more subtle, no more baffling consideration than that one. We must not forget the words of the woman who was, unhappily for her, in the best position to know him—the words of his wife, Lady Byron: 'His character is a labyrinth; but no clue would ever find the way to his _heart_'.[1] At all events, Lady Byron—accomplished, irreproachable, in every respect a superior being—never found that clue. Was it even ever in the possession of Augusta herself, the Astarte of _Manfred?_ And above all, supposing it was, would she ever have possessed it if she had not been the half-sister, if—all-potent for Byron—the philtre of incest had not been at work? That question will have to be answered later on; but one thing is certain—Byron's heart was 'mad' in so far as that, when women were concerned, it could not function apart from anomaly. When the conditions were normal, Byron's heart stopped dead; I mean to say that it never went out to women, that he was never drawn to them by a spontaneous impulse, by what the hackneyed but extremely apt expression calls 'a leap of the heart' (_élan du coeur_). Let us understand each other. In more than one circumstance of his life, for instance in the Lady Frances Webster episode, or later in his behaviour to the Countess Guiccioli, Byron performs, often not without courage and always to the detriment of his own preferences, what we might call the rites of the heart; yet he performs them by virtue of the survival in him of a code of honour, and even of chivalrous honour, but a quite objective code, into the observance of which there enters at the time no personal sentiment whatever. At such moments it is precisely because he does not feel that Byron acquits himself, and wants to acquit himself; for with women he was sometimes capable of generous actions which counterbalanced and (even more important to him) redeemed in his own eyes the absence of feeling; sometimes again, as in the case of Claire Clairmont, he was equally capable of a radical, an indefensible harshness; and too often, as we saw a few pages back, of a

[1] _Astarte_, p. 10.—The sentence was written by Lady Byron about 1817.

brutal tactlessness. It is true that with men he was different, but for that there is more than one reason. For in his relations with men, remote from all anomalies, Byron is quite unsophisticated; in friendship his heart functions normally, though like all his other feelings, his friendships were at the mercy of moods and his native moroseness; on the whole, however, there are no complications here.[1] In Byron's life men-friends stood for ease, relaxation, and a sense of security; that is why they alone—Hobhouse and Moore pre-eminently, but also Hodgson, Douglas Kinnaird, John Murray, and the man about town, Scrope Davies—saw what we must call the 'good chap', the Byron who laid down, and enjoyed laying down, the glittering but somewhat oppressive panoply of the Fatal Being. 'The Man's Man': so Ethel Colburn Mayne entitles one of her chapters; and Byron, who maintained that he was the martyr of women, *was* a man's man—I do not mean fundamentally, in the turbid and concentrated zone where his genius found its food, but in his potentialities for, if not happiness at any rate enjoyment, sense of high spirits. In this chapter Ethel Colburn Mayne, commenting on an anecdote of Moore's, makes some very illuminating remarks on that aspect of Byron:

[1] I let this sentence stand, but the few following pages are those which appear to me the most open to question since the publication by Maurois of these two notes of Hobhouse's: 'Regarding Lord Grey, Hobhouse writes on the margin of a letter of Moore's: "And a circumstance occurred during this intimacy which certainly had much effect on his future morals" '.—'On Byron's friendships at Harrow, Hobhouse notes: "M. knows nothing or will tell nothing of the principal cause of all these boyish friendships".' (Maurois, *Byron*, English edition, p. 443). If a shade less reticent than Hobhouse, in his narrative of the episodes relating to Eddleston, to Nicolo Giraud and to Loukas, Maurois' *esprit de finesse* shows itself faithful to the saying of Vauvenargues: '*La finesse emploie des termes qui laissent beaucoup à deviner*'. Yet if Byron was what we call to-day a bi-sexual, if he remained so after schooltime and even until the end, the fact will have to be taken account of, for it is impossible that it should not bear upon his psychology as a whole: it is just conceivable that, when debarred from and even cured of the incest, the bi-sexual element afforded some solace to his nature: anyhow, the fact would show to what a degree Byron was essentially the outlaw. But this theme may be handed over to future workers in the field.

'In the diary for 1813 Byron records a criticism made by Mme de Staël. "She told Lewis ... that I was affected, in the first place; and that in the next place, I committed the heinous offence of sitting at dinner with my *eyes* shut, or half-shut. I wonder if I really have this trick. I must cure myself of it, if true. One insensibly acquires awkward habits, which should be broken in time. If this is one, I wish I had been told of it before". Thus we see that an apparent affectation of a peculiarly irritating kind was quite unconscious. The truth is, I think, that the Byronic poise suffered from an excess of the qualities of both poises and poses. It was at once too sincere and too effective. Precisely as Byron looked, he felt—alone in a crowd; but then self-consciousness arrived to show him how sublime he appeared in this betrayal of his feeling, and thenceforth, though sincerity survived, it was sincerity under the limelight—hardly, like a good actor in a similar plight, to be recognised for the thing it was'.

' "Nothing", says Moore, "could be more amusing and delightful than the contrast which his manners afterwards when we were alone, presented to his proud reserve in the brilliant circle we had just left. It was like the bursting gaiety of a boy let loose from school, and seemed as if there was no extent of fun or tricks of which he was not capable. Finding him thus invariably lively when we were together, I often rallied him on the gloomy tone of his poetry, as assumed; but his constant answer was (and I soon ceased to doubt of its truth) that, though thus merry and full of laughter with those he liked, he was, at heart, one of the most melancholy wretches in existence".[1]

Here—as so often happens with complex human nature— Byron, Moore, and Ethel Colburn Mayne are all three right. The Byronic basis is, in very truth, that inborn melancholy, due perhaps to a heart (if I may so express myself) essentially static, which could not feel its own pulsations unless they were accelerated to fever-point. Now, if on the one hand it

[1] *Byron*, Ethel Colburn Mayne, p. 193.

seems that Byron could not obtain that acceleration in his
love-affairs unless he felt and imagined himself to be outside
the law, on the other he was 'merry and full of laughter with
those he liked' precisely because friendship was in him a
normal sentiment, sane and sound, stopping short of passion
in the strict sense of the word—the sentiment which alone, in
my view at least, raises friendship between man and man to
an emotional category, and that a category by itself, wholly
differentiated, subject to its own laws. (For, even in the sphere
of friendship, between men and women the problem assumes
other forms, and connotes many more complications). I recognize that my view of friendship thus conceived and defined, sins (or more precisely, may seem to sin) by excess of
sobriety; but I am persuaded, and this is what most concerns
us here, that such was Byron's own view. And in such friendship the principal part is played by what I might call *the
heart of the brain*—which, I hasten to add, does not by any
means signify a lack of the emotional elements in that heart.
Everything springs from, is sustained by, the emotional elements—sentiments of friendship as well as all the rest; only,
in friendship, those elements attain to clear consciousness,
group and rank themselves into valid motives for caring, are
able to render account to themselves, not indeed of the
original impulse, too remote and too mysterious, but of the
legitimacy of this impulse, its constant justification in and by
the facts. Here enters in that kind of pragmatism which is the
stuff of all friendship, in which its history is registered, and
which ensures its duration. Whence friendship predisposes
to actions in favour of its objects—actions which are at once
spontaneous and the fruit of reflection, but in which the
emotion itself tends ever to increase the part played by reflection; actions considered, weighed, objective, one might even
say dispassionate, so much does the idea of efficiency—of
efficiency for the sake of others—dominate all the rest. To do
service—assuredly I should not go so far as to say that this is
the whole of friendship; but it forms a guarantee, in the sense

that Ramón Fernandez gives to the word when speaking of sentiments; and it is also the healthy element, the sign that other elements have not insinuated themselves under the guise of friendship. Friendship renders service; passion serves itself.

Byron knew how to be a friend in this sense; and knew all the better because, without cherishing illusions on that point any more than on any others, he was careful not to leave out of his reckoning the irreducible minimum of complacency and unconscious self-seeking which lurks at the bottom of most services rendered. 'It has lately been in my power to make two persons (and their connections) comfortable, *pro tempore*, and one happy, *ex tempore*—I rejoice in the last particularly, as it is an excellent man. I wish there had been more inconvenience and less gratification to my self-love in it, for then there had been more merit. We are all selfish—and I believe, ye gods of Epicurus! I believe in Rochefoucault about men, and in Lucretius . . . about yourselves'.[1] Significant words! It was because Hodgson was an excellent man that Byron was particularly glad to have been able to do him a service; in friendship, both our objective judgments and our judgments of value come into play. What I have ventured to call 'the heart of the brain' is as sane, as sound in Byron as the brain itself.

But does this give us the right to assume the existence in him of a heart in the strict, the normal sense of the word? I am not sure; and if I am not—but I recognize this to be a personal view, perhaps a hazardous one, on which adepts in passionate friendship will be justified in frowning—it is because for my part I do not believe that the kind of friendship I have attempted to define can be a quite infallible index to the existence of a heart in normal human beings. Precisely because normal friendship seems to me to stop short, and rightly to stop short, of passion, it does not give us any certain indication of what is to be found in the ultimate regions of the being in question; and if Byron turned into a 'good chap',

[1] *Letters and Journals*, ii. p. 325.

merry and full of laughter with those he liked, it was because, feeling about them as he did, they were never allowed to penetrate to the zone where the innate melancholy of which he spoke was immovably seated.

And yet I grant that I am but partly right; for if in masculine friendships the Byron of maturity came, and that pretty quickly, to the quite normal standpoint, he did not begin there; on the contrary, he began with the passionate type of friendship, and his own words supply the indispensable corrective. I allude to Fragment 91 of the *Detached Thoughts* (the Ravenna Journal):

'My school friendships were with *me passions* (for I was always violent), but I do not know that there is one which has endured (to be sure some have been cut short by death) till now. That with Lord Clare began one of the earliest and lasted longest, being only interrupted by distance, that I know of. I never hear the word '*Clare*' without a beating of the heart even *now*, and I write it with the feelings of 1803-4-5-*ad infinitum*.'[1]

The importance of this passage cannot be discounted; but on the other hand we must not forget that the passionate character of school friendships is itself an eminently normal fact—normal to banality—and all the more to be expected in those violent Byronic natures which will eventually find another outlet for their violence, and then assuage themselves all the more in the zone of their first passions. This once stated, there can be no doubt that among masculine friendships Byron's passionate feeling for Lord Clare is of a quite exceptional order; and as, besides, it has a poetic quality and beauty, and reveals a certain background and certain resources very rarely encountered in the Byronic sensibility, I here transcribe two relevant passages. The first, dated at Pisa on November 5, 1821, comes from the *Detached Thoughts*; it is Fragment 113:

'There is a strange coincidence sometimes in the "little

[1] *Letters and Journals*, v. p. 455.

things of this world, Sancho", says Sterne in a letter (if I mistake not), and so I have often found it. On page 128, article 91, of this collection of scattered things, I had alluded to my friend Lord Clare in terms such as my feelings suggested. About a week or two afterwards, I met him on the road between Imola and Bologna, after not having met him for seven or eight years. He was abroad in 1814, and came home just as I set out in 1816.

'This meeting annihilated for a moment all the years between the present time and the days of *Harrow*. It was a new and inexplicable feeling, like rising from the grave, to me. Clare, too, was much agitated—more in appearance than even myself; for I could feel his heart beat to his fingers' ends, unless, indeed, it was the pulse of my own that made me think so. He told me that I should find a note from him, left at Bologna. I did. We were obliged to part for our different journeys—he for Rome, I for Pisa; but with the promise to meet again in Spring. We were but five minutes together, and in the public road; but I hardly recollect an hour of my existence which could be weighed against them. He had heard that I was coming on, and had left his letter for me at B., because the people with whom he was travelling could not wait longer.

'Of all I have ever known, he has always been the least altered in everything from the excellent qualities and kind affections which attached me to him so strongly at school. I should hardly have thought it possible for Society (or the world as it is called) to leave a being with so little of the leaven of bad passions. I do not speak from personal experience alone, but from all I have ever heard from others during absence and distance.'[1]

The Countess Guiccioli is our second witness, when telling of a visit paid to Byron by Lord Clare in 1822, at Leghorn:

'Lord Clare's visit also occasioned him great delight. He had a great affection for Lord Clare, and was very happy dur-

[1] *Letters and Journals*, v. pp. 462-463.

ing the short visit he paid him at Leghorn. The day on which they separated was a melancholy one for Lord Byron. "I have a presentiment that I shall never see him more", he said, and his eyes filled with tears. The same melancholy came over him during the first weeks that succeeded to Lord Clare's departure, whenever his conversation happened to fall upon his friend'.[1]

But the proof that this passionate friendship was of quite an exceptional order in Byron lies in another passage, where Byron himself puts Clare apart from all the rest of his experience; and since this reveals the central truth, as regards friendship, about the Byron of maturity, it is well to give it here. The letter in question happens to have much to excite our curiosity, for in the first place it bears no date, and in the second we cannot be quite sure to whom it was addressed, though everything leads us to suppose that this was Mary Shelley. If so, the fact is obviously of importance, and perhaps my readers, like myself, will long oscillate between the desire, wholly inspired by human pity, that Shelley's widow should not have had to read these lines, and an obscure, substantial, if somewhat perverse sort of satisfaction, that Byron's individuality could assert itself to the point of presuming so to write to her.

'As to friendship, it is a propensity in which my genius is very limited. I do not know the *male* human being, except Lord Clare, the friend of my infancy, for whom I feel anything that deserves the name. All my others are men-of-the-world friendships. I did not even feel it for Shelley, however much I admired and esteemed him; so that you see not even vanity could bribe me into it, for, of all men, Shelley thought highest of my talents—and perhaps of my disposition.

'I will do my duty by my intimates, upon the principle of

[1] *Letters and Journals*, vi. p. 112. I may add that one of Byron's last letters (March 31, 1824) is addressed to Clare, and contains these words: 'I hope you do not forget that I always regard you as my dearest friend, and love you as when we were Harrow boys together; and if I do not repeat this so often as I ought, it is that I may not tire you with what you so well know'.

doing as you would be done by. I have done so, I trust, in most instances. I may be pleased with their conversation—rejoice in their success, be glad to do them service, or to receive their counsel and assistance in return. But as for friends and friendship, I have (as I already said) named the only remaining male for whom I feel anything of the kind, excepting, perhaps, Thomas Moore. I have had, and may have still, a thousand friends, as they are called, in *life* who are like one's partners in the waltz of this world—not much remembered when the ball is over, though very pleasant for the time. Habit, business, and companionship in pleasure or in pain, are links of a similar kind, and the same faith in politics is another.'[1]

If space permitted, my comments on that text would run the risk of becoming inexhaustible. We need not dwell on the lordly, the much too lordly, unsuitability of his writing those lines to Shelley's widow; rather let us pity—for indeed we must—pity Byron for having been able to enjoy the intimacy of the most adorable of men without adoring him, without even loving him; and we may pity him too for the fact that such an incredible deficiency cannot but figure henceforward in our judgment of him. To tell the truth, his adverse balance seems to me here so heavy that I am reluctant to leave him in so bad a position; and to restore the equilibrium in some degree, I must cite the admirable tribute which Byron wrote to Murray, a month after this same Shelley's death: 'You were all brutally mistaken about Shelley, who was without exception the *best* and least selfish man I ever knew. I never knew one that was not a beast by comparison'. Observe—this time to Byron's advantage—that, as is often the case with him, his first reaction had sounded the true, full note that the event always wrings from those who in any form or measure have the sense of what constitutes greatness—in spite of themselves, and their own limitations and pettinesses; but afterwards, when the first shock is over, these limitations and

[1] *Letters and Journals,* vi. p. 175.

pettinesses reassert themselves, take their former place, adhere like barnacles, and we then have no right to discount them, if it is true that everyone is to be judged by what he is at ordinary times, and not by his exceptional moments.

This parenthesis is long, but my parentheses are always long when Shelley comes into them. Anyhow, in this series of abrupt smiting statements, so cumulative in effect, Byron's own words give us the ultimate truth about his mature view of friendship; we can have no further doubts concerning his sentiments for the male sex. True, his school-friendships were passions—and that is why Harrow and everything connected with those years is always idealized in memory by Byron, and keeps to the end a poetic quality; but with the single exception of Lord Clare, they gradually faded out, and could offer no further nourishment to the most violent of violent natures.

Remained the women; and assuredly—as we shall see—they never were less chary of themselves; but we must not forget that, present though they were, they had to do with a creature whose heart, on the one hand, never went out to them, and who, on the other hand, needed them, could not do without them, as 'partners'—not in 'the waltz of this world' (men played that part with Byron), but in the conflict with the perpetual renewal, springing from the sub-soil of his nature, of that sense, that as it were solid sense of the nothingness of all things to which I referred just now. Until Augusta, until the incest, in Byron's life, women are, essentially, the indispensable distraction, but distraction is here to be understood in the deep sense that Pascal gives to the French word *divertissement*. And that distraction was rarely, almost never, a thing for which Byron had to go in search—it came to him from every side. There is here an inversion of the usual rôles which I certainly do not put forth as unique, for after all Byron is not the only man who has been courted by women;

but I do not think that in any other case this has been so conspicuous, so general, the attraction so irresistible and so sudden.

It is the suddenness which makes it so impressive, akin to some grand natural phenomenon, inevitable as weather conditions. 'I awoke one morning and found myself famous.' Who does not know the phrase, illustrious as Byron himself? The morning was that of March 10, 1812, when the first two cantos of *Childe Harold* made their appearance. Byron was just twenty-four. We shall resolutely ignore these first two cantos: the lines that are so full of sublime conviction—quoted at the head of a previous chapter—belong to Canto IV, which dates from the exile and was written at Venice in 1817. Besides, as I said in my opening chapter, Byron's work concerns us here—and, as I think, matters to us—only as a function of his personality, in so far as that utters itself with the power, the authority, of which I have spoken. Now in the two first cantos of *Harold*, and indeed in all the works anterior to the incest (say until the middle of 1813),[1] it happens that Byron falls short of his real powers. The treatment is ineffective, two-dimensional, lacking in the plastic depth which only an experience lived and realized to the full can supply. And though the first *Harold* must interest those literary historians who elect to study the *Zeitgeist*, the intellectual, emotional, and social currents which traversed and penetrated the age, together with the marks of their influence on the poem, this lack is the reason why, not only for the artist but for anyone who aims at reaching an ultimate conclusion on Byron's psychology, those two cantos are relatively of little importance. We all know, only too well, that for these instantaneous triumphs, these fulminating rapes of public opinion (of which the first *Harold* is a typical example), it is almost never the quality of the work, but the accident of time, which is accountable; in such the factors of

[1]Except the letters. In that line Byron was so great that from the first he is completely himself in his letters.

form and expression are well-nigh negligible; the necessary condition is to be, at the given moment, in possession of that soul which awakes the echo because fundamentally it is itself an echo—of that soul which made Henri de Latouche say of George Sand: 'C'est un écho qui double la voix'. Now that echo-soul was in the supreme degree possessed by Byron, though he—and it is the beauty of his case—did not know that he possessed it. When he gave the public the first Childe Harold, he gave it in total ignorance of the sort of effect it might make. In fact, it was his friends who wrested it from him; he himself would rather have published his Hints from Horace, of which the sub-title was: 'An Allusion in English verse to Horace's Ars Poetica, conceived as a sequel to English Bards and Scotch Reviewers'—the retort he had made to those who had attacked his first juvenile collection of verses, Hours of Idleness. Byron's inclination would have led him to pursue this satirical, epigrammatic vein, which was to reappear at the close of his life, then transposed into his masterpiece, Don Juan; for at heart Byron detested the 'new poetry', the very poetry which he incarnated, could not but incarnate for his contemporaries. All his tastes tended to the classical in the limited, almost the conventional, sense of the word. Neither Shelley nor Keats nor Wordsworth nor Coleridge could in his eyes be compared with a Horace or a Pope; and, as concerns Childe Harold, he yielded to his friends' urgencies only because they assured him that he could publish Hints from Horace immediately afterwards, which is enough to show that he had still to attain, not only to his true means of expression, but to that pregnant sense of fatality which was peculiarly his.

But everything was altered on the 10th of March, 1812, when Byron woke up and found himself famous; and the problem then was to know when and how he should be able to sleep again. Truth to tell, it did not too greatly absorb him. We have seen that in the deeper, the almost meta-physical, sense of the word, Byron was the sleepless being;

and there is another sense, not so deep, and in no way metaphysical, in which this applies to him. Let me recall Toulet's exquisitely worded saying: 'L'homme cherche des conseils le plus loin, les femmes le plus près possible. Et la métaphysicienne est encore à découvrir'. Byron had no objection whatever to keeping vigil in feminine company, and, where he was concerned, women were vigilance itself; moreover, the triumph of *Childe Harold* made him for a time the idol of English society—that English society which, four years later, in one of those formidable attacks of cant to which it is subject, and which are the more pronounced when they constitute reactions, was to condemn him as unanimously, as irresistibly, as it had enthroned him. . . . And with that triumph, the quality and rank of his feminine companions underwent a drastic change. We left Byron in convulsive despair, caused by vexation at the marriages of the two Marys, Mary Duff and Mary Chaworth; but these were the last victories to be registered by women—the hour for reprisals had struck. Reprisals, it is true, at first paltry enough, so paltry that his lordship was obliged, in *Harold*, to dress them up a little. Describing in the opening stanzas the abode of the Fatal Being, that Childe with whom it is impossible not to identify him, he depicts it as a monastic dome condemned to uses vile, and adds:

'Where superstition once had made her den,
Now Paphian girls were known to sing and smile'.

Effective; in the circumstances perhaps even too effective, for if the religious Paphos of antiquity was a den of prostitution, it was of a prostitution sumptuous and almost sacred, as is evident by the magnificent temple there erected by the Greeks, wherein the chariot of Venus was displayed. The Byronic reality was devoid of all sacred character, and took place on a plane sensibly more modest. The monastic dome was indeed the quite authentic Newstead Abbey; but the Paphian girls with whom the youthful Byron and his guests consorted were merely, we are told, the women-servants.

If we except the few somewhat commonplace affairs which marked the two years of his Eastern trip (1809-11)—affairs moreover earlier in date than the so-called Paphian epoch, but in fact of less importance—Byron, by virtue of the *Childe Harold* triumph, passed from his women-servants to Lady Caroline Lamb. Here both the quality and the rank of his feminine partner were altogether of another order. And his lordship leaped into the saddle with the dazzling mastery which was his in exploits of the kind; but I do not propose at once to emulate him—in the first place because the Caroline episode is too fine in itself to be relegated to the end of a chapter; and in the second, and still more cogently, because it is fitting for those less expert in such glittering feats of horsemanship to leave a decent interval for oblivion of the rather too rustic nymphs of Newstead Abbey, before introducing the most distraught, most pathetic of Byron's victims.

CHAPTER IV

'All her errors hurt only herself.'

THE more one reflects on the fate of Caroline Lamb, the more one inclines to see in those words the final truth about her. And they were said, or rather written, by her husband in an obituary notice in the *Literary Gazette*, a few days after she had died in his arms at the end of January, 1828. I know few things more honourable, not only to the husband and wife but to the married state itself, few which give a better idea of its inexhaustible resources, its reserves of pardon.

But indeed no one ever was able to feel any real animosity towards Caroline Lamb—no one, that is, except Byron, who never forgave a woman's insistence, and could always and instantly find himself in possession of an impeccable sense of the proprieties when oblivion of them did not coincide with his good pleasure. There again he shows himself to be the Man's Man, in the sense that has been defined—one who cannot do without women, of course, but who resents the fact, and for that very reason does not forgive them if at the right moment they cannot contrive to do without *him*. As with all men for whom women are merely a *divertissement* (even when, as with him, it is in the deeper, the Pascalian sense of the word), and love, as in the well-known definition, is 'the exchange of two whims and the contact of two epiderms', feminine insistence was for him the unpardonable crime. And doubtless in a woman the most exquisite of attributes is reserve even in the embrace of passion—we have only to remember *La Princesse de Clèves*, and nearer to our own day, in a register less inaccessible, the heroine of *Le Bal du Comte d'Orgel*. But passion, after all, does not necessarily foster reserve : and if a Byron sometimes, when it suits him, can heartily admire that virtue in others, and even (in this respect very sincerely) value it

71

much as a horse-breeder values the points of a thoroughbred, on the other hand he often displays, confronted with passion, such irritable impatience as almost amounts to scorn. Not for the sheer animal promptings, the short-lived explosions of temperament which we have seen that he appreciated in the Venetian women of the people (and I doubt not that, in that kind, certain aristocratic Englishwomen gave him similar satisfactions); but for the passion which sways the whole being, and above all for an enduring passion. In virtue of an anomaly explicable by the fact that, shrewd judge of character though he was, Byron was essentially—to repeat Ethel Colburn Mayne's consummate phrase—'an immovable nature', he who, where himself was concerned, had in such a degree the sense and the need of fatality, was never able to believe in the fatality of others, above all in the fatality of love. He did not believe in feminine passion; and the less because, though directed by undeviating instinct, it is often accompanied by a whole network of puerile and excessive manifestations which Byron's massive sense of nothingness (as I have called it) very soon stripped bare for him—with the result that being healthily averse from the manifestations themselves, he mistook the nature and intention of the impulse behind them, sometimes 'on purpose', but, as I think, much more often inevitably.[1]

Now, if Lady Caroline was puerile and excessive in all her manifestations, she was none the less a genuinely passionate woman, and wholly straightforward in her obedience to instinct. In the somewhat restricted company—much more restricted than is commonly supposed—of genuinely passionate

[1] And yet there was a day when, concerning Lady Caroline, Byron had seen the truth, and that to the point of formulating it once for all. In a letter, undated but probably of April, 1812, when their intimacy began, he wrote to her: 'Every word you utter, every line you write, proves you to be either *sincere* or a *fool*. Now as I know you are not the one, I must believe you the other' (*Letters and Journals*, ii. p. 116). Only, as too often happens when a person who oppresses and bores one will not let one alone, Byron lost sight of the truth he had perceived; he ceased to believe in it—'sincere' was dropped, only 'a fool' remained, and a fool who, in his eyes, was unfortunately not Augusta.

women she takes her place by lawful right; and it would be an even higher one were it not for the something a little deliberate, a little too wilfully picturesque, too airily graceful, not entirely unaware of its effect, which makes her—to borrow an image from her favourite disguise—the page of a very real but slightly frivolous fatality.

When Lady Caroline Ponsonby (as she then was) was married at twenty to William Lamb, there was among her men-friends a more than usual degree of the general mourning attendant on the nuptials of an exceptionally brilliant girl; and one of them wrote to his mother: 'I cannot fancy Lady Caroline married. I cannot be glad of it. How changed she must be —the delicate Ariel, the little Fairy Queen, become a wife and soon perhaps a mother! She is under the laws of a Man. It is the first death of a woman. They must die twice, for I am sure all their friends, their male friends at least, receive a pang when they change character so completely'. To which his mother, seeking to reassure him, at once replied: 'You may retract all your sorrow about Caroline Ponsonby's marriage, for she is the same wild, delicate, odd, delightful person, unlike everything'. Her training and education had been at first entirely neglected: we are told that at ten she could not even read; but when at fifteen she began to learn, she showed exceptional eagerness and talent. Modern languages were not enough for her; she mastered Latin and Greek, and one of her later triumphs was the recitation of that Ode of Sappho which she was so sadly to realize in her own person. All this was accompanied by a certain preciosity, so entirely unpedantic as to be the very grace of the state—she is, indeed, an admirable example of the difference between preciosity and pedantry, and the more because she has every mark of the blue-stocking without the slightest trace of studiousness; in that as in everything else, including life itself (which took so cruel a revenge on her), essentially the improvisatrice. Like all girls of her age, she kept a diary; and the egotism of which she cannot be absolved, since everyone who knew her agrees in saying that she could hardly ever talk of anything but herself, led her to make a list on the first page of the pet-names she had been given: 'Sprite, Squirrel, Fairy-Queen', and that one adapted from her courtesy-title, 'Her Lavishship'. But hers was a disarming egotism, the guileless egotism of exuberance, of youth intoxicated by its own vitality; and the pet-names seem to set before us the tiny, ardent, slender creature with her 'fawnflaxen hair shot with gold', her great dark eyes, and low caressing voice. When William Lamb—he who, long after Caroline's death, was to become that Lord Melbourne, adored Prime Minister of the youthful Queen Victoria, of whom Lytton Strachey has given us an unforgettable portrait—first proposed to her, she refused him and afterwards told us why: 'I knew I was a fury, and I would not marry him'. Like everything she said, this remark gives the whole of her, and moreover prefigures her inevitable destiny. William Lamb, who did not inherit the title until some years later, on the death of his elder brother Peniston, was then only a young barrister with no great prospects, as it seemed; and so that he might have no doubt of her entire attachment, Caroline, though she refused to marry him, offered to go with him anywhere as his clerk, thus anticipating the 'page' who was so frequently to invade the rooms of Byron, just as the proposal 'to go anywhere' anticipates those which she so often made to him. But when William Lamb's offer was renewed in 1805, she did accept it; she was then nineteen-and-a-half, and he twenty-six.

Till 1812 the marriage was a happy one, though there were storms—but they were those violent storms, followed by radiant sunshine, which in the conjugal state are proof that love is not yet out of court. Then came the day of March, 1812, on which Byron woke up famous. In literary matters, as indeed in everything, Caroline was queen of the drawingrooms, and the poet Rogers took care to lend her one of the very early copies of *Childe Harold*.

She read it, instantly summoned Rogers, and said: 'I must see him—I am dying to see him!'

74

'He has a club-foot', said Rogers, 'and he bites his nails'.

'If he is as ugly as Aesop, I must see him!'

Two days later, at Lady Westmorland's, she did see him. Her hostess led her up to be introduced—a reversal of English custom which sufficiently shows the state of delirium then reached by the Byron Fever. But when on coming nearer to the god, she beheld 'all the women throwing up their heads at him', a swift revulsion seized her. She gazed at him an instant, then turned on her heel and walked away.

That night she wrote in her diary these wise words—which, like so many other wise words, are the surest forerunners of sentimental disaster, if it be true that sometimes love celebrates its own birth by a tribute to lucidity; the words I have already quoted: 'Mad, bad, and dangerous to know'.

Two days later she was calling at Holland House when Byron was announced. This time custom was observed; he was presented to her, and using one of the direct approaches of that perfectly spontaneous sincerity, which I have analysed, and which was one of his most irresistible effects, he said: 'This offer was made to you the other day—may I ask why you declined it?' We do not know what she replied; but it is only too probable that that evening the diary recorded the other saying: 'That beautiful pale face is my fate'.

Byron had at once asked permission to visit her, and next morning presented himself at Melbourne House, where the Lambs lived with their mother and mother-in-law, the amazing Lady Melbourne of whom we shall soon have to speak; but he found her with two friends of his who were also friends of hers—the poets Rogers and Moore. And here there is an incident which shows us that the most elegant society of the day, even in those circles where our blue-stocking exercised her graceful preciosity, did not flinch from calling things by their right names, employing—they too—that direct mode of speech so dear to Byron himself. Lady Caroline had just come in from her morning ride, and she tells us: 'I was on the sofa, filthy, heated. When Lord Byron was announced, I flew to

75

change my habit. When I came back, Rogers said: "Lord Byron, you are a lucky man. Here has Lady Caroline been sitting in all her dirt with us, but as soon as you were announced, she fled to make herself beautiful".'

But the *partie carrée* was not entirely to his lordship's taste; he asked Lady Caroline if he might not come to see her when she was alone, and by preference at dinner-time. She said he might, and 'for more than nine months afterwards he almost lived at Melbourne House'—where, moreover, as was his wont, he did away with all the established customs. The waltz had only just been introduced, and Melbourne House was the chosen centre of the dancing-set: from one day to another 'it was swept aside'. Where Byron had failed with Mary Chaworth, he instantly succeeded with Caroline Lamb.

One day in the early spring of 1812, before the season of flowers, Byron came in with a rose and a carnation in his fingers, and presenting them to Caroline, he said: 'Your Ladyship, I am told, likes all that is new and rare—for a moment'. The remark is invested with the Byronic magic—and might well be applied to himself, defining as it gracefully and concisely does his attitude towards, and his relations with, women; to it, moreover, Caroline's passion lends a poignancy for us, and it drove her to write a letter that is one more proof of how even passion revels—perhaps consoles itself beforehand—in that preciosity which then becomes one of the favourite ways of caressing the beloved. Here it is:

'The Rose Lord Byron gave Lady Caroline Lamb died in despight of every effort made to save it; probably from regret at its fallen Fortunes. Hume, at least, who is no great believer in most things, says that many more die of broken hearts than is supposed. When Lady Caroline returns from Brocket Hall, she will dispatch the *Cabinet Maker* to Lord Biron, with the Flower she wishes most of all others to resemble, as however deficient its beauty and even use, it has a noble and aspiring mind, and having once beheld in its full lustre the bright and unclouded sun that for one moment condescended to shine

76

upon it, never while it exists could it think any lower object worthy of its worship and Admiration. Yet the sunflower was punished for its temerity; but its fate is more to be envied than that of many less proud flowers. It is still permitted to gaze, though at the humblest distance, on him who is superior to every other, and though in this cold foggy atmosphere it meets no doubt with many disappointments, and though it never could, never will, have reason to boast of any peculiar mark of condescension or attention from the bright star to whom it pays constant homage, yet to behold it sometimes, to see it gazed at, to hear it admired, will repay all. She hopes, therefore, when brought by the little Page, it will be graciously received without any more Taunts and cuts about "Love of what is New". Lady Caroline does not plead guilty to this most unkind charge, at least no further than is laudable, for that which is rare and is distinguished and singular ought to be more prized and sought after than what is commonplace and disagreeable. How can the other accusation, of being easily pleased, agree with this? The very circumstance of seeking out that which is of high value shows at least a mind not readily satisfied. But to attempt excuses for faults would be impossible with Lady Caroline Lamb. They have so long been rooted in a soil suited to their growth that a far less penetrating eye than Lord Byron's might perceive them—even on the shortest acquaintance. There is not one, however, though long indulged, that shall not instantly be got rid of, if Lord Byron thinks it worth while to name them. The reproof and abuse of some, however severe and just, may be valued more than the easily gained encomiums of the rest of the world. . . . March 27th, 1812, *Good Friday*.[1]

[1]*Letters and Journals*, ii. pp. 446-447.—Better perhaps than any other instance we have, this letter shows how completely the usual parts were reversed when Byron was in question. A woman seldom writes in this way; while on the other hand, it is a perfect specimen of the language used by those masculine lovers who are much less concerned to succeed than to envelop, enwind with tender attentions, as it were spread wings over, the beloved.

77

Beneath the grace, here so self-indulgent, of her preciosity, nothing is more indicative of her genuine passion than the mention (in italics) of Good Friday at the close of a letter which from beginning to end is an act of the most profane idolization. In passionate love-affairs, it is infrequent enough for any man to escape idolizing the woman—except in Byron's case, for we must do him the justice to say that he never idolized anyone, and called even the indispensable Augusta a fool (how right he was!); but it is almost unexampled for a woman to escape idolizing a man—or it would be better to say that she feels an imperious, an almost irresistible desire so to do. When this kind of sacrilege is committed by a woman deeply in love, it is often the sign of a nature as sincerely religious as in that sphere it is completely astray. How many a feminine passion has an origin quite unknown to itself—that incurable human thirst by virtue of which, if God remains unfound, a mortal must be enthroned. And that mortal (whence the recurrent tragedy) must be *visible*, endowed with all the attributes, all the charms of actuality: moreover, to make things worse, and even irremediable, with women the imagination comes into play so swiftly that the intrinsic worth of the chosen object is of little consequence—of so little that sometimes their idolization is never more instantaneous and more exhaustive than when there is nothing to account for it. We need only remember the genius of *personality* possessed by Byron, all his visible and actual attributes, his unequalled prestige, to see that in the doomed Caroline, with her tendril-like ardour, we behold the victim of a fatality, not complex as was Byron's, but on the contrary most appealing in its simplicity.

'I grew to love him better than virtue, Religion—all prospects here. He broke my heart, and still I love him—witness the agony that I experienced at his death, and the tears your book has caused me.' These words come from the letter to Medwin in November, 1824—that cry, so overwhelming in its sincerity, which was wrung from Caroline on reading the original edition of the *Conversations with Lord Byron*, which

Medwin had just published. There Byron had spoken of her in terms both unjust and insulting, which seemed to have no other purpose than to dishonour her; and there too appeared, for the first time printed in all the atrocity and baseness of their revengeful hatred, the stanzas addressed to her by name and entitled *Remember Thee, Remember Thee*. On receiving her letter Medwin cancelled, in the second edition of a few months afterwards, every word that related to her. . . . Observe that Caroline, as women often do, shrank from admitting how soon she had lost her head about Byron: 'I *grew* to love him better than virtue, etc.'. In reality, as I think, the whole letter of March 27, 1812, shows that already she not only loved Byron 'more than Religion', but that he was himself her religion.

But, involved in a fatality akin to his own, what was Byron's reaction? It seems certain, both from the contemporary records and the study of the facts themselves, that at no time did he love Caroline. There is one fact, one only, which seems to contradict this assertion—the undated letter of August, 1812. But first let us examine the circumstances in which this was written. For some months there had been a liaison between Caroline and Byron[1]—wished for and almost insisted on by her, on Byron's part little more than endured, though it hardly seems to have encroached upon his liberty, for we are told that he was never faithful to her. But she conducted herself with so flagrant, so eloquent a disregard of Society's susceptible code that Society—all the stricter about forms because it so took its ease about acts—was scandalized. With their usual readiness, family and friends had at once intervened, and Byron had given his word that he would leave

[1] Of contemporary witnesses, Rogers seems to have been alone in always believing that their relations were platonic. Probably they were at first, and (for reasons we shall see) would have continued to be so, if it had depended on Byron only; but a passion like Caroline's, though in the early days it may ask no more (and especially as platonism is favourable to a lavish display of the tenderest sort of preciosity), is by its very nature incapable of stopping there.

London. He did leave town, but only for a few days; and no sooner was he back than, thanks to one of those concoctions which represent the favourite dainty of the world, the rumour was abroad that the lovers were on the eve of elopement. This was imparted to Lady Bessborough, Caroline's mother, and she—a slave to maternal duty—manifested her sentiments by breaking a blood-vessel. In this rupture Byron refused to believe (and indeed it was difficult for him, faced with Caroline's example, to believe in the reality of any kind of rupture) until he was convinced by the arrival of Caroline herself, who had come to tell him on the one hand that the news was true and that therefore they must part; and on the other, to implore him to fly with her. He refused, escorted her back to Melbourne House; and it was on that very night that he is supposed to have written her the letter in question[1]: 'My dearest Caroline,—If tears which you saw and know I am not apt to shed,—if the agitation in which I parted from you,— agitation which you must have perceived through the *whole* of this most *nervous* affair, did not commence until the moment of leaving you approached,—if all I have said and done, and am still but too ready to say and do, have not sufficiently proved what my real feelings are, and must ever be towards you, my love, I have no other proof to offer. God knows, I wish you happy, and when I quit you, or rather you, from a sense of duty to your husband and mother, quit me, you shall acknowledge the truth of what I again promise and vow, that no other in word or deed, shall ever hold the place in my affections, which is, and shall be, most sacred to you, until I am nothing. I never knew till *that moment* the *madness* of my dearest and most beloved friend; I cannot express myself; this is no time for words, but I shall have a pride, a melancholy pleasure, in suffering what you yourself can scarcely conceive,

[1]My account of the facts was based on Ethel Colburn Mayne (*Byron*, 2nd edition, revised, p. 158).—Maurois has since had access to documents which enabled him to give us the exact bearing and sequence of the events (*Byron*, English edition, pp. 158-159); but in both cases the result is the same and does not affect the interpretation.

for you do not know me. I am about to go out with a heavy heart, because my appearing this evening will stop any absurd story which the event of the day might give rise to. Do you think *now* I am *cold* and *stern* and *artful*? Will even others think so? Will your *mother* even—that mother to whom we must indeed sacrifice more, much more on my part than she shall ever know or can imagine? "Promise not to love you!" ah, Caroline, it is past promising. But I shall attribute all concessions to the proper motive, and never cease to feel all that you have already witnessed, and more than can ever be known but to my own heart,—perhaps to yours. May God protect, forgive and bless you. Ever and ever, and even more than ever, your most attached   Byron.

'P.S.—These taunts which have driven you to this, my dearest Caroline, were it not for your mother and the kindness of your connections, is there anything on earth or heaven that would have made me so happy as to have made you mine long ago? and not less *now* than *then*, but *more* than ever at this time. You know I would with pleasure give up all here and all beyond the grave for you, and in refraining from this, must my motives be misunderstood? I care not who knows this, what use is made of it—it is to *you* and to *you* only that they are *yourself* [*sic*]. I was and am yours freely and most entirely, to obey, to honour, love—and fly with you when, where, and how yourself *might* and *may* determine.'[1]

I say 'is supposed to have written', because the letter is not only so contradictory of Byron's whole attitude towards Caroline, but so unlike any other he ever wrote, that Ethel Colburn Mayne has put forth the hypothesis that it may not have been written by him, but by Caroline herself. In a searching analysis she shows that if the language is the antipodes of Byron's language, on the other hand the letter represents Caroline's very dream of what she would have wished him to write; and she justly adds that if Caroline had really received it, had been in possession of so plain and unconditional an

---

[1] *Letters and Journals*, ii. pp. 135-139.

offer to 'fly with her', it is highly improbable that she, being what we know her to have been, would have consented to be taken to Ireland by her family—she would instantly have fled with Byron. The hypothesis gains strength from the fact that in January, 1813, Caroline did forge a letter in Byron's name to Murray, so skilfully that she obtained possession of his miniature. Thus it has every plausibility; nevertheless I remain persuaded that Byron really wrote the letter. Even when we do not love, the love felt for us by another, and throbbing visibly before us, will so penetrate us with its quality as to give birth to a not ignoble impulse of emulation, under the influence of which all insincerity is dissolved in an ardent desire to reciprocate. Moreover, it has already been said that the less his personal feelings were involved, the more Byron held himself bound to perform the rites of the heart; and as he had the most cogent reasons for refusing Caroline's proposition, as he was determined *not* to fly with her, he would be particularly desirous to acquit himself of those rites on this occasion, to give that ultimate pledge which he could not but have known would prove to be no pledge at all—since family, friends, and public opinion were leagued together against such a flight; and since a woman, even though she plead to be abducted, will hesitate at the last moment when she is aware that it is only from chivalrous obligation or (still worse) from pity that the man consents to be carried off.

Now, though she never would admit it, Caroline knew—in those flashes of lucidity when the dark night of throbbing passion is shot through by lightnings—knew in the uttermost depths of her being that Byron did not love her. Finally, and especially—and now we are back in Byron's personal atmosphere—in this letter the Byronic sincerity is not, as I think, to be questioned because the letter was wrung from him in one of those moments when, quite spontaneously, his feelings were stirred, written, expressed in the region of *myth*, not in that of reality. Caroline might be an object of complete indifference to him save in so far as that, by the passionate love she bore him, she was willingly or unwillingly enthralled to the Byronic fatality. For Byron, as I have already said, nothing was more powerful in effect; it transcended indifference, aversion, perhaps even hatred. Just as we saw with Mary Chaworth and *The Dream*, as we shall see with the central myth of Augusta, and that of Lady Byron herself, the enigmatic letter of August, 1812, symbolized Caroline's one *mythical* moment; and if we keep in mind that the more mythical a fellow-creature was, the nearer that creature approached Byron's mythical centre, the letter may be regarded as—if not a victory, at any rate a consolation prize for Caroline.[1] But when she fell short of that mythical region—and it was only once that she did not—not only did Byron not love her, but he had two very definite reasons for resenting her. The first (and we could wish it were not Byron himself who had revealed it, and still more that Caroline had not perceived it and felt constrained to make the humiliating avowal) is that she did not physically attract him.[2] Bad enough when love enters in; utterly unforgivable when it does not. The second reason is that passion deprived Caroline of all sense of the ridiculous; and though this is one of passion's noblest attributes, it is also one of its most exasperating for those who have to endure passion without in the smallest degree returning it. The result was that Byron was made ridiculous, and

[1]Maurois, in his *Byron*, does not allude to this letter because, still more definitely than Ethel Colburn Mayne, he regards it as a forgery, as emanating from Caroline herself. I admit that the tone of the letter is wholly in their favour, and that, hypothesis for hypothesis—for there can be no certainty in either case—mine is much the more hazardous. If nevertheless I let it stand, this is because in my view it accords with a deep-lying strain in Byron's nature, and, even if it was never translated into action, represents a Byronic *potentiality*.

[2]Her avowal was made in the letter to Medwin: 'As he and you justly observe, I had few personal attractions'; and elsewhere, in one of those piercing, ultimate perceptions which the very intensity of their sufferings wring from women, Caroline said that Byron was ashamed to be in love with her because she was not beautiful—'an expression', says Galt, 'at once curious and just, evincing a shrewd perception of the springs of his lordship's conduct'. This is where Byron's two grievances against her join hands—physical aversion and fear of ridicule.

Byron felt it: very likely this was the liveliest feeling that Caroline ever aroused in him; and thoroughly English in that as in so much else, there was almost nothing he could less bear than being made ridiculous.

Caroline had lost the game, and she must at the very least have divined this during the three months she spent in Ireland with her mother;[1] but what she did not foresee was the tone of the letter from Byron which awaited her at Dublin on the return journey to England. The skein is here so tangled that the best way to unravel it will be to produce the brief for the prosecution before making any comments.

Our sole text for this letter is Caroline's *Glenarvon*, the *roman à clef* which she could not resist publishing in May, 1816, a month after Byron had left England for an exile which proved to be final; but Byron himself acknowledged that the passages quoted by her had formed part of the letter actually sent. The date—November 9, 1812—as given in *Glenarvon* must very closely correspond with reality, for Byron spent October and November at Eywood with Lady Oxford, whose coronet and initials adorned the seal. He was at that time her lover—and also, for the occasion, her secretary, if it is true (as stated by our sole authority[2] on the subject) that Lady Oxford herself dictated the letter we are now to read: 'Mortanville Priory, November 9. Lady Avondale,—

---

[1] Three months, according to her own statement in the letter to Medwin; but it seems that in fact the 'three' were only one. 'The Bessboroughs', writes her cousin Harriet Leveson Gower, as Harriet Cavendish had become, from her house in Staffordshire on September 12, 1812, 'have been unpacked about a couple of hours. My aunt looks stout and well, but poor Caroline most terribly the contrary. She is worn to the bone, as pale as death, and her eyes starting out of her head. She seems indeed in a sad way, alternately in tearing spirits and in tears ... to see her poor careworn face is dismal. . . . She appears to me in a state very little short of insanity, and my aunt describes it as at times having been decidedly so . . .' (*Letters of Harriet, Countess Granville*, i. 40-41).

[2] The authority is a certain C. Lemon who in 1816, after *Glenarvon* had been published, wrote to Lady H. Frampton: 'This letter she really dictated to Lord Byron to send to Lady Caroline Lamb, and is now very much offended that she has treated the matter so lightly as to introduce it into her book' (*Journal of Mary Frampton*, p. 161).

84

I am no longer your lover; and since you oblige me to confess it, by this truly unfeminine persecution . . . learn that I am attached to another, whose name it would be dishonourable to mention. I shall ever remember with gratitude the many instances I have received of the predilection you have shown in my favour. I shall ever continue your friend, if your ladyship will permit me so to style myself; and, as a first proof of my regard, I offer you this advice; correct your vanity, which is ridiculous; exert your absurd caprices on others; and leave me in peace.—Your most obedient servant, Glenarvon.' A letter so insulting in its cruelty, so unqualifiable in every sense, that it at all events disqualifies Byron by depriving him of the prerogative to which the most modest of Englishmen invariably aspires—that of being a gentleman; while at the same time robbing him of the one advantage he might have had in the fact that certain 'persecutions' *are* 'truly unfeminine'; for no feminine persecution could possibly justify any man for daring so grossly to insult a woman—especially when only four months earlier he had assumed, and to such an extent, the chivalrous attitude.[1]

However we regard it, there is nothing to be said of this letter but that it is inexcusable, and remains one of the ineffaceable blots upon his lordship's scutcheon. That granted, it is not the least of Caroline's tragedies that at the very moment when we would fain unreservedly sympathize with her, we are nevertheless compelled to admit that, though he had no right to say it to her, though a gentleman would never have said it to anyone, Byron *had* some excuse for calling her persecutions truly unfeminine. We must not forget her own confession: 'I knew I was a fury'; and with Byron she oscillated incessantly between the parts of loving slave and raging tigress, consistent only in what least becomes a woman—in importunity.

[1]This of course on the assumption, which I still cling to, that the letter of August, 1812, is authentic; but even if Byron did not then assume, and to the utmost extent, the chivalrous attitude, the Glenarvon letter remains inexcusable on the ground of mere humanity.

In March, 1813, her state of health was so alarming that not only her mother-in-law, Lady Melbourne (who was so hostile towards her), but all concerned yielded to her entreaties and allowed her to have a final interview with Byron —at which, in view of her unaccountability and her revengeful feelings, it was thought indispensable that a third person should be present. The witness chosen by Byron—in all this incredible affair perhaps the most incredible circumstance— was Lady Oxford. But even the imperturbable Lady Melbourne found this too much for her, and reproached him for it, adding: 'Why did you not ask me? I would have left the room if she was calm'. Byron answered thus on March 14: 'My wish that Lady O. should be the third person was to save you a scene, and I confess also—odd as it may seem—that it would have been less awkward for me. You will wonder why —and I can't tell you more than that she might make some brilliant harangue to which Lady O. would be a less embarrassed listener than you could possibly be.'

I do not deny that in the conscious sphere the motives invoked by Byron may have played a part; but I am persuaded that on this occasion there was an element of the sub-conscious enjoyment in stirring up troubled waters which alone fed his emotional faculties, and that to confront Caroline with Lady Oxford promised him one of his favourite sensations. In the event he was denied it; for, less complex than he, taking her pleasures in a simpler spirit, Lady Oxford declined the suggestion. It seems, though there is no actual proof of this, that the projected interview between Byron and Caroline did take place, but not until May; if it did, Lady Melbourne seems to have been present, for on May 7 Byron wrote to her: 'You must be present; it will make you laugh, which will be some consolation'.

Since 1922, when the letters to Lady Melbourne were published, covering all the period from September 16, 1812, to November 13, 1814 (shortly before his wedding), we have been in possession of the final truth about Byron's sentiments, and can follow his life from day to day—or better (so great is here his genius for self-presentation) can feel that we are actually sharers in it. Taken in themselves, I consider the Letters to Lady Melbourne Byron's masterpiece; but besides, they are of inestimable value for our present zoological purpose, because by supplying the indispensable 'other side' to his idea of and need for fatality, they give us Byron's genius in the nude—I mean as pre-mythical, non-mythical, even anti-mythical. Now, though Byron is spontaneous and remains sincere even when fabricating the myth, in these letters we find a spontaneity and sincerity quite otherwise naked and radical; never has the sincerity of moods been carried further. With that headlong rapidity, that brutal brevity which are the very stuff of life, but which expression always aims at—and succeeds in—disguising, his sentiments are set forth with a far-ranging cynicism which I do not hesitate to describe as Shakespearean in quality. The truth is, indeed, that by virtue both of this and of the knowledge, no less final than serene, of human motives displayed in them, these letters are perhaps the nearest approach we can imagine to what certain letters of Shakespeare's may have been.

Now—though they cannot, I repeat, justify a proceeding which nothing could possibly justify—to study the facts is to be obliged to admit that Byron's line of conduct was almost inevitable, and that though he was responsible for his own share in the business, he was also in no negligible degree the instrument of Lady Caroline's family. When I say that, I am thinking particularly of Lady Melbourne. Though on occasions, when it was convenient to him, Byron made a great point of William Lamb ('Thou *false* to him, thou *fiend* to me'), and with his brutal tactlessness reproached Caroline for having deceived her husband, he was not so much troubled by that aspect of the affair as he would have us believe; and if he ostensibly regulated his proceedings with Caroline by consideration for the health of Lady Bessborough (whose absurdities were frequently the subject of his raillery), this was because, feeling as he did, the arrangement suited him very well; for did he not write to Lady Melbourne:

'Do you suppose that at my *time* of *life*, were I so very *far* gone, that I should not be in Ireland, or at least have followed into Wales, as it was hinted was *expected*. Now they have crossed the Channel, I feel anything but regret.'[1]

On the other hand, what Lady Melbourne thought was of great importance to him. At the end of November, 1813, he wrote in his diary:

'To Lady Melbourne I write with most pleasure—and her answers, so sensible, so *tactique*—I never met with half her talent. If she had been a few years younger, what a fool she would have made of me, had she thought it worth her while, —and I should have lost a valuable and most agreeable *friend*. Mem. a mistress never is nor can be a friend. While you agree, you are lovers; and, when it is over, anything but friends.'[2]

Here Byron takes a somewhat modest attitude, for as she was sixty-two, he twenty-four, she would have had to be more than 'a few years younger'. But, as Ethel Colburn Mayne has remarked, 'this is not the only instance of Byron's feeling the spell of a woman much older than himself'. She points out that Lady Oxford, the only one of his mistresses to whom he refers with gratitude, was nearly double his age at the time of their liaison. He said that the autumn of a beauty like hers was preferable to the spring in others; and Ethel Colburn Mayne pursues: 'Whatever may have been the truth of his intercourse with Lady Melbourne—by himself described in his diary as friendship, but to his wife as something very different indeed —there is no question that the magic she still possessed was potent for him as it had been for many other men. He wrote to her in a strain of enchanted admiration, well laced with his characteristic ribaldry, but unmistakably sounding the lover's note. Of course she enjoyed it; a woman who could write her delightful, mockingly tender letters, does not refuse herself that diversion, even at sixty-two. But in one of them

[1] *Corr.* i. p. 74.   [2] *Letters and Journals*, ii. p. 343.

she said:"I told you I would teach you friendship, and so I will". His diary of 1813 seems proof that she did, despite the obscene boastings he was afterwards (by some accounts) to make. They belong to the period of pseudo-insanity in 1815.'[1]

Ethel Colburn Mayne does not tell us what Byron said to Annabella during the period of pseudo-insanity; but it is easily imagined, and besides, whatever it was, addressed to his wife and at that time, I could give it no other credence than consists in seeing the truth to be the exact opposite of what he offered for belief. For the rest, I own that for once I am not in entire agreement with Ethel Colburn Mayne. When Lady Oxford resembled 'a landscape by Claude Lorrain', she was forty; and if for Byron 'the autumn of a beauty like hers' was 'preferable to the spring in others', I think we may be sure that spring would have regained all its attractions against the finest of winters—that of Lady Melbourne at sixty-two. I may add that, to my sense, Byron's letters to Lady Melbourne do not 'sound unmistakably the lover's note'; true, he enjoys paying court to her and is captivated by her cleverness, but she cannot have had much difficulty in teaching him friendship, for (as I see it) what he specially prized in his intercourse with her was the having at last encountered a woman with whom he could be wholly sincere, to whom he could tell everything; and, as the Journals splendidly testify, with Byron the sincerity of moods was the supreme sincerity. This is why I continue to hold that in the Letters to Lady Melbourne there is almost as little to be discounted as in the Journals, and in those there is nothing.

On her side Lady Melbourne, even with Byron's collaboration, would probably not have made a fool of herself: amorous follies were not much in the line of that discreet but finished disciple of the Marquise de Merteuil; but she would assuredly have had with him, not the most glorious (since she had been a Royal mistress), but the most congenial, of her numerous liaisons. They understood each other perfectly in

[1]*Life of Lady Byron*, pp. 46-47.

every way; Lady Melbourne was (as all their correspondence shows) the one human being by whom Byron not only allowed himself to be guided, but wished to be guided. Now in Lady Melbourne's eyes—apart from all family considerations, or rather bringing these to bear when the general and her own private peace were disturbed—Caroline was irredeemably in fault because she had not conformed to the rules of the game of love, had flaunted what ought to have been conducted in the serene and comfortable atmosphere of secrecy.

In the letter to Medwin of November, 1824, Caroline says, 'I went to Ireland, and stayed three months there. He wrote, every day, long kind entertaining letters'. No doubt he did—but what was his reason? Open the Melbourne Correspondence. The second of his letters to Lady Melbourne—written as soon as he felt sure that she was no less sincere than he in desiring that the rupture with Caroline should be final—that of September 13, 1812, nearly a month after Caroline's departure, contains this passage:

'Grant me but till December, and if I do not disenchant the Dulcinea and Don Quichotte, both, then I must attack the windmills, and leave the land in quest of adventures. In the meantime I must, and do write the greatest absurdities to keep her "gay", and the more so because the last epistle informed me that "eight guineas, a mail, and a packet could bring her to London", a threat which immediately called forth a letter worthy of the Grand Cyrus or the Duke of York, or any other hero of Madame Scudéry or Mrs Clarke.'[1]

This passage—and there are so many more of its kind in the Melbourne Correspondence from September to November, 1812, that one's difficulty is to choose; for Byron and Lady Melbourne were in this matter leagued together, and he kept her posted at every stage . . . this passage gives us the key not only to Byron's sentiments, but to the motives which were to culminate in the flagrant Glenarvon letter. For on the one hand there is nothing more contradictory, more impos-

[1]*Correspondence*, i. p. 74.

sible, than to try both to 'disenchant' a woman and to 'keep her gay'; and on the other, the boredom everyone feels when writing insincere letters could not but turn to exasperation in a creature endowed to the extent we have just seen Byron to be, with the most formidable kind of sincerity—that of moods. As we follow this period from day to day, as we feel Byron upheld by the support and complicity of Lady Melbourne, and are confronted with the incessant appeals and importunities of Caroline, we end—assuredly not by approving, but by understanding, the Glenarvon letter. And we understand it still better because we know that during Byron's stay with the Oxfords at Eywood, Caroline incessantly pestered not only him but Lady Oxford with frantic letters, and moreover that Lady Melbourne, in writing to Byron, was given to stressing the harm that Caroline might do him: 'if I know her, *vous n'en êtes pas quitte*'. (This feminine cruelty is aptly commented on by Maurois: 'It is only women who are ferocious in denouncing the lies of other women'.) Hence we must realize that Caroline, Lady Melbourne and Lady Oxford (who very likely did dictate it) are all responsible for the outburst represented by the Glenarvon letter. I am in complete agreement with Maurois' masterly analysis of the situation.[1]

But its actual effect was such that Caroline believed she might go mad.[2] She fainted. 'They bled me', she told Lady Morgan afterwards, 'and applied leeches, and I had to stay a week at the filthy *Dolphin* hotel, at Rock.' And yet so incurable was her passion that it was after this that the most distressing incidents took place—her importunity, against which nothing could prevail, in obtaining interviews with Byron, the

---

[1] In his *Byron*, English edition, pp. 166-168.

[2] She said to Lady Morgan that for a while it did deprive her of reason. However that may be, she was more than once on the borderland of insanity; it is very probable that this was so in December, 1812, when at Brocket Hall, surrounded by young village girls, whom she dressed in white, while she herself was attired as a page and recited some verses of her own, she burned Byron in effigy. And after Byron's departure from England, between 1816 and her death in 1828, she had more than once to be kept in seclusion.

forgery for the miniature, the letters threatening suicide, and finally the deplorable occasion when, lost to all dignity, shedding even the page's graceful disguise, she dressed up as a carman and penetrated to Byron's rooms, to find a woman with him.[1]

But we do not wish to see the last of her in such a situation. She shall speak for herself once more; let us recur to the letter to Medwin, and from that hurried panting cry (how many more than one!) of a passion so real in spite of all, let us listen to these final accents, as we look our last on Caroline Lamb:

'I was brought to England a mere wreck; and in due time, Lady Melbourne and my mother, being seriously alarmed for me, brought me to town and allowed me to see Lord Byron. Our meeting was not what he insinuates—he asked me to forgive him; he looked sorry for me; he cried. I adored him still, but I felt as passionless as the dead may feel.—Would I had died there!—I should have died pitied, and still loved by him, and with the sympathy of all. I even should have pardoned myself—so deeply had I suffered. But, unhappily, we continued occasionally to meet. Lord Byron liked others, I only him.—The scene at Lady Heathcote's is nearly true—he had made me swear I was never to waltz. Lady Heathcote said, "Come, Lady Caroline, you must begin", and I bitterly answered: "Oh, yes! I am in a merry humour". I did so—but

[1]To be quite fair to Byron, I must mention that the real reason for the hatred he felt for Caroline from the time of his exile was that he held her to be the originator of the rumours current in London about the incest. Augusta shared his view, and from that time the mere sight of Caroline caused her positive horror. It is certain—and given her character and the situation, it was almost inevitable—that at first Caroline was very imprudent in what she said; but it is not less certain that, once she realized the effect, she was equally eager to retract; and though in the nature of things, such retractations are almost invariably futile, and sometimes even make the matter worse, we have no right to doubt her good intentions. I allude to this fact only for the sake of an almost abstract desire to be fair, and I hasten to add that in this respect no one is less qualified to be severe than Byron was: for not only did he confide in several women about the incest, but in general conversation at fashionable parties he took an evident delight in introducing the subject, and maintaining the most audacious views on the relations between brothers and sisters.

whispered to Lord Byron, "I conclude I may waltz *now*", and he answered sarcastically, "With everybody in turn—you always did it better than anyone. I shall have a pleasure in seeing you".—I did so, you may judge with what feelings. After this, feeling ill, I went into a small inner room where supper was prepared; Lord Byron and Lady Rancliffe entered after; seeing me, he said, "I have been admiring your dexterity". I clasped a knife, not intending anything. " Do, my dear", he said. "But if you mean to act a Roman's part, mind which way you strike with your knife—be it at your own heart, not mine —you have struck there already." "Byron", I said, and ran away with the knife. I never stabbed myself. It is false. Lady Rancliffe and Tankerville screamed and said I would; people pulled to get it from me; I was terrified; my hand got cut, and the blood came over my gown. I know not what happened after—but this is the very truth. After this, long after, Lord Byron abused by every one, made the theme of every one's horror, yet pitied me enough to come and see me; and still, in spight of every one, William Lamb had the generosity to retain me. I never held my head up after—never could. It was in all the papers, and put not truly. It *is* true I burnt Lord Byron in Effigy, and his book, ring and chain. It *is* true I went to see him as a Carman, after all that! But it is also true that, the last time we parted for ever, as he pressed his lips on mine (it was in the Albany) he said, "poor Caro, if every one hates me, you, I see, will never change—No, not with ill usage!" and I said, "Yes, I *am* changed, and shall come near you no more".—For then he showed me letters and told me things I cannot repeat, and all my attachment went. This was our parting scene—well I remember it. It had an effect upon me not to be conceived—3 years I had *worshipped* him.'

* * *

On July 12, 1824, convalescent from the feverish attack (lasting two months) which the news of Byron's death had caused her, Caroline Lamb went out for her first drive in an

93

open carriage. Her husband preceded her on horseback, and on coming to the gate he encountered a funeral procession.

'Whose is it?' he asked.

'Lord Byron's', they told him.

The two carriages passed one another.

One can but recall the *Quarterly's* comment on Byron's behaviour on the day of his mother's funeral. Not Shakespeare himself could have conceived the circumstances in which, for the last time, those two fatalities passed one another.

CHAPTER V

'She resembled a landscape by Claude Lorrain, with a setting sun, her beauties enhanced by the knowledge that they were shedding their last dying beams, which threw a radiance round: the autumn of a beauty like hers is preferable to the spring in others.'

THUS, towards the end of his life, Byron described to Lady Blessington that Lady Oxford who is said to have dictated the Glenarvon letter; and it is certain that she is the only woman whom he remembered with—we can hardly say pure, but let us say unalloyed, pleasure; so much so that in another conversation with Lady Blessington it led him to commit one of those blunders to which even the most cultivated foreigners are liable when they use a proverbial expression, whose literal sense is quite clear to them but carries implications which on occasion make it impossible. I mean the following remarks: 'A woman is only grateful for her first and last conquests; the first of poor dear Lady Oxford's was achieved before I entered on this world of care; but the last, I do flatter myself, was reserved for me, and a *bonne bouche* it was'. Whence we may deduce that when one wishes to be precise about the pleasure a woman has afforded one, it is better not to make use of a foreign idiom. Anyhow, it was to be expected that, like all realists, Byron should have preferred the fruit to the flower, the flavour to the fragrance.

Lady Oxford was the daughter of a clergyman—a circumstance which, by virtue of that rhythmic reaction governing all things, perhaps predisposed her to what we shall see to have been a zealous and practical cult of the Lucretian gods. Further, she had been married from the schoolroom to the fifth Earl of Oxford—'sacrificed', said Byron, 'almost before she was a woman to one whose body and mind were equally contemptible in the scale of creation'; and she was the mother of several children (on the rhythmic principle) of whom

Byron said that they were 'perfect angels, and to whom the law gave Lord Oxford the right to be called father'. The law alone, for in *Astarte* Lord Lovelace tells us that these angelic children were called the Harleian Miscellany.

Proudly, as becomes the mention of a fact in itself exceptional, Byron informed Medwin that he had had an uninterrupted liaison of eight months with her. 'She told me that she was never in love until thirty; and I thought myself so with her when she was forty. I never felt a stronger passion, which she returned with equal ardour.' There is nothing here to contradict my assertion that Byron was averse from passion, for passion in this instance is to be taken in the most elementary physical sense—that which later made him say of the Venetian women of the people: 'I like these splendid animals'; and when the splendid animal was of the aristocratic English species, his sense of breeding and lineage was pleasantly affected. At the meridian of this mutual ardour, Lady Oxford one day said to Byron: 'Have we not passed our last month like the gods in Lucretius?' The allusion is to a passage in the first book of *De Rerum Natura* which, veiled in the terminology proper to the Epicurean Philosophy, seems in fact to refer—let me make use of Lucretius' own title—to 'the nature of things' in the most primitive of all possible acceptations. Quoting Lady Oxford's remark in the Journal of 1813, Byron adds: 'And so we had'. That he was really happy in this liaison is proved by his confession that he had great difficulty in breaking with her, even when he knew she was unfaithful to him—a confession which, as Ethel Colburn Mayne observes, does not chime with his declaration that he was the last of her conquests; but it does emphasize the value he attached to the liaison.

But as things turned out, it would have been better for everyone if Byron had continued to be Lady Oxford's lover and, as he long hoped to do, had accompanied her on her yachting trip to Sicily; for she left England on the 28th of June, 1813, and it is shortly after that date that, relying on

documents which admit of no refutation, Lord Lovelace in
Astarte places the beginning of Byron's incestuous intercourse
with his half-sister Augusta.

★   ★   ★

As we have seen, Augusta was four years older than Byron,
and the daughter of 'Mad Jack's' first marriage with that
Marchioness of Carmarthen whom he had run away with. Did
her mother die at her birth, or not until a year afterwards?
Witnesses disagree; but it is certain that until Augusta was
four years old she lived with her father and step-mother in
France, and that Mrs. Byron brought her back to England in
1788, on the return to London for Byron's birth. It was
doubtless for this reason that Mrs. Byron handed her over to
her maternal grandmother, Lady Holderness; and as Lady
Holderness, like most other people, would not have anything
to do with Mrs. Byron, Augusta was completely separated
from her father's family until her grandmother died in 1801.
After this event Mrs. Byron, wishing to renew their intercourse, wrote to Augusta (October 18, 1801) in these terms:

'As I wish to bury what is past in *oblivion*, I shall avoid all
reflections on a person now no more; my opinion of yourself I
have suspended for some years; the time is now arrived when
I shall form a very *decided* one. I take up my pen now, however, to condole with you on the melancholy event that has
happened, to offer you every consolation in my power, to assure you of the inalterable regard and friendship of myself and
son. We will be extremely happy if ever we can be of any service to you, now or at any future period. I take it upon me to
answer for him; although he knows so little of you, he often
mentions you to me in the most affectionate manner, indeed
the goodness of his heart and amiable disposition is such that
your being his sister, had he never seen you, would be a sufficient claim upon him and ensure you every attention in his
power to bestow.

'Ah, Augusta, need I assure you that you will ever be dear
to me as the Daughter of the man I tenderly loved, as the sister

of my beloved, my darling Boy, and I take God to witness you *once* was dear to me on your own account, and may be so *again*. I still recollect with a degree of horror the many *sleepless* nights, and days of *agony*, I have passed by your bedside drowned in tears, while you lay insensible and at the gates of death. Your recovery certainly was wonderful, and thank God I did my duty. These days you cannot remember, but I never will forget them. . . . Your brother is at Harrow School, and if you wish to see him, I have now no desire to keep you asunder.'[1]

Augusta, however, did not share the Byron abode; till her marriage in 1807 she lived with her mother's people; nevertheless from 1802 the brother and sister frequently met, and in 1804 began the correspondence from which I have given some extracts. In this, Augusta was Byron's confidante regarding the quarrels with his mother, and in January, 1805, there is a letter which proves that they were on intimate terms of affection, for Augusta wrote to Hanson, the family solicitor (Byron was then under age): 'You will not be surprised to hear that Byron *is a very great favourite of mine*, and I may add that the more I see of him, the more I *must* love and esteem him'.[2]

So Byron was fourteen when the normal relations of brother and sister began to be established between them. The date is not entirely negligible, for doubtless we must assign some importance to the fact that they had never known as children that daily companionship which, by the tissue of habits it weaves—I shall go so far as to say, by the element of healthy indifference latent in affections that are taken for granted—forms so natural an antidote to anomalous sentiments. When in the years of puberty the aspirations of the heart and the curiosity of the senses first take shape, finding, as they do, a special stimulation in the thrill of novelty, the charm of mystery, it is scarcely likely that they will crystallize round one who has always been at one's side. If as a child he

[1] *Letters and Journals*, i. pp. 18-19.   [2] *Letters and Journals*, i. p. 39.

had played with Augusta, he would probably never have felt for her anything more than the sentiment—in him, it is true, exceptionally strong—which he accorded to all who were linked with him, whether closely or remotely, by ties of blood, and whom he prized as a species of satellites.[1] In the normal circumstances of brother and sister, he would have felt for Augusta the esteem which belonged by right to Lord Byron's half-sister, but beyond that would have treated her with the salutary good-humoured derision induced by her 'foolishness'; while, coming as a girl of eighteen into the life of an adolescent four years younger, and with the familiarity conferred by her being his sister, Augusta did, at the very least, possess the attraction of novelty. But I hasten to add that I am envisaging this hypothesis in a spirit of almost abstract justice; a scrupulous desire to exhaust every conjecture is my sole reason for putting it forward—for whether it is or is not applicable to other cases, I am unalterably persuaded that it does not apply to Byron's, and that before June, 1813, not only was there no incestuous undercurrent, but no sentiment

[1] It is true that in *Astarte* Lord Lovelace tells us that Byron used to say: 'In our early days we were separated by Lady Holderness on account of some apparent impropriety'; but that is the kind of Byronic assertion which does nothing to convince me—for to pose as precocious, especially in the matter of incest, is what he was sure to do. Lord Lovelace also says: 'Byron recollected having asked his mother why he should not marry Augusta, the question being suggested by some *germana Jovis* in Roman history'; but, considering the sort of questions children ask, this seems to me of still smaller importance. I should be tempted to give more weight to this fragment from one of the many letters from Byron which Augusta destroyed—a fragment coinciding in date with *Manfred* (1816): 'When I was "gentle and juvenile—curly and gay", and was myself in love with a certain silly person—and who was she—can *you* guess?' (*Astarte*, p. 78). But even if Byron did at one time feel that kind of calf-love, he completely forgot it until June, 1813. He loved Augusta from the period of the incest, and essentially (as we shall see) because of the incest; he had never loved her *till then*.—Since this passage and its accompanying note were written, Ethel Colburn Mayne (*Life of Lady Byron*, p. 248) has informed us that Augusta told Annabella that from the time Byron was sixteen, he had been a source of misery to her 'on that account'. Ethel Colburn Mayne's admirable analysis of Augusta's feelings should be read very carefully: both Augusta's statement and the writer's comments supply the indispensable corrective to the view I have here proposed (Note of 1931).

other than is born of the most ordinary fraternal affection; and what makes this, in my opinion, certain is the tone of all Byron's letters to her before this date. Their relation was then so normal that it was with what I may perhaps call a cordial indifference, devoid even of the slight shock usually felt by a brother at the news of his sister's engagement, that Byron regarded Augusta's to Colonel George Leigh—who, following the family tradition, was her cousin-german. The marriage did not take place until 1807, but there must have been a long engagement, for it was on March 22, 1804, that Byron wrote thus: 'When you see my Cousin and future Brother George Leigh, tell him that I already consider him as my Friend, for whoever is beloved by you, my amiable Sister, will always be equally Dear to me'.[1]

But it seems that during the long engagement there were troubled periods, in which the precocious sceptic in matters of love that Byron was at sixteen spoke with the voice of reason, and a rather sardonic sort of reason:

'That you are unhappy, my dear Sister, makes me so also; were it in my power to relieve your sorrows you would soon recover your spirits; as it is, I sympathize better than you yourself expect. But really, after all (pardon me, my dear Sister), I feel a little inclined to laugh at you; for love, in my humble opinion, is utter nonsense, a mere jargon of compliments, romance and deceit; now, for my part, had I fifty mistresses, I should in the course of a fortnight, forget them all, and, if by any chance I ever recollected one, should laugh at it as a dream, and bless my stars for delivering me from the hands of the little mischievous Blind God. Can't you drive this Cousin of ours out of your pretty little head (for as to *hearts* I think they are out of the question).'[2]

As a letter-writer Byron is unmatched for precocity, but never more so than when love is the topic.

Once Augusta was married, Byron made use of Colonel Leigh in the interest of one of his military friends; but he did

[1] *Letters and Journals*, i. p. 21.   [2] *Letters and Journals*, i. p. 35.

not go so far as to court his brother-in-law's acquaintance for here is what he wrote to her on November 30, 1808:

'I saw Colonel Leigh at Brighton in July, where I should have been glad to have seen you; I only know your husband by sight, though I am acquainted with many of the Tenth. Indeed my relations are those whom I know the least, and in most instances, I am not very anxious to improve the acquaintance.'[1]

Colonel Leigh (by whom Augusta had no fewer than seven children) was a personal friend of the Prince Regent's, and as such in high favour at Court; and the one advantage he brought his wife was this connection with Royalty, and the privileges attaching to it—privileges which, more even than other peoples, English men and women prize so dearly, and which Byron thoroughly appreciated, for when alluding to his sister in letters he rarely fails to mention her distinctions in that kind. But excepting the seven children—and if there is an act which tells, which proves, precisely nothing, it is that of procreation—this access to Royalty was indeed the only benefit conferred by Colonel Leigh upon his wife. The testimony of all contemporary witnesses is striking enough, and these words of Lord Lovelace's complete the impression:

'She was abominably married to a first cousin—impracticable, helpless, tiresome and obstructive. She was more than anyone sensible how intolerable her husband was with his debts and selfishness, which had a large share in bringing on the ruin of the whole family. He was little with her, being generally at race-meetings or on long visits to Lord Darlington[2] and other reprobates, protectors and boon companions. When

---

[1]*Letters and Journals*, i. p. 203.

[2]Of this Lord Darlington, here is what the future Lady Byron's mother wrote in 1797: 'Lord D. plunges deeper and deeper in low Amours, and got into a terrible scrape at Dunbar when there with his Regiment—he went into the room of a Servant Girl at the Inn and attempted violence; the poor Girl threw herself out of the window and was so much hurt that She will be a cripple for life, this is one of many stories equally to his credit' (*Astarte*, p. 27).

Newmarket Races brought Colonel Leigh home, Mrs. Leigh went off on a holiday if she could. He was a trying and exacting inmate. Everything had to be done for him, not the least of which was his turfy correspondence. He was *quite* capable of acquiescing in her going away for any purpose, temporarily or otherwise.'[1]

In short, Colonel Leigh was a finished specimen of the husband who exists only to give trouble, and whose degree of existence varies in proportion to the degree of trouble he gives—in that respect, but only in that, it is true that Colonel Leigh often existed to excess.

Not only did Byron feel no particular desire to make his brother-in-law's acquaintance, but for nearly three years he quite forgot Augusta herself—she is absent from his correspondence from November 30, 1808 to August 21, 1811; and when they again exchanged letters, it was she who wrote first. Nor did Byron answer quickly; and when he did, the tone was conventional, manifestly inspired by a feeling of duty, so that the letter is most reassuringly a 'family' one:

'*My dear Sister*,—I ought to have answered your letter before, but when did I ever do any thing that I ought? I am losing my relatives and you are adding to the number of yours; but which is best, God knows;—besides poor Mrs. Byron, I have been deprived by death of two most particular friends within little more than a month; but as all observations on such subjects are superfluous and unavailing, I leave the dead to their rest, and return to the dull business of life, which however presents nothing very pleasant to me either in prospect or retrospection. I hear you have been increasing his Majesty's Subjects, which in these times of War and tribulation is really patriotic. Notwithstanding Malthus tells us that,

[1]*Astarte*, pp. 26-27. In a letter from the Hon. Mrs. Villiers, Augusta's intimate friend, to Lady Byron (May 18, 1816), written at the time when Mrs. Villiers feared that Augusta would flee to Byron in exile, this is what she says: 'He may propose to her to go abroad to him, she may think it a better alternative than starvation (believing the world ignorant) and Colonel Leigh is *quite capable* of acquiescing in it' (*Astarte*, p. 206).

were it not for Battle, Murder and Sudden Death, we should be overstocked, I think we have latterly had a redundance of these national benefits, and therefore I give you all credit for your matronly behaviour. I believe you know that for upwards of two years I have been rambling round the Archipelago, and am returned just in time to know that I might as well have staid away for any good I ever have done, or am likely to do at home, and so, as soon as I have somewhat *repaired* my *irreparable* affairs I shall een go abroad again, for I am heartily sick of your climate and everything it *rains* upon, always save and except *yourself* as in *duty bound*. I should be glad to see you here (as I think you have never seen the place) if you could make it convenient. . . . You say you have much to communicate to me, let us have it by all means, as I am utterly at a loss to guess; whatever it may be it will meet with due attention. . . . By the bye, *I* shall marry, if I can find anything inclined to barter money for rank within six months; after which I shall return to my friends the Turks. In the interim I am, dear Madam, [Signature cut out.]'[1]

Augusta replied on August 27 from Six Mile Bottom, her home at Newmarket:

'*My dearest Brother*,—Your letter was stupidly sent to Town to me on Sunday, from whence I arrived at home yesterday; consequently I have not received it as soon as I ought to have done. I feel so *very* happy to have the pleasure of hearing from you that I will not delay a moment answering it, altho' I am in all the delights of *unpacking*, and afraid of being too late for the Post.

'I have been a fortnight in Town, and went up on my *eldest* little girl's account. She had been very unwell for some time, and I could not feel happy till I had better advice than this neighbourhood affords. She is, thank Heaven! much better, and I hope in a fair way to be quite *herself* again. Mr. Davies flattered me by saying she was exactly the sort of child *you* would delight in. I am determined not to say another

[1]*Letters and Journals*, i. pp. 332-333.

word in her praise for fear you should accuse me of partiality and expect too much. The youngest (*little* Augusta) is just 6 months old, and has no particular merit at present but a very sweet placid temper.

'Oh! that I could immediately set out to Newstead and shew them to you. I can't tell you *half* the happiness it would give me to see it and *you*; but, my dearest B. it is a long journey and serious undertaking all things considered. Mr. Davies writes me word you promise to make him a visit by-and-bye; *pray do*, you can then so easily come here. I have set my heart upon it. Consider how very long it is since I have seen you. I have indeed *much* to tell you; but it is more easily *said* than *written*. Probably you have heard of many *changes* in our situation since you left England; in a *pecuniary* point of view it is materially altered for ye worse; perhaps in other respects better. Col. Leigh has been in Dorsetshire and Sussex during my stay in Town. I expect him at home towards the end of this week, and hope to make him acquainted with you ere long. I have not time to write half I have to say, for my letter must go; but I prefer writing in a hurry to not writing at all. You can't think how much I feel for your griefs and losses, or how much and constantly I have thought of you lately. I began a letter to you in town, but destroyed it, from the fear of appearing troublesome. There are times, I know, when one cannot write with any degree of comfort or satisfaction. I intend to do so again shortly, so I hope you won't think me a bore. . . . Your letter (some parts of it at least) made me laugh. I am so very glad to hear you have sufficiently overcome your prejudices against the *fair sex* to have determined upon marrying; but I shall be most anxious that my future *Belle Soeur* should have more attractions than merely money, though to be sure *that* is somewhat necessary. I have not another moment, dearest B., so forgive me if I write again very soon, and believe me,—Your most affectionate sister, A. L.

'Do write if you can.'[1]

[1]*Letters and Journals*, ii. pp. 10-11.

Let us not anticipate upon what that letter shows us regarding Augusta herself and her incomprehension, or rather (for, as we shall soon see, the act of comprehension was not her strong point: she nearly always fell short of that) her ignorance of Byron's real nature, an ignorance that was never dispelled by manifestations which would have enlightened anyone else. This time Byron answered at once, and we learn a good deal from his reply:

'Newstead Abbey, August 30th, 1811.

'*My Dear Augusta*,—The embarrassments you mention in your last letter I never heard of before, but that disease is epidemic in our family. Neither have I been apprised of any of the changes at which you hint, indeed how should I? On the borders of the Black Sea, we heard only of the Russians. So you have much to tell, and all will be novelty.

'I don't know what Scrope Davies meant by telling you I liked children, I abominate the sight of them so much that I have always had the greatest respect for the character of Herod. But, as my house here is large enough for us all, we should go on very well, and I need not tell you that I long to see *you*. I really do not perceive any thing so formidable in a Journey hither of two days, but all this comes of Matrimony, you have a Nurse and all the etcaeteras of a family. Well, I must marry to repair the ravages of myself and prodigal ancestry, but if I am ever so unfortunate as to be afflicted with an heir, instead of a *Rattle* he shall be provided with a *Gag*. . . . As you won't come, you will write; I long to hear all those unutterable things, being utterly unable to guess at any of them . . . I will now take leave of you in the Jargon of 1794. "Health and *Fraternity!*"—Yours alway, B.'[1]

But the same evening (for both letters are dated August 30th), urged by one of those second thoughts which in him alternate oddly between good and bad impulses—and, be it said to his honour, it was nearly always a good one when a practical, and especially a pecuniary, matter was in question

[1] *Letters and Journals*, ii. pp. 10-12.

—Byron, feeling perhaps that he had gone too far about the children and not far enough about anything else, wrote again:

'*My dear Augusta,*—I wrote to you yesterday, and as you will not be very sorry to hear from me again, considering our long separation, I shall fill up this sheet before I go to bed. I have heard something of a quarrel between your spouse and the Prince, I don't wish to pry into family secrets or to hear anything more of the matter, but I can't help regretting on your account that so long an intimacy should be dissolved at the very moment when your husband might have derived some advantage from his R.H.'s friendship. However, at all events, and in all Situations, you have a brother in me, and a *home* here.

'I am led into this train of thinking by a part of your letter which hints at pecuniary losses. I know how delicate one ought to be on such subjects, but you are probably the only being on Earth *now* interested in my welfare, certainly the only relative, and I should be very ungrateful if I did not feel the obligation. You must excuse my being a little cynical, knowing how my *temper* was tried in my Non-age; the manner in which I was brought up must necessarily have broken a meek Spirit, or rendered a fiery one ungovernable; the effect it has had on mine I need not state.

'However, buffeting with the World has brought me a little to reason, and two years' travel in distant and barbarous countries has accustomed me to bear privations, and consequently to laugh at many things which would have made me angry before. But I am wandering—in short I only want to assure you that I love you, and that you must not think I am indifferent, because I don't show my affection in the usual way.

'Pray can't you contrive to pay me a visit between this and Xmas? or shall I carry you down with me from Cambridge, supposing it practicable for me to come? You will do what you please, without our interfering with each other; the premises are so delightfully extensive that two people might live together without ever seeing, hearing or meeting,—but I can't feel the comfort of this until I marry. In short it would be the most amiable matrimonial mansion, and *that* is another great inducement to my plan—my wife and I shall be so happy,—one in each Wing. If this description won't make you come, I can't tell what will, you must please yourself. Good night, I have to walk half a mile to my Bed chamber. Yours ever,—Byron.'[1]

At this time they exchanged three more letters which on both sides are identical in tone—one from Augusta of August 31 to which Byron replied on September 2; then, on September 9, when he heard that she could not possibly come to Newstead before Christmas, he wrote to tell her that he would by that time have left the Abbey, and added: 'However, I shall endeavour to see you somewhere, and make my bow with decorum before I return to the Ottomans. I believe I shall turn Mussulman in the end'.[2]

So little was he destined to turn Mussulman that he was to die in the service of Greece after having fortified Missolonghi against those very people.

Probably he considered that, as he did not in the event leave England, the 'bow with decorum' could wait; at any rate Augusta vanishes completely from his correspondence, and apparently from his life, till March 26, 1813; and the letter written to her on that day is a reply to a request for money. In the definitive edition of the Letters, by an unintentional irony of arrangement the text is faced by a reproduction of Hoppner's very fine portrait of Lady Oxford, so velvety in treatment that it makes Byron's preference for the fruit still easier to understand. Just then, in fact, his liaison with her was ripening to the full.

'*My dearest Augusta*,—I did not answer your letter, because I could not answer as I wished, but expected that every week would bring me some tidings that might enable me to reply better than by apologies. But Claughton has not, will

[1] *Letters and Journals*, ii. pp. 13-14.   [2] *Letters and Journals*, ii. p. 31.

not, and, I think, cannot pay his money, and though, luckily, it was stipulated that he should never have possession till the whole was paid, the estate is still on my hands, and your brother consequently not less embarrassed than ever. This is the truth, and is all the excuse I can offer for inability, but not unwillingness, to serve you.

I am going abroad again in June, but should wish to see you before my departure. You have perhaps heard that I have been fooling away my time with different *"régnantes"*; but what better can be expected of me? I have but one *relative*, and her I never see. I have no connections to domesticate with, and for marriage I have neither the talent nor the inclination. I cannot fortune-hunt, nor afford to marry without a fortune. . . . I am thus wasting the best part of my life, daily repenting and never amending. On Sunday, I set off for a fortnight to Eywood, near Presteign, in Herefordshire—with the *Oxfords*. I see you put on a *demure* look at the name, which is very becoming and matronly in you; but you won't be sorry to hear that I am quite out of a more serious scrape with another singular personage which threatened me last year, and trouble enough I had to steer clear of it, I assure you. I hope all my nieces are well, and increasing in growth and number; but I wish you were not always buried in that bleak common near Newmarket. I am very well in health, but not happy, nor even comfortable; but I will not bore you with complaints. I am a fool, and deserve all the ills I have met, or may meet with, but nevertheless very *sensibly*, dearest Augusta, Your most affectionate brother, Byron.'[1]

Silence once more reigns until June 26, 1813, the opening date of the cardinal period. Before entering on the interpretation of the facts—a process second to none in complexity—I will set forth the two facts regarding which the publication of *Astarte* has removed all doubt: namely, that there was an incestuous relation, and that we have both Augusta's and Byron's avowals: Augusta having confessed the whole truth

[1] *Letters and Journals*, ii. pp. 196-199.

to Lady Byron in September, 1816, and Byron having spoken out—not only in *Manfred* which, though myth illuminated, casts its own flood of evidential light and is a triumph of what we must call the *veracious myth*; not only in the verses directly addressed to Augusta:

'I speak not—I trace not—I breathe not thy name',

verses which contain the most moving, most convincing, most persuasive accents of his sense and need of fatality; but also (and this time wholly uninfluenced by the poetic mood) in the letter written to her from Venice on May 17, 1819,[1]—a letter so revealing, so outspoken, and, fatalistically regarded, so beautiful in its radical sincerity. And the event took place between June 26 and July 15, 1813, for the daughter of Byron and Augusta, Medora Leigh, was born on April 15, 1814.[2]

In the eyes of all who are not, like Mr. Edgcumbe, wilfully blind, there has never been the slightest doubt of Byron's paternity, and since the publication of the Melbourne Correspondence we have Byron's own evidence. He wrote to Lady Melbourne on April 25, 1814: 'Oh! but it is "worth while", I can't tell you why, and it is *not* an "Ape",[3] and if it is, that must be my fault.' But these two certainties once stated, the process of interpretation begins, and here I must proceed step by step. The long series of documents which I have made a point of producing establishes, as I think, irrefutably the perfectly commonplace nature of the relations between this brother and sister until June, 1813. On his side, nothing be-

---

[1]*Astarte*, pp. 81-83.

[2]The essential facts concerning Medora Leigh had been given in Appendix III of Ethel Colburn Mayne's *Byron* (2nd edition); but since then the same writer has dealt exhaustively with the subject in Chapter XXIII of her *Life of Lady Byron*.

M. Roger de Vivie de Régie's *Le Secret de Byron* (Paris, Emile-Paul, 1927) supplies many facts concerning Medora's life in France and the fate of her children, from numerous documents belonging to the family-papers of the Waroquier de Puel Parlan.

[3]Ethel Colburn Mayne tells us that the phrase 'It is not an ape' is an evident allusion to the mediaeval idea that the child of incest must be a kind of monster (*Byron*, p. 453).—*Corr.* i. p. 125.

yond a sort of abstract sense (and even that, as we have seen,
sometimes on second thoughts) of what is due to her who has
the honour to be Lord Byron's only surviving near relative;
on hers, when one thinks of her customary effusiveness—
and that almost equally with everyone, so extraordinarily
muddled was her nature—the most moderate, as it were ritual,
flow of family affection. And now, when documents would be
most needed, they of course fail us well-nigh completely, so
that too often conjecture must take the place of proof.

At the beginning of June, Byron had made up his mind to
set out on a prolonged trip: he wrote on the 8th to Lady Melbourne: 'I shall now be but little in London, as I must see my
sister, etc., and it is not impossible I may embark finally without taking leave of you';[1] but on the 29th he told the same
correspondent that Lady Oxford had sailed the day before,[2]
and he adds: 'To tell you the truth, I feel more *Carolinish*
about her than I expected. They went at last so suddenly,
the day I was to have met her on the coast—all the fault of
my sister's arrival.' What had happened was that, thanks to
Colonel Leigh's progressive virtuosity in the art of getting
into debt, there had been a financial crisis at Six Mile Bottom
which rendered the situation untenable, and Augusta had
taken refuge with her brother in London for an indefinite
period. This caused Byron to abandon the Portsmouth farewells; but from that fact no conclusions can be drawn, for he
may very well have given up his plan in order to show Augusta
the consideration which we have seen that he held to be due

[1] *Corr*. i. p. 159.

[2] It had at first been arranged that Byron should accompany the Oxfords
on their yachting trip to Sicily, but we now know why that plan had had
to be abandoned: 'They were forming pleasant plans for travelling *à trois*
in Sicily when Lord Oxford, alarmed by an absurd family, took it into his
head—as always happens—to grow jealous of Lord Byron just when the
latter himself had the strongest reasons for jealousy. His wife had taken
instant steps to calm the senile storm by reassuring lies, but it was decided
that she should leave for the Mediterranean alone with her husband, and,
as Byron wrote, that they would 'live happy ever after' (Maurois, *Byron*,
English edition, p. 171). So it was not the cruise, but what I later call 'the
Portsmouth farewells', which Augusta's arrival caused Byron to renounce.

to her. At any rate, the remark in his second letter to Lady Melbourne, 'It is all the fault of my sister's arrival', seems to point that way. When he laid such stress upon the 'Carolinish' sentiments inspired by Lady Oxford's departure, was Byron falling short of the absolute sincerity with which he honoured Lady Melbourne? We shall answer that question according to the degree of awareness or unawareness that we impute to him regarding that which, at this very moment, was preparing itself within the depths of his being; and it is here especially that conjecture has to take the place of proof. We do, it is true, possess notes from Byron to Augusta, dated June 26 and 27, where the tone modulates, in a singularly revealing manner, to something quite different from what we have been accustomed to till now: 'June 26, 1813. My dearest Augusta,—Let me know when you arrive, and when and where and how you would like to see me—anywhere in short but at *dinner*. I have put off going into ye country on purpose to *waylay* you. Ever yours, Bn.'[1]—'June, 1813 [the letter has no more precise date, but from the context it follows immediately upon the first one]: My dearest Augusta,—And if you knew *whom* I had put off besides my journey—you would think me grown strangely fraternal. However, I won't overwhelm you with *my own praises*. Between one and two be it—I shall, in course, prefer seeing you all to myself without the incumbrance of third persons, even of *your* (for I won't own the relationship) fair cousin of *eleven page* memory, who, by-the-bye, makes one of the finest busts I have seen in the exhibition or out of it. Good night! Ever yours, Byron.

'P.S.—Your writing has grown like my attorney's, and gave me a qualm, till I found the remedy in your signature.'[2]— 'Sunday, June 27th, 1813. My dearest Augusta,—If you like to go with me to ye Lady Davy's to-night, I *have* an invitation for you. There you will see the *Staël*, some people whom you know, and *me* whom you do *not* know, and you can talk to

---

[1]*Letters and Journals*, ii. p. 225.   [2]*Letters and Journals*, ii. p. 226.

which you please, and I will watch over you as if you were un-married and in danger of always being so. Now do as you like; but if you chuse to array yourself before or after half-past ten I will call for you. I think our being together before 3d persons will be a new *sensation* for *us both*.'[1]

These three notes form an arresting sequence; and yet the special and almost insurmountable difficulty in interpreting them is born of the fact that it is now well-nigh impossible for us to read them otherwise than in the light of what followed. 'Strangely fraternal'—that clearly strikes the note of incest, but strikes it perhaps too clearly in our ears, may here mean no more than the Byronic trick of always gibing at himself when he was doing something intrinsically meritorious. But it is above all in the phrase, 'I think that to be together before third persons will be a novel *sensation* for *us both*', that one feels the very heart of the mystery to lie. I have asked my-self over and over again—I sometimes ask myself still—what it covers, what significance we should properly attach to it. Whether written *before* or *after* the incest, in both cases equally the phrase is so intimately the one that would have come to Byron that hesitation is thereby increased. At first, abounding in the sense peculiar to Byron, but possibly going too far in that direction, I was ready to see in it the proof that incest was even then an accomplished fact. To-day I am in-clined to believe[2] that though it forms the most amazing of indications—let us even say, illuminations—this is, on the contrary, because it is a *prefiguration*, because it comes from the deepest-lying zone of the subconscious, from that wherein potentialities, things that are yet to be, have their quivering existence. It is not a record—it is a pointer, but so much so

[1]*Letters and Journals*, ii. p. 227.

[2]Perhaps we may also see some symptomatic value in the words: 'and *me* whom you do *not* know', if we remember that in the only letter (it is true a contested one) written under emotional stress to Caroline Lamb, Byron uses the same expression: 'for you do not know me'. It seems that with Byron both the sense of his individuality and the desire to make others aware of it are the sign of a stirring within him of obscure emotions then beginning to make themselves felt.

that its effect is that of an announcement. It signifies little though the message it bore was not yet transmitted so that Byron could decipher it; in the subterranean regions of his being, which are here the essential ones, the germ of incest had been deposited.[1]

This is what I imagine the curve of events to have been. Byron, at first obedient only to a sense of duty, resigns his 'week-end' and awaits his sister in London; but at any rate she is to know that he has been so kind, and the sacrifice is to have its natural outcome in an immediate meeting:—the first of the three notes. Augusta fixes the day in a reply which unfortunately we do not possess, for, with a very few exceptions, all her letters to Byron have been destroyed—some by herself, others by her descendants. . . . Except for the signature, her letter is difficult to read; whence a flash of impatience of the kind which, when it takes place, is sometimes a stimulant

[1] In the order of facts, what inclines me to think as I do, and to adhere to my interpretation, is first and foremost the question of dates. For the phrase to come after the incest, it would have to have been written on the same day—that is to say, the day on which Byron first saw Augusta again. Master of realism though he was, we can scarcely suppose that matters were brought so quickly to a point; and it is later on, in a letter of July 8 to Thomas Moore, that we find the following words: 'The Oxfords have sailed almost a fortnight, and my sister is in town, which is a great comfort—for, never having been much together, we are naturally more attached to each other' (*Letters and Journals*, ii. pp. 229-230). Now we have seen that, after Lord Clare, Thomas Moore was the only member of the male sex for whom Byron confessed that he felt real friendship; and, after Lady Melbourne, the correspondent with whom he was always at his sincerest. If the incest had taken place, I am persuaded that in a letter to Moore Byron would not have thus expressed himself, but would have said nothing about his sister. When at the beginning of this chapter I advanced the general hypothesis (but added that I did not think it applicable to Byron's case) that the lack of daily companionship might have had some influence on the nature of the future relations between brother and sister, I had forgotten these words to Moore. They are a rather curious confirmation and reinforcement of the hypothesis itself; and I now perceive in them a not unimportant signpost, for they possibly mark the final moments of a fugitive phase—that of innocence at its zenith. The two have divined their mutual attachment, the discovery intoxicates them; but already the spell which is to prove all-powerful is at work, and it is between the 8th and 15th of July, 1813, that we may most probably place the incest.

to curiosity, or at any rate electrifies the atmosphere. Byron lays stress on his good behaviour, his sacrifice: that it is not merely a pleasant visit, but a certain person, that he has given up for Augusta's sake, and if Augusta knew *who she was*, would she not think he had grown strangely fraternal—but as he writes that 'strangely', we can guess that he is very far from wondering how it will strike Augusta; we feel as though witnessing the sub-conscious reaction that overtakes him as he writes. That is the second note. He sees her on June 27 between one and two—for though the second note bears no date, it fully justifies the conjecture that the meeting took place that day.[1] Let us bear in mind that in all probability (for no document informs us) they had not seen one another since 1808; so that it was the moment when Augusta was invested with that attribute of novelty which, when joined with the familiarity of a sister, I have said to be so inducive of false sentiment in normal relations—and this attribute was exercised upon a Byron who, in the same five years, had been shown only too clearly that his power over women was unlimited, and who (by reason of the inversion of rôles that we have analysed) had been implored by women themselves to make use of it. Well, he sees her, and she attracts him—attracts him physically. To borrow the expression that he was, ten months later, to use in the letter to Lady Melbourne where he spoke of his child, she is 'the sort of woman' he 'prefers', and 'has never got before'.[2] We must remember that he never forgave Caroline her want of physical attraction for him; and remember too that, as concerns Lady Oxford, he

[1] We now know that 'Byron received her in his Bennet Street apartments, in the early afternoon of June 27, 1813' (Maurois, *Byron*, English edition, p. 172).

[2] "You must however allow that it is absolutely impossible I can ever be half so well liked elsewhere, and I have been all my life trying to make someone love me, and never got the sort that I preferred before' (*Correspondence*, i. p. 251). The passage is instructive in more than one respect: first, because Byron there acknowledges that all his life he has been trying to make himself loved; and then because he avows that, until with Augusta, he has never got the sort he prefers; which on the one hand—since nothing is more annoying than to receive from one undesired the

had just been shown by her that even fruits have their infidelities. And here he was, in presence of a woman who was not only a novelty, but 'the sort he preferred', and with whom he enjoyed the privileges of a brother—a brother whom all women idolized; moreover, she was 'abominably married', a prey to the worst kind of material anxieties, this sister who had taken refuge with him as her sole protector; he not only could be, but was bound to be, both her support and her escort in society . . . was not this indeed a situation to stir the depths of the Byronic sub-consciousness?

But we must not any longer intrude on this first tête-à-tête; rather let us picture Byron to ourselves after Augusta had left him that day. What is he doing this evening? Why, to be sure, he is going to Lady Davy's—it will be the usual sort of party . . . suppose he takes Augusta? To escort and chaperone her there will be an amusing change. We do not know whether the sub-conscious had been so beforehand with its task as to have already secured an invitation for her; anyhow, nothing is easier than to get one—and Byron sits down to write the third note, and as he writes it the sub-conscious pursues, accelerates its work . . . so well that in his concluding words, where past, present, and future combine into a single indivisible projection, by one of those acts of the imagination which, in the sphere of emotion, are so often the veritable acts, the incest is accomplished:—'I think that to be together before third persons will be a novel *sensation* for *us both*.'

When the act of imagination has been accomplished, the material act can take its time; it may even indulge in the

very thing that *is* desired—explains his aversion for Caroline's passion, and on the other proves that Augusta did physically attract him.

Despite appearances, I do not think that there is any real contradiction between Byron's confession: 'I have been all my life trying to make some one love me', and the view put forward by me that Byron was not a deliberate seducer; for the seducer *in spite of himself* is much more likely to try, half-unconsciously, half-consciously, to make himself loved; to the deliberate seducer what matters is, not so much being loved, as getting what he wants.

luxury of a little postponement, well knowing that its day will come. We need not question the sincerity of the letter of June 29 to Lady Melbourne; nothing could be less surprising than that Lady Oxford's departure should leave Byron in a 'Carolinish' mood. We know that at the moment when, like a bird forsaking the nest, a feeling detaches itself from us, we pay it the tribute of a self-pitying dejection. For the time being Byron is in a state of desuetude, but he devotes himself wholly to Augusta, and very soon he perceives that he is no longer in that state; they mutually discover their attachment—this is the hour marked by the words to Moore: in that discovery, for a moment, the unconscious lets them delight, then, precipitating the pace, it flings them into one another's arms.

Now this conjunction was of such a nature that, for a Byron, once it had taken place, it could not but become, and never cease to be, irresistible. For though with Lady Oxford he had known the fulness of sensual accord, what he experiences with Augusta is a deepening,[1] and especially an incalculable aggravation, of that accord, from the mere fact that its origin was incestuous. We are here at the core of the central Byronic theme. As yet—it will be relevant later—the word

[1]That with Augusta this sensual accord went deep in a sense quite different from that of even Lady Oxford's 'autumn', is sufficiently proved by the verses, themselves so sincere and quick with genuine emotion, composed for Lady Oxford:

> Thou art not false, but thou art fickle,
>   To those thyself so fondly sought;
> The tears that thou hast forced to trickle
>   Are doubly bitter from that thought:
> 'Tis this which breaks the heart thou grievest,
> *Too well* thou lov'st—*too soon* thou leavest.
>
> The wholly false the *heart* despises,
>   And spurns deceiver and deceit;
> But she who not a thought disguises,
>   Whose love is as sincere as sweet—
> When *she* can change who loved so truly,
> It *feels* what mine has *felt* so newly.

Contrast these with the panting accents of those lines to Augusta which

love may be held in reserve: Byron loved Augusta, but (by virtue of another essential trait, to be touched on at the close) it was especially in absence, after she was lost—in every sense of the word—and for that very reason. To speak quite precisely, he began to love her truly on the day before he left England, during that poignant evening spent alone with her, when at last he was visited by remorse, when at last his tears flowed. But at the point we have reached—the beginning of their incestuous intercourse—what he loved irresistibly was the unique sensation given him by the incest, that which it alone could give him; and this is why the unconscious impulse which dictated the final phrase of the third note expresses the very essence of his nature. Byron could not live without sensations, and novel sensations, sensations ceaselessly renewed; it is not enough to say that he quickly becomes *blasé*, he seems to have been born *blasé*, and not to have been able truly to feel unless outside the law. Thus, if we regard as factitious, conventional, the innumerable portraits of himself as the outlaw drawn by him, we make the most irremediable of mistakes about him; for these portraits all emanate from, all have their source in, the inmost regions of his sincerity. Within the law, he feels nothing; outside it, he feels to the depths.

So that, at first, what Byron loved in Augusta was the incest: not *though* she was his sister, but *because* she was, she attracted, fascinated, held him, was to become indispensable to him. We are now as far as can be from the external fatality

we feel so certain that he would never even have thought of addressing to Lady Oxford:

> Too brief for our passion—too long for our peace—
> Was that hour—can its hope—can its memory cease?
> We repent—we abjure—we will break from our chain—
> We must part—we must fly to—unite it again!

And in a rough draft of the same poem there are these two most revealing lines:

> And thine is that love which I would not forego,
> Though that heart may be bought by Eternity's woe.

The poem was written in April, 1814—thus at the very time of their daughter Medora's birth. Byron enclosed it in a letter to Moore of May 4 (*Astarte*, p. 328).

which I defined at the outset, 'the antique fatality which is repulsed with horror by him on whom it falls, from which it is his dearest wish to escape'; we are at the very heart of the self-induced deliberate fatality, exultantly embraced and pro-claimed. The importance, the value of Augusta are, above all, of the order I shall venture to call *familial*; they are even doubly so, for if on the one hand, thanks to the incest, they saturate in Byron the outlaw, on the other they correspond to a strange but fundamental need of his nature, that of never committing himself to the outer world—or to speak more bluntly, of never going outside the family. It seems there was a mysterious localization, which defies analysis, of pride in Byron, so that he could never be stirred to the depths by any but those of his own blood—even in the sphere of 'the out-law', there was to him no outlawry but that which brought him back to them. To such a degree was he an immovable nature that even for love he could not depart from himself; and if Augusta was the only woman he loved, this was really because in loving her he could concentrate wholly on himself and on his race.

But except for the inestimable privilege of being *the sister*, what was Augusta herself? Ah! here the problem grows com-plex—by dint of its excess of simplicity. Numerous are the questions which we cannot answer because they are beyond any answer; this question baffles for a motive ideally opposite: because it falls short of the plane where answers begin to be given,—or at any rate answers in the least corresponding in scale to the issue here raised. Between the reality of Augusta and the things which happened to her, the disproportion is cruel—would be positively crushing if, fortunately, the degree of her frivolity did not redress the balance. Whatever the fatality in which one may be involved, one must, to feel it, carry some weight of one's own. Augusta—a water-colour sketch by Isabey, with a touch of Romney in the pose—was in very truth the thistle-down that evades all capture; and, to those for whom incest is not an abiding, or even a passing, obsession, her attractions are very debatable. True, in Hayter's drawing of 1812, there is the charm of a beauty at once regular and languorous; but the miniature by Holmes— Holmes of whom Byron said that he made 'inveterate likenesses', and who did in fact, at the same period, execute a most convincing portrait of Byron himself—shows, fifteen years later, a face with features wholly inexpressive, a face which incest has as it were petrified without informing it. But we need not insist on the physical side, which is always a controversial matter. Augusta seems to me one of the most finished specimens of that type of great lady whose ingrained foolishness does not prevent her from spreading protective wings, and who thereby secures a quite special authority in English society. Her most certain attribute is an insignificance uniformly diluted, pouring out all the effusions of vapid sentimentality, and traversed from time to time by the terrible archness of the fine lady playing the child. And if one proceeds (or rather, in the circumstances, tries to proceed) from the intellectual to the moral plane—why then, the last word has been said by Lady Byron who, after having for nearly thirty-five years upheld and rescued her in every way, was compelled to declare that Augusta's conduct could be explained only by 'a kind of moral idiocy from birth'. Now let us hear Lord Lovelace, who has drawn a masterly portrait of her, the essential passages of which are all I need give here: 'She was a woman of that great family—often very lovable— which is vague about facts, unconscious of duties, impulsive in conduct. She was of a sanguine and buoyant disposition, childishly fond and playful, ready to laugh at anything, loving to talk nonsense. The great charm of her society was a refined species of comic talent. She had kind feelings and good intentions without principles; she had received a strict moral and pietistic training, but its influence on her life was limited to a prodigal and sometimes inappropriate use of devout phrases. . . . Her moral ideas were to the greatest degree confused. She did not feel that there was much harm in anything which made no one unhappy'. (Lady Byron once wrote that between Byron and his sister, she had 'observed the remarkable difference that his feelings, distinct from practice, were much more sensitive and correct on all moral questions than hers'.) Lord Lovelace continues: 'There was always a blend of artificial sentiment. She excelled in simulation; herself she could persuade of almost anything. She feigned without thinking, perhaps felt what she feigned, unmindful of tangible truths at unsuitable seasons. There was apparently an absence of all deep feeling in her mind, of everything on which a strong impression could be made. . . . For years and down to her death, she was under the necessity of acting what she did not feel. She was almost always collected and prepared to repel suspicion, and at the same time her horror of the crime was already not too great. She was strangely insensible to the nature and magnitude of the offence in question, even as an imputation. She did not appear to think these transgressions of consequence. . . . Outwardly she affected extreme prudery, and after alighting on one unlucky passage, said she would not open *Don Juan* again, for fear her delicate feelings should be shocked by stumbling again on a Shipwreck'. (On which Byron wrote to her: 'I am delighted to see *you* grown so *moral*. It is edifying'.) 'She had a language of her own,[1] that of half-fact, half-fiction; that in which the most definite actions are

[1]Of this 'language of her own' Augusta was such a mistress that—like masterpieces, but again for a motive ideally opposite—it defies translation. One would have to give in facsimile, with its multitudinous crosses and interjections, the note (one of the few we possess) which she wrote to Byron on December 15, 1814, nineteen days before his marriage—a note in which tone and language, by their incurably puerile sentimentality, would seem to proclaim her guilty at the very time when she was beyond all question innocent. When Augusta's notes contained these ambiguous effusions, Byron exulted; and of course showed his tact by bringing that of December 15 to his wife, and presenting it as a tribute—to which, incidentally, we owe its preservation. But when he had left England, and desired beyond all else to obtain from Augusta the open avowal of her unalterable love, and more generally to be told exactly what was happening, her language exasperated him; and to describe it, he retrieved the ruthless Byronic downrightness.

blurred or obliterated under an ambiguous mist of hints, parentheses, innuendoes, etc. . . . . In Augusta's idiom blood-shame is translated into, 'I have been most unfortunate in all my nearest connections'. When she writes 'None can know *how much* I have suffered from this unhappy business'—the real meaning is that detection of her secret is imminent. . . . If a fact grew into an obstruction, it must no longer be a fact. Some women can thus delete their own past in good faith, or very nearly so'.[1]

In the sphere of sentiments, no less than in that of works of art, 'precision is the sign of the master'; and as muddle was Augusta's native element, it follows that—incredible though it seems, considering what her action implies of passion—not only do we never succeed in representing her feelings to ourselves, but we have to ask ourselves how far feeling, in the strict sense of the word, can be said to enter in at all. Did she love Byron—by which I mean, did she love him in any other way than that in which she was so lavish at so little expense to herself, and to which a brother—and such a brother—had a natural right? We do not know and never shall, convinced though I may be that here too Lady Byron said the last word, and that the answer is to be found in 'absence of deep feeling'. When there is 'nothing in a mind on which a deep impression could be made', the person of such a mind will nearly always, even when living or acting on her own account, even when she follows her bent, still be equally incapable of receiving and still more of originating deep impressions. It is only too evident that the sense and need of fatality in the Byronic, and indeed in any, acceptation of the phrase was always entirely beyond her range; but we must go farther than that, for we can divine that at the very time of her surrender she had no sort of realization of what incest signified, either as a fact or as an idea.[2] Women's letters by their whole manner, the kind

[1] *Astarte*, pp. 25-29; and from Lady Byron's letters to Mrs. Villiers in 1816.

[2] To be quite fair, let it be said that before 1816, before the time when Lady Byron gradually led her to reflection and confession, there is a

of phrases used in them, give countless evanescent indications of sensual potentialities—in Augusta's I can find no least trace of any. Even for sensuality—and above all when it is outside the law—a minimum of attention, of concentration, of gravity even, is requisite. If she ever felt any fulfilment of passion, it can only have been entirely passive in its nature—not the less real for that, the contrary indeed, for the state of passivity is the one positive pole of her being. Augusta exists but in yielding, and I should be inclined to believe that the keenest sensation given her by the incest was that of the degree of yielding that it implied. Was Byron bragging when he said that it cost him very little time or trouble to seduce her, that Augusta was very willing?[1] I am sure he was telling the truth. When one thinks that there is not much harm in anything which does not make anyone unhappy, why not yield, since 'it does not matter', to the desires of a brother who, when bills are raining at home, has offered one hospitality? When such a brother, swayed by a star to which one is even more blind than to the others, suddenly displays the sentiments of Phaedra, is there any reason why—being no more a devotee of Diana than of Venus—one should encounter him in the spirit of Hippolytus? The only pity is that if such facility enables one to enter into every kind of part, it does not always permit one to give them up; and once involved—Lady Anne Wilmot's words to Lady Byron are far-reaching—poor Augusta 'was under the necessity of acting what she did not feel'.

From the mental standpoint, Byron regarded Augusta very

document, one only, in which she shows some consciousness of her predicament. Moved by his constant desire to divulge and proclaim the incest, Byron one day showed a woman-friend who was with him in his rooms at the Albany (which places the date in 1813 or 1814) some letters from Augusta in which there were frequent allusions to it. The general tone seems to have been frivolous and silly, but from time to time there were evident symptoms of remorse, such as: 'O! B.—if we loved one another as we did in childhood—*then* it was innocent'. But the rest of the letters were less and less expressive of any remorse. See *Astarte*, pp. 35-36.

[1] *Astarte*, p. 35.

much as we do, and had no hesitation whatever in telling her to her face that she was a 'fool'. But this attribute of hers was entirely to his taste; for in the first place there was nothing he objected to—or even scorned—more than intelligence in women, or at any rate in those with whom his relations were on another plane; and though in such relations he greatly preferred the mute activity of the 'splendid animals', on the other hand (as we have seen) he liked sometimes to lay down the panoply of the Fatal Being, and then he sought relaxation and amusement in masculine company, becoming the Man's Man whom we have studied. Now the presence of Augusta was very decidedly favourable to an atmosphere of relaxation and amusement, and was enhanced by her comic talent, which was peculiarly congenial to both the easy-going and the psychological strains in him; so that when he said: 'She is a fool, but no one loves me as well as she does, or can keep me in better humour', he gave us the key to several Byronic doors. *Mythic*, *familial*, and *comic* (comic, too, both involuntarily and purposely), wearing a triple diadem surmounted by the crown of incest, Augusta was indeed an unhoped-for prize.

Byron had drunk of the philtre, but it was not until January, 1814, that the drink became wholly poisonous; and the period immediately following the incest—from July to September, 1813, up to the first stay with the Wedderburn Websters—is perhaps the most difficult of all to interpret. It seems that at first Byron himself underwent a violent revulsion; at any rate he buried in silence the dread secret which afterwards he was never to weary of parading. Even with that unique confidante to whom he told everything, even with Lady Melbourne, he held his tongue, and wrote to her less frequently. On the other hand, as though he entertained and even welcomed the after-thought that as yet incest was only an accident that might be got over, he began again to think of marriage. Until the day when experience undeceived him,

Byron indeed always considered the married state to be the natural solution of all difficulties—it is one of the *naïvetés*, exceptional in him, which he cherished in common with most men. He even tried to crystallize it on the person of Lady Adelaide Forbes. On July 13, five days after the letter which contains that characteristic remark about his sister, he again wrote to Moore, and in these terms: 'Do you know, Moore, I am amazingly inclined—remember I say but *inclined*—to be seriously enamoured with Lady A(delaide) F(orbes)—but this *** has ruined all my prospects. However, you know her; is she *clever*, or sensible, or good-tempered? either *would* do— I scratch out the *will*. I don't ask as to her beauty—that I see; but my circumstances are mending, and were not my other prospects blackening, I would take a wife, and that should be the woman, had I a chance. I do not yet know her much, but better than I did.'[1]

What do the series of asterisks stand for, followed by 'has ruined all my prospects'? It is much to be wished that, now the truth has come to light, the asterisks which abound in the definitive edition might disappear. Most of them refer to Augusta, and designate her most plainly when the intention is most evidently the opposite. That here they refer to the incest I am persuaded, and I see a confirmation of this in the other phrase, 'were not my other prospects blackening'. We should then be obliged to conclude that the incest took place between July 8 and 13, and that in a letter either destroyed or suppressed, Byron had at once confided in Moore. In view of the very particular friendship and sincerity always shown by him to Moore, this is by no means impossible, and does not even imply any contradiction with the silence observed towards Lady Melbourne; for there are certain confidences, and this is among them, of which a male friend may well be the first depositary. However it may be, this letter, by reason of its alterations and hesitations, is an important document, and reinforces my view that Byron had then fastened on the idea

[1] *Letters and Journals*, ii. pp. 230-231.

of marriage as his only means of salvation. But another letter to Moore on July 25 begins thus: 'I am not well-versed enough in the ways of single women to make much matrimonial progress'. The fact was that, feeling Lady Adelaide's sister, Lady Rancliffe, to be opposed to the match, Byron had gone no further—the first attempt at 'salvation' had failed. We may, I think, suppose that this failure did not leave Byron disconsolate, for there is only one satisfaction greater than that of doing one's duty—namely, finding that the duty refuses to be done. It is true that Augusta had been obliged to make a reappearance at Six Mile Bottom, but she wrote industriously; and just now we find a passage in a letter to Lady Melbourne from Byron, on July 30, which is of a nature to interest us. Lady Melbourne, who knew Byron as no one else did, felt pretty sure that his recent reticence meant no good; she reproached him for it, and he answered: ' "I don't tell you anything!" Very good, everybody rates me about my confidences with you. Augusta, for example, writes to-day, and the last thing she says is: "This must not go to Lady M." and to punish you, it *shan't*.'[1]

The punishment must have been light for Lady Melbourne which so fed the clear-sightedness that she prized above everything else; and the mere fact that Byron, who admired her perspicacity and even loved her for that very reason, should have said so much was a proof both that he was ripening for avowal, and that he was already feeling that itch for playing with fire which henceforth was to rule all his references to incest. He did not send the letter he spoke of, but he did go down on a visit to the writer, and brought her back with him to London, for on August 5 he informed Lady Melbourne: 'My sister, who is going abroad with me, is now in town, where she returned with me from Newmarket. Under the existing circumstances of her lord's embarrassments, she could not well do otherwise, and she appears to have still less reluctance at leaving the country than even myself. Lady C.

[1]*Corr.* i. p. 167.

may do as she pleases. If Augusta likes to take her, she may; but in that case she will travel by *herself*. Nugent does not know I am in town, and if he did, I could not at present accept his invitation, though your presence is a strong temptation, indeed much stronger for not being a new one.'[1]

Whence it appears that Lady Melbourne, wanting both to separate him from Augusta and to provoke an explanation, had tried to arrange a meeting in society, and that for once Byron had preferred some one else's company to hers. Byron and Augusta stayed in London throughout August; in his letters he still harps upon going abroad with his sister, but Lady Melbourne returned from the country towards the end of the month, and it is then that Byron must have made full confession, for on August 31 he wrote to her, and his letter begins thus: 'Your kind letter is *unanswerable*; no one but yourself would have taken the trouble; no one but me would have been in a situation to require it; I am still in town, so that it has as yet had all the effect you wish'.[2]

What exactly had taken place? Here I turn to Lord Lovelace: 'Augusta had consented to go with him to Sicily, but Lady Melbourne dissuaded him from taking "this fatal step," saying: "You are on the brink of a precipice, and if you do not retreat, you are lost for ever—it is a crime for which there is no salvation in this world, whatever there may be in the next"'. She told him that, whatever he might affect, she knew how susceptible he was to opinion, and would he do that which must utterly destroy his character? She told him that, though destitute of principle, she believed him naturally generous and honourable, and remonstrated with him on the cruelty of depriving of all future peace or happiness a woman who had hitherto, whether deservedly or not, maintained a good reputation—and even if their distresses, after he had taken this fatal step, should arise from external causes, they would always reproach themselves for their reciprocal wretchedness. His comment on this advice of Lady Melbourne's

[1]*Corr*. i. p. 168. [2]*Corr*. i. p. 177.

was: 'She is a good woman after all, for there are things she will stop at'. He followed her advice in part (as to Sicily), but not altogether. The day came when he said: 'I wish I had'.[1]

Having, this time, done half his duty, Byron was to feel a perilous satisfaction. Augusta was back at Newmarket, and though—faithful to the promise he had probably given (and probably of his own accord) to Lady Melbourne—he made himself stay a week in London, by September 8 he could hold out no longer, and with the honesty he always showed towards her, he informed Lady Melbourne of his departure in these terms: 'I leave town to-morrow for a few days, come what may; and as I am sure you would get the better of my resolution, I shall not venture to encounter you. If nothing very particular occurs, you will allow me to write as usual; if there does, you will probably hear of, but not *from*, me (of course) again'.[2]

Lady Melbourne instantly replied, and wishing—in pursuance of the wise method employed by all great spiritual directors—to preserve contact at any price, she begged Byron to go on writing to her, whatever happened. So next day (September 9) came another note: 'I did not receive your note till midnight, having gone out immediately on writing my own, or you may feel assured that I could have as little resisted your *conjuration* as any other spell you may think proper to cast over me. Something has occurred which prevents my leaving town till Saturday—perhaps till Sunday; later than that day-I cannot well remain. Without, as A.[3] says, being in a state of *despondency*, I am, nevertheless, very much perplexed; however, that must end one way or another. You say "Write to me at all events"; depend upon it, I will, till the moment arrives (if it does arrive) when I feel that you ought not to acknowledge me as a correspondent—in that case, a

[1] *Astarte*, pp. 33-34. Lord Lovelace's text is here based on one of Lady Byron's Narratives—that marked F.

[2] *Corr.* i. p. 179.

[3] 'A.' here refers not to Augusta, but to Annabella, the future Lady Byron.

sense of what is due to yourself, and a very grateful remembrance of all you have done to save one not worth preserving,
will of course close our correspondence and acquaintance at
once—the sincerest and only proof I could then afford of the
value I set upon your friendship'.[1]

His correspondence with her was interrupted between
September 9 and 21, and the letter of the 21st is dated from
Aston Hall, Rotherham, the Wedderburn Websters' house,
where Byron had just arrived. During this interval, though we
know nothing of his feelings, we can (thanks to *Letters and
Journals*) follow his movements and pick up a few hints.
Though he could not resist casting anchor at Newmarket, it
was only the briefest of landings; for on the 13th, at eight
o'clock in the evening, he was at Cambridge with Scrope
Davies, his faithful boon companion, and two days later he
informed Augusta that that night, at eleven o'clock, they had
between them disposed of six bottles of Burgundy and Bor-
deaux—a well-deserved reward for the effort he had had to
make in tearing himself away from Six Mile Bottom. He
returned to London on the night between the 14th and 15th;
and in his letter of the 15th to Augusta, describing the stay at
Cambridge, he adds: 'To-night I shall leave it again, perhaps
for Aston (the Wedderburn Websters) or Newstead. I have
not yet determined, nor does it much matter. As you perhaps
care more on the subject than I do, I will tell you when I know
myself. When my departure is arranged, and I can get this
long-evaded passage, you will be able to tell me whether I am
to expect a visit or not, and I can come for or meet you as you
think best'.[2]

We are so entirely ignorant not only of Augusta's attitude
towards the incest, but also of the real nature of her feelings
for Byron, that it is impossible to interpret this letter. Was she
in favour of Aston or of Newstead? Was she devoutly hoping
for some distraction that might cure him, or on the contrary
for the solitude which could have no effect but to fix his

[1] *Corr.* i. pp. 179-180.   [2] *Letters and Journals*, ii. pp. 264-265.

thoughts—fix them on herself? Here our perplexity is her triumph, for so transcendent is her inexpressiveness that it utterly transcends interpretation.

But no sooner had Byron written this letter—and doubtless because, however guileless in intention, the mere fact of having written it revived in him so much of the old feeling —than he decided for Aston, and on the same day wrote to Webster, accepting his invitation and announcing immediate arrival.

The first stay at Aston Hall did not last more than a week; Byron was back in London on September 26; but the Websters asked him again, and again he accepted, returning to Aston at the beginning of October, and that month may be said to belong to Lady Frances. Lady Melbourne had been at Brocket Hall in September, so that she and Byron had not met; but, in her correspondence no less than in tête-à-tête, Lady Melbourne was always very much to the point, and though we have no letters of hers belonging to this particular period, other documents enable us to guess at their contents. Lady Melbourne's position with Byron had become embarrassing: she had got her way about the trip to Sicily, but she was aiming at more than that—at nothing less than the rupture of Byron's liaison with Augusta. Now it is all very well to be endowed with some of the qualities appertaining to the part of a great spiritual director, to know and practise the method, to possess the adequate wisdom; but it is uncommonly difficult to make use of these things when in the first place religious issues are on both sides out of court, and when in the second, the spiritual director has a past so peopled as to make any resort to the moral argument a precarious course, above all when confronted with the piercing Byronic scrutiny. Between two evils there is nothing for it, as the adage says, but to choose the lesser: Lady Melbourne, in her need, remembered her admiration for the Marquise de Merteuil and, mobilizing all that personage's experience in the service of the triumph of virtue (relatively speaking), she dispatched to

Byron some instructions which might be called a detailed code of the art of seduction.[1] We do not know the exact date on which he received them, but it must have been before September 28, for on that day, on his return to London from the first visit to Aston, he wrote to her: 'I have tried, and hardly too, to vanquish my demon; but to very little purpose, for a resource that seldom failed me before did in this instance. I mean *transferring* my regards to another, of which I had a fair and not *discouraging* opportunity at one time. I willingly would, but the feeling that it was an effort spoiled all again; and *here* I am—*what* I am you know already. As I have never been accustomed to parade my thoughts before you in a *larmoyante* strain, I shall not begin now'[2]. And next day, fearing he had not been sufficiently explicit, he added: 'The letter I have written you will not please you, as I think you will perceive from its tone that I have no *newer* attachment'.[3] The 'not discouraging opportunity' bore the name of Lady Frances; but during his earlier visit Byron had held so completely aloof that the encouragement had been no more than implicit. It was during the second stay—when all October was spent at Aston, except for a flying visit, with the Websters, to Newstead—that the episode with Lady Frances (which, in the order of actual life, has the quality of a perfect elegy) came to birth, described its fluctuating tangent, reached a brief but pure and moving climax, then drooped and died. This episode would deserve separate treatment, but that would mean giving the whole series of letters written by Byron from Aston—which in their combination of sincerity, fair-mindedness, and unformulated nobility are the masterpiece within the masterpiece of the correspondence with Lady Melbourne. With Lady Frances for heroine—a sister to those youthful patrician ladies of Van Dyck's who have ac-

[1]*Astarte*, p. 34: 'Lady Melbourne, in order to get him out of this "*worse* business", encouraged him to start on a fresh intrigue, and gave him the most minute instructions about seducing another woman, almost in the style of the Marquise de Merteuil; in *Les Liaisons Dangereuses*'.

[2]*Corr.* i. p. 183.   [3]*Corr.* i. pp. 184-185.

quired a fallacious reputation for coldness, not to say insensibility, by reason of their pale cheeks, their elegant but re-
strained dignity—it would be attractive to examine what is
the most difficult of all emotional stirrings to analyse, namely,
that felt by a virtuous-minded woman. But space forbids, and
I must here confine myself to what we can learn from Byron
himself, which is the more important because the climax of
the episode shows him as irreproachable, while the general
course of his behaviour towards Lady Frances during the
second stay at Aston reveals a background to his nature which
flatly contradicts the accepted views about him. Despite the
'reputation of a rake' which had preceded him to Aston[1] and
which successes with women, whether sought or offered, are
always enough to secure, Byron was *not* a seducer. He is the
seducer in spite of himself—which to me (but I grant that I
may be inclined to push the antithesis too far) represents the
exact contrary. In every born seducer there is something of
the military man, who in the act of seduction sees a warlike
operation in which it is important to be first in the field, in
which the offensive is the sole course, and which will culminate in an assault. This is why the far from complex temperament peculiar to the Frenchman of the *ancien régime*—a
temperament which is often that of the soldier out of work—
was so marvellously adapted to the task of the born seducer.
With such an one, if he cannot make war on the grand scale,
there is nothing for it but to revert to the little war, and conduct it in such a way that it shall compensate for the default of
the other—to which, moreover, when he gets the opportunity
(let me recall the many instances of this between 1914 and
1918), he returns with an ardour and a heroism that com-

---

[1]Alluding to his first stay at Aston, Byron wrote from London to Lady
Melbourne on October 1st: 'I am not exactly cut out for the lady of the
mansion; but I think a stray dandy would have a chance of preferment.
She evidently expects to be attacked, and seems prepared for a brilliant
defence; my character as a *roué* has gone before me, and my careless and
quiet behaviour astonished her so much that I believe she began to think
herself ugly, or me blind—if not worse' (*Corr.* i. p. 186).

pletely redeem him. Of the born seducer Valmont is the consummate type, because amid the languor and bucolics of Louis XVI's reign he intensifies this little war to the point of creating an illusion of the great one. But Valmont is the very antitype of Byron, and nothing proves it better than this passage in the letter of October 5 to Lady Melbourne, soon after the return to Aston: 'But I never should think of her, nor anyone else, if left to my own cogitations, as I have neither the patience nor presumption to advance till met half-way'.[1] Everything here is the antipodes of the born seducer. In the first place, Byron is wholly sincere when he says that he asks only to be left to his cogitations; as I have often emphatically said, of his own accord he is never moved to depart from himself; if he does so depart, and he incessantly does, it is only because he cannot bear the burden of those cogitations, of all that ebbs back in solitary brooding. For on the one hand, his 'massive sense of nothingness' gets too quickly to the bottom of things; on the other (once incest had taken place) remorse was at the core of all—a remorse, it is true, which he begins by savouring to the full in its 'morose delectation', but which soon becomes intolerable even to himself. The born seducer, on the contrary, has no desire to be left to his cogitations—for the best of reasons, because he has none; I mean to say, none but those which are shaped by a possible action, and fasten at once upon that; for *he* exists but in departing from himself, but in pursuit. Presumptuous he is by definition, since presumptuousness is an indispensable professional quality, a falsified and degraded survival from the soldier's daring—and he is patient too, in the degree that any enterprise of seduction implies a special kind of patience. The born seducer must, of course, feel : otherwise he could never establish contact with the opposite partner; but anything he may feel is confined to those general, almost abstract, feelings—the pulse of desire and the love of conquest for its own sake, though to be sure all his art consists in bringing the woman to perceive and receive

[1] *Corr.* i. p. 189.

the warmth which emanates from those feelings as inspired by
her alone, addressed to her alone. Now of all the forms of
pride and vanity, there is perhaps only one from which Byron
is exempt, and that is this very presumptuousness. In all good
faith, he was always surprised, even scandalized, by both his
literary and his amorous conquests. His modesty as an author
is admirable—say rather his moderation (for moderation is
the surest sign of genuine modesty); and if, as concerned
women, he was obliged to succumb to the evidence, he did
it with the shrug we keep for childishness—a shrug which
meant: 'I am the fashion; it's absurd, but it is so, and I can't
help it'. Moreover, if even for the born seducer the patience
implied in an enterprise of seduction proves wearisome and
oppressive, for a being higher in the scale of creation—and
especially when, as with Byron, there is already a strain of
fierce impatience, eruptive as a volcano—that business will
have, in addition to its baseness and silliness, a tediousness
which redoubles the normal state of ennui, and makes him even
disinclined to insist in any way. Finally, and especially, one
who never feels disposed to advance unless the other has come
half-way is not a born seducer, but he runs the risk of being
predestined to the part of seducer in spite of himself; and it is
just there that resides the drama included in the Byronic prestige. For if it is easy to refrain from playing a part which is
not your own, there is nothing more difficult—and nothing,
in this instance, more honourable to Byron—than to refuse
one that obviously falls to your lot. The more because—we
must not forget this—Byron's difficulty far surpassed that of
his spiritual director; for to undertake on what might (by a
stretch) be called Platonic lines the part of the Marquise
de Merteuil, costs no more than a few letters, which for an
accomplished correspondent merely means taking the trouble
of a pleasure; while Byron who, as he has told us in so many
words (and he never said anything truer about himself),
'could not exist without some object of attachment', and had
at last found the one for which he was born—Byron, who

nevertheless confessed that nothing worse could have befallen him and was sincerely seeking some means of altering the situation, now found himself in the fantastic position (comic, if you will, but I have already hinted that Byron is sometimes at his greatest where with other men the element of comedy would prevail), and a position from which he could not extricate himself, of realizing that the triumph of the only virtue left to him depended on the fact that for once Valmont's antitype could turn into Valmont himself. The first result and, for Byron, the first chastisement of incest was that the hero of *Les Liaisons Dangereuses* could, beyond his obligations as born seducer, figure as the personification of a duty that had to be regarded as a moral one.

Here I must transcribe the passage, so important in every respect, from the Aston letter of October 13, where Byron frankly says: 'Anything, you will allow, is better than the *last*; and I cannot exist without some object of attachment. You will laugh at my perpetual *changes*, but recollect the circumstances which have broken off the last, and don't exactly attribute their conclusion to caprice. I think you will admit, whatever C. may assert, that I did not use her ill; though I find *her own* story, even in this part of the world, to be the genuine narrative; as to Lady O., that I did to please you, and luckily, finding it pleasant to myself also and very useful to C.; it might have lasted longer but for the voyage. I spare you the third.'[1] A document that gorges us with information. In the first place it enables us, better than any other, to gauge the unique influence exercised upon him by Lady Melbourne; it shows us precisely what brought about the liaison with Lady Oxford, which was certainly, at first, the work of Lady Melbourne, resolute for the sake of her family's and her own peace to confront Caroline with the *fait accompli*; and (which matters still more to us) it establishes the fact that, though

[1]*Corr.* i. p. 198.

events caused it to be but momentary, Lady Melbourne did obtain the rupture with Augusta, and that in October, 1813, Byron was at his sincerest in his desire, and even his resolve, to break away from the incestuous relation—all circumstances which only make his conduct towards Lady Frances the more admirable. That he 'could not exist without some object of attachment' may be explained by many factors of which I have already had something to say—the impossibility of enduring the results of solitary rumination; the need, sometimes stronger in one who cannot depart from himself, of devoting to somebody the overplus of suffocating emotion, at once letting it flow and canalizing its outbursts by enlisting them under the banner of the heart; above all and as it were including everything else, the temperament of the man of action who has nothing to do, for whom (as Byron always, and so truthfully, declared) the act of composition is nothing but a makeshift, the indispensable safety-valve.

We must now do justice to the good will of Lady Frances. With a singular intuition of the Byronic propensities, she came more than half-way; since—let us once for all dismiss the fictitious coldness, insensibility of Van Dyck's youthful patricians, and salute instead their daring candour—she was able to ask Byron 'how a woman who liked a man could inform him of it when he did not perceive it'.[1] For (Byron was, as I have said, genuinely modest) he had *not* perceived it. When he talked of a 'not discouraging opportunity', when he depicted the hostess who 'evidently expects to be attacked, and seems prepared for a brilliant defence', he was observing the phenomenon in a general sense, as an opportunity offered to the born seducer, and concerning him, Byron, in no wise. Not being presumptuous, it had not occurred to him that her attitude might be interpreted as the outcome of a sentiment for himself. This is evident from a passage in the letter fol-

[1] *Corr.* i. p. 191.

lowing that in which he tells of her daring candour: 'She says she is convinced that my own declaration was produced solely because I perceived her previous *penchant*, which by-the-bye, as I think I said to you before, I neither perceived nor expected. I really did not suspect her of a predilection for anyone, and even now in public, with the exception of those little indirect, yet mutually understood—I don't know how and it is unnecessary to name or describe them—her conduct is as coldly correct as her still, fair aspect'.[1] Lady Frances was both right and wrong. She was right in thinking that it was the discovery of her own *penchant* (to which discovery, as woman-like she prefers to forget, she was the instigator) that made Byron declare himself; but she was wrong in imagining that this diminished the sincerity of his declaration. Byron was, in truth, among those who must feel and even know themselves beloved before they make any advance—and then they make it as sincerely as can be. And he did from that moment begin to love Lady Frances, though not in the fullest sense until the moment when he spared her, and *after* that he loved her more utterly still—thus for once in his life taking high, very high, rank in the sphere of sentiment.

I cannot resist the temptation of giving the climax; but if Byron's letter is to be read in the key of the episode as it was lived—and that, I repeat, is the key of elegy—we must also have in memory a phrase in a later letter which reveals a fundamental trait of his character, one so constantly misunderstood that even Lady Melbourne could mistake him: 'You really *wrong* me if you do not suppose that I would sacrifice everything for Ph—' [his designation for Lady Frances]. 'I hate sentiment, and in consequence my epistolary levity makes you believe me as hollow and heartless as my letters are light'.[2] And now here is what he wrote on October 17, this time from Newstead, where the Websters were his guests: 'One day, left entirely to ourselves, was nearly fatal—another such victory, and with Pyrrhus we were lost—it came to this.

[1] *Corr.* i. p. 195.   [2] *Corr.* i. p. 213.

136

"I am entirely at your *mercy*. I own it. I give myself up to you. I am not *cold*—whatever I seem to others; but I know that I cannot bear the reflection hereafter. Do not imagine that these are mere words. I tell you the truth—now act as you will." Was I wrong? I spared her. There was something so very peculiar in her manner—a kind of mild decision—no scene—not even a struggle; but still I know not what, that convinced me she was serious. It was not that mere "No", which one has heard forty times before, and always with the same accent; but the *tone*, and the aspect—yet I sacrificed much—the hour *two* in the morning—away—the Devil whispering that it was mere verbiage, etc. And yet I know not whether I can regret it—she seems so very thankful for my forbearance—a proof at least that she was not playing merely the usual decorous reluctance, which is sometimes so tiresome on these occasions. You ask if I am prepared to go all lengths. If you mean by "all lengths" anything including duel or divorce, I answer *Yes*. I love her. If I did not, and much too, I should have been more selfish on the occasion before mentioned. I have offered to go away with her, and her answer, whether sincere or not, is "that on *my account* she declines it".[1] That letter is the record of Byron's finest moment in the sphere which, at bottom, alone was of import to him—that of actual life. In such a case, some inner process must have been carried to its utmost limit if a man is *not* to act; and it is moving to see the temperament of the man of action with nothing to do thus finding, in the most noble inaction, his mode of achievement. A virtuous-minded woman, when emotionally stirred—and especially when, as here, she is only twenty, with all the persuasive charms which are at the moment her helpless abettors—will deeply touch a 'generous nature'; and in spite of all (as Lady Melbourne had told him, scarcely two months earlier) Byron's nature was that. And Lady Frances' power extended much farther than this, since for the first and only time it led Byron, in writing of her, to use in all their

[1] *Corr.* i. pp. 203-204.

137

obvious simplicity, their eternal banality, the three little words: 'I love her'[1]; and to use them *after* he had spared her, perhaps even only to dare to utter them (to himself and to Lady Melbourne) because he had spared her. By this, of course, I do not mean to say that Byron did not feel for Augusta a sentiment quite differently potent and passionate (without considering at all the question of duration) from that which Lady Frances inspired; but only that the latter was the normal, universal sentiment, which irresistibly expresses itself by the simple and limpid 'I love you'.

Once Lady Frances, whether 'sincerely or not', whether for his sake or her own, had declined Byron's offer, the circumstances were such that the episode could not but droop and die; and the facts now concern us only in so far as we can distinguish their reverberations. Except for the letters to Lady Melbourne, which are all full of the affair, Byron's correspondence between October 12 and November 8 completely lapsed, and for us who have seen what the year 1813 portended for him, there could be no more eloquent testimony to the degree in which Lady Frances absorbed, even confiscated, his thoughts. But there is another proof, still more significant: this silence of his intervened between two very short notes to Augusta,[2] from both of which there is much to learn. The first is of October 10, about five or six days after his return to Aston; it is a reply to one of hers and—reminiscent of the pre-incestuous ways and manners—a tardy reply. 'My dearest Augusta, I have only time to say that I am not in the least angry, and that my silence has merely arisen from several cir-

[1]The three little words oblige me to apologise for the passage in which I said that in the Lady Frances episode Byron accomplished the rites of the heart. I was then too much inclined to believe that from the first the incest had been the poison for him which it did not become until January, 1814. Consequently I could not attach the proper importance to the Lady Frances episode, nor read in its true light the letter of October 17, 1813.

[2]To be quite accurate, I should mention that there does exist a short note of October 12 addressed to Murray, but this refers only to certain slips that Byron had let pass whilst correcting the proofs of *The Giaour*.

cumstances which I cannot now detail. I trust you are better, and will continue *best*. Ever, my dearest, Yours B.'[1] Whence it would seem in the first place that Augusta was afraid he was angry with her—which in any other woman might possibly give some clue to her own sentiments, might faintly indicate the desire to avoid a rupture, but which in her has no great bearing, for mere automatic family-feeling has always to be reckoned with in Augusta's case; and in the second place, and very especially, that Byron (whose cursory superlatives about her health are, like all such, so unmistakably casual), having to break off a tête-à-tête with Lady Frances in order to catch the post, had felt that even incest, especially when one is trying to eliminate it, does not authorize such intrusions, and that if one runs the risk of so intruding, one runs at the same time the risk of meeting with the treatment reserved for Caroline Lamb. But Augusta was not of those who read between the lines, even when it was so easy as in this instance; probably she wrote again, but this time got no answer at all; for on October 13, when the Lady Frances episode was working up to its climax, Byron informed Lady Melbourne: 'All my correspondences, and every other business, are at a standstill'; and it was not for nearly a fortnight after his return to London that Augusta received the second note: 'November 8, 1813. My dearest Augusta, I have only time to say that I shall write to-morrow, and that my present and long silence has been occasioned by a thousand things (with which *you* are not concerned). It is not Lady C. nor O.; but perhaps you may *guess*, and if you do, do not tell. You do not know what mischief your being with me might have prevented. You shall hear from me to-morrow; in the mean time don't be alarmed. I am in *no immediate* peril. Believe me, ever yours, B.'[2] The 'peril', which hovered for some time, was the possibility of a duel with Webster, in case he had intercepted a letter of Byron's to Lady Frances. It was real enough, for Byron had no intention of drawing upon Webster, should they have

[1]*Letters and Journals*, ii. p. 276.   [2]*Letters and Journals*, ii. p. 277.

fought. . . . I regret being obliged to deny myself even the hastiest sketch of that exquisitely typical *mari de comédie*, James Wedderburn Webster. Enough, perhaps, to say that after having several times assumed the classical attitude of jealousy, and made it impossible for Byron to prolong his stay at Aston, Webster accompanied him to London, and there received from him a loan of £1000, arranged for before they left.

Lady Frances had, in fact, invited Augusta to share Byron's second stay at Aston, and Augusta had declined; we know no more. Lady Frances of course knew nothing about Byron's relations with his sister; and we, as usual, are totally ignorant of Augusta's motives for refusing. Did Byron himself—before events took the turn we have seen—desire or dread her presence at Aston? All these are insoluble enigmas. One thing is certain—he was back in London on October 21, and during the fortnight preceding the second note to Augusta, was going through the paroxysm of divided emotions to which he was to be condemned until January, 1814, when the circle of incest closed for good around him. Let us try to represent his feelings to ourselves, for never did they more deserve our serious sympathy. As soon as the incest is committed, and before he even confides in Lady Melbourne, when in fact he is absolutely alone, with nothing to depend on but a will-power in itself of the weakest,[1] and, in this particular predicament, all the more difficult to exert, he makes a first move in the direction of marriage,—oh! feeble enough, no doubt, but which after

---

[1] "You will believe me, what I sometimes believe myself, mad, when I tell you that I seem to have *two* states of existence, *one* purely contemplative, during which the crimes, faults, and follies of mankind are laid open to my view (my own forming a prominent object in the picture), and the other *active*, when I play my part in the drama of life, as if impelled by some power over which I have no control, though the consciousness of doing wrong remains. It is as though I had the faculty of discovering error without the power of avoiding it'. (Quoted in *Astarte*, from Lady Blessington's Journal, p. 10). Such a duality is very frequent in introspective and even spiritual natures; but Byron's nature was not introspective, though his keenness of scrutiny and his volcanic outbursts sometimes gave birth to prodigies in that kind. And in no degree was he spiritual.

all, when we consider that he has just drunk of the philtre, counts for a good deal. The attempt fails; he tells Lady Melbourne all; he gives up the trip with Augusta, and even breaks with her for a while: without any zest, he envisages the part which awaits him, that part of seducer now more than ever uncongenial to him,—that part which presents itself under the aspect of a mere duty, most chilling of aspects, and most unlikely to lead to any success in it. And, instead of seduction, it is love that he encounters : a love which he inspires not only without having courted it but without even having suspected it, and to which he at once responds—responds to such a degree that for a moment a perspective seems to open itself of salvation, of a life re-made and consecrated to the 'object' of a sincere, a perfectly real 'attachment'. The perspective fades—first as a result of his 'native generosity', then because Lady Frances refuses his offer.[1] How one understands that when back in London he should write to Lady Melbourne : ' I have thrown away the best opportunity that ever was wasted on a spoiled child, and when it may occur again is not

Feebleness, paralysis, even complete failure of volition are, despite appearances, in him simply the result of his craving for action—action at any price; but that craving is associated with the quasi-impossibility of joining hands, or rather of knowing how to join hands (here we retrieve the 'uncertainty of touch' that Ethel Colburn Mayne has pointed to) with the kind of action which at the same time would give him the consciousness of acting rightly. As the best judges had always perceived, and as Mr. Harold Nicolson has recently demonstrated in his *Byron: The Last Journey* (1823-4), Byron had to be almost driven to embark for Greece, where he found—and even there not, strictly speaking, in action but (once more) in that most heroic inaction represented by death—a glorious and fruitful realization of *right-doing*.

[1]At the end of the letter of October 17 we discern a touching wistfulness towards the vanished perspective: 'Poor thing—she is either the most *artful* or *artless* of her age (20) I ever came across. . . . She throws, or seems to throw, herself so entirely upon my discretion in every respect, that it disarms me quite; but I am really wretched with the perpetual conflict with myself. Her health is so very delicate; she is so thin and pale, and seems to have lost her appetite so entirely, that I doubt her living much longer. This is also her own opinion. But these fancies are common to all who are not very happy. If she were once my wife, or likely to be so, a warm climate should be the first resort, nevertheless, for her recovery' (*Corr.* i. pp. 204-205).

in my calculation'; and on the very day of his return to town he adds these words: 'Perhaps after all I was her dupe—if so, I am also the dupe of the few good feelings I could ever boast of, but here perhaps I am my own dupe too, in attributing to a good motive what may be quite otherwise.' Let us not here make the mistake of thinking that the second thought in any way annuls the first; for with Byron the La Rochefoucauld vein is likewise, in its way, allied to his 'native generosity'— an effluence from integrity alone, from the piercing eye he kept upon himself. On the first page of the Journal I am about to talk of, Byron quotes the proverb: 'Virtue is its own reward', and makes this comment: 'It certainly should be paid well for its trouble'. At this precise moment, he had every right to think and feel that he was paying a heavy price for his virtue.

Byron, both abandoned and haunted, was besides torn in two—and that in the supreme degree. Though as far as facts went he had lost, one after the other, his two objects of attachment, in the sphere of sentiment on the contrary they for a time amalgamate in a fashion singularly revealing, and (when we remember all that was at stake, for this is the grand climacteric of Byron's destiny) here truly poignant. At the end of October and beginning of November, it seems that, in the conscious zone at any rate, Lady Frances reigns alone, and his delay in writing to Augusta is no negligible fact. But we possess, besides, an essential piece of information in the only letter belonging to that fortnight, which is (as we might expect) addressed to Lady Melbourne, and contains the following passage: 'For the last three days I have been quite shut up; my mind has been from *late* and *later* events in such a state of fermentation, that as usual I have been obliged to empty it in rhyme, and am in the very heart of another Eastern tale—something of the *Giaour* cast—but not so sombre, though rather more villainous. This is my usual resource; if it were not for some such occupation to dispel reflection during *inaction*, I verily believe I should often go mad.'[1]

An important document, because *The Bride of Abydos* was written at such a pace—it was finished in four nights[2]—that it is a cardinal example of that process of expulsion and 'getting away from himself', which alone drove Byron to composition, and ruled him throughout its course. Composition, for Byron, was a fourfold process in which all the four factors were at war with one another, but without any one of them having anything to do with literature or, even in the broadest acceptation of the word, with art. In his case to write was at once to express and to forget himself, to soothe his inmost soul by emptying it of the overdose of poison, and at the same time to 'keep the wound alive'.

'To withdraw *myself* from *myself* (oh! that cursed selfish-ness!) has ever been my sole, my entire, my sincere motive in scribbling at all; and publishing is also the continuance of the same object, by the action it affords to the mind, which else recoils upon itself.'[3] Reflection in the strong and etymo-logical sense of the word, the reflux of the mind upon itself (which nevertheless the solitary rumination of the Byronic Journal invests with the stamp of genius)—this Byron not only did not love, but, being unable to endure his own thoughts, objected to beyond all else; and perhaps nothing more clearly defines his temperament as that of the man of action, places him more unmistakably apart from the *artist*, the *introspective*, and the *contemplative*, who all love the 'recoil upon itself'—the first in view of bringing his work to per-fection, the second because it sounds the psychological depths, the third because it sheds an increase of light.

[1] *Corr.* i. p. 214.

[2] Either four nights or a week, for Byron's statements vary; but even a week would be a remarkably short time in which to be delivered of 1500 lines, however unimpressive.

[3] *Letters and Journals*, ii. p. 351, Journal of November 27, 1813.

Now when, as in *Manfred*, all the four factors in Byron's process of composition attain their utmost intensity, the outcome is a masterpiece of 'outlawry', as much beyond the law as its progenitor. But, as a matter of course, such conditions are not favourable to the purity, beauty, completeness, and, above all, perfection of a work—and equally as a matter of course, Byron knows this better than anyone, and does not in the least care. If he could read my words when I say here that, moved by a purely professional sense of duty, and having re-read *The Bride* from beginning to end, I have for my sole reward the austere satisfaction of having accomplished that duty,—that indeed I can but wonder how an outpouring so insipid in its futile vehemence could have soothed its perpetrator . . . why, he would remind me that of this very poem he wrote to Murray: 'I care no more for my poetry than for a lump of sugar', and would rightly add that *The Bride of Abydos* had fulfilled its function in giving him 'employment', and 'wringing his thoughts from reality'.[1] Before such an avowal, what can one do but bow the head as before all the kindred mysteries presented in literature by the incommensurability between the results and the solace they bring? But though intrinsically worthless, *The Bride of Abydos* has a symptomatic value, and that is all we are here concerned with. It was to have been a tale of incestuous love; but in the work as it actually exists the illusion of incest disappears as soon as it gets under way, and the sentiments become as conventional as can be. Byron wrote to Galt on December 11, 1813: 'Something still more singular is, that the *first* part, where you have found a coincidence in some events within your observations on *life*, was *drawn* from *observations* of mine also,[2] and I meant

[1] *Letters and Journals*, ii. p. 293. Letter to Moore of November 30, 1813.

[2] It is said that during his first Eastern trip (1809-11) Byron had known of a drama of incestuous love which took place in a harem. Are we therefore to conclude that this incident, so remote as it was, prepared his imagination for the theme? Since the Byronic imagination was of the type which broods to the maximum on a minimum of themes, it may be so; but though worth mentioning, in the absence of any documents we had better not make too much of this indication.

to have gone on with the story, but on second thoughts, I thought myself *two centuries* at least too late for the subject; which, though admitting of very powerful feeling and description, yet is not adapted for this age, at least this country, though the finest works of the Greeks, one of Schiller's and Alfieri's in modern times, besides several of our old (and best) dramatists, have been grounded on incidents of a similar cast. I therefore altered it as you perceive, and in so doing have weakened the whole, by interrupting the train of thought: and in composition I do not think *second* thoughts are the best, though *second* expressions may improve the first ideas'.[1] Very sensible remarks, and, objectively regarded, beyond argument; but we may go deeper and ask ourselves whether another fact was not still more decisive than that of coming two centuries too late, and whether the incestuous strain in *The Bride of Abydos* was not, if not two years (*Manfred* belongs to 1816), at any rate two months too soon, and its symptomatic value wholly that of the strange amalgamation, already referred to, of Byron's two objects of attachment. The original conception belongs by right to Augusta; but in those first days of November, 1813, it was Lady Frances who still ruled Byron's secret thoughts, and of whom the recent memory forbade return to the incestuous relation; and to her alone *The Bride of Abydos* more and more addressed itself, to culminate in the White Rose rhapsody at the end of the poem. But the rose was *white*, and it blossomed on a tomb; and here we come upon another reason why the Lady Frances episode could not but droop and die. On August 28, 1813, here is what Byron wrote to Moore: 'I have been thinking of a story, grafted on the amours of a Peri and a mortal—something like, only more *philanthropical* than, Cazotte's *Diable Amoureux*. It would require a good deal of poesy, and tenderness is not my forte.'[2] 'Tenderness is not my forte.' No; no more than *bêtise* is that of the author of *La soirée avec Monsieur Teste*, was tenderness Byron's forte. If one uses the

[1] *Letters and Journals*, ii. p. 305.   [2] *Letters and Journals*, ii. p. 255.

word 'demon' in the entirely profane sense of the temptation which is not native to the tempted, tenderness is Byron's demon; and it is pathetic to see how, on the one occasion that he quite sincerely yielded to it, the punishment falls upon his work, which then becomes irredeemably weak and insipid.

The 'Lady Frances cycle', in the canon of Byron's works, comprises (besides the reminiscent inspiration of *The Bride*) the piece 'Remember him whom Passion's Power' and the two sonnets *To Genevra*. In the former the feeling is so sincere and fine that it redeems the technical weaknesses; but the two sonnets are among the most detestable we owe to many centuries of Petrarchism. And Byron thought so himself, for when he had written them on December 17, 1813, he noted in his Journal: 'Redde some Italian and wrote two sonnets on . . . I never wrote but one sonnet before, and that was not in earnest, and many years ago, as an exercise—and I will never write another. They are the most puling, petrifying, stupidly platonic compositions. I detest the Petrarch so much that I would not have been the man, even to have obtained his Laura, which the metaphysical whining dotard never could.'[1] The tone here regarding Platonism and Petrarch seems to show that this was an important date in the decline of Lady Frances' star; not only does the Petrarchian mode lend itself admirably to what one might call the tribute of the last hour, but on the very next day—doubtless to deplatonize himself— Byron began *The Corsair*. Now at first, by reason of the way in which a sentiment will sometimes insist on surviving itself (thus becoming the very indication of the inward detachment), the heroine of *The Corsair* bore the transparent name of Francesca; on January 6, 1814, she is, as in the sonnets, Genevra; but on January 7, as we see in the postscript of a letter to Murray (that is to say, four days before the decisive letter to Lady Melbourne), she receives her final appellation, Medora (as the corrected proofs of January 15 testify)—thus anticipating the name chosen by Byron for his daughter in

---

[1] *Letters and Journals*, ii. p. 379.

days to come, and alluded to by him when in the following months, mysteriously bruiting abroad the incest, he said: 'There is a woman I love so passionately: she is pregnant by me, and if it is a girl, I shall call her Medora'.[1] With *The Corsair*, the part played by Lady Frances in the amalgam ceases, and it is only logical for her name to have vanished with her—for by the tone, which with Byron always signifies more than the story, the plot, *The Corsair* belongs to Augusta. It exactly foreshadows the incestuous cycle; in those few thousand lines —written, they too, in less than three weeks, and significant of Byron's return to his native vein, his escape to the manner which was truly his—we find some awkward, hesitating attempts at the hammerstroke which was to beat throughout *Lara*. In the order of poetry, it was not until May, 1814, that with *Lara* Byron entered into possession of his genius.

That Byron was conscious of the feebleness which marks the Lady Frances cycle, he has just told us himself; but I hasten to add that in his case the perception of this kind of feebleness could not, from interested motives touching literature or art, have played any part in the return to the incest; for Byron never allowed solicitude about his work to have any sort of influence upon the march of his destiny. In him there is not the smallest vestige of the man of letters; not only did he scorn—and very sincerely scorn—his work, and above all, it seems, when it came from the depths of his being; but he was entirely exempt from that contemporary taint which, as with the war-profiteers in their peculiar sphere, has produced, and day by day increasingly produces, what I can only call the life-profiteers. True—as I shall presently show—Byron's genius, the explosion of that genius, owes nearly everything to the central event of his life; but here the intention is all, and to Byron it was the event itself which signified, signified *as* event. Oppressed by that, he wrote to relieve his mind; but in no degree did he live the event so as to be able subsequently

[1]Probably Augusta's pregnancy played a part in the resumption of the incest; but it is impossible to say to what extent.

to write of it. It would be an insult to my readers were I further to emphasize the difference between him and too many of our contemporaries. ...

All I need say here is that tenderness was not Byron's native element, and that the adage says: '*Chassez le naturel, il revient au galop*'. And this was why, soothed by the composition of *The Bride of Abydos*, but soothed in a way which was not truly congenial to his spirit, the Byronic sub-consciousness, beginning on November 8 to dwell again on Augusta, dictated the phrase: 'You do not know what harm your being with me might have prevented'. Though Byron set the incest going, it is only fair to recognize that he opposed to it that after-resistance which is the most difficult of all to wrest from one's-self. But the elements conspired against him—so far as to engage his 'native generosity' in the service of his defeat. From that moment, since he 'could not exist without some object of attachment', Byron is thrown back on the incestuous relation. In the overcharged, dense, leaden-lowering atmosphere of the first prodigious Journal, begun on November 14, 1813—wherein a man huddled, immobile, seems to watch an invisible ceiling slowly descend on him—one foresees that the fatality required by his nature is about to claim him in good earnest; and on January 11, 1814, a letter to Lady Melbourne confronts us with the accomplished fact: 'In the present circumstances, it is impossible I should feel anything beyond friendship for her[1] or anyone else; and the kind of feeling which has lately absorbed me has a mixture of the terrible, which renders all others, even passion (*pour les autres*), insipid to a degree; in short, one of its effects has been like the habit

[1]*Corr*. i. p. 228. The 'her' is Mrs. Musters (once Mary Chaworth) who, very unhappily married, had just renewed contact with Byron in letters begging him to befriend her in her matrimonial distresses. Urged by motives similar to those in the Lady Frances episode, Lady Melbourne was advising Byron to see Mary again—probably with her own ideas as to the possible outcome. In a note to *Astarte* (pp. 314-317), designed to refute Mr. Edgcumbe's impossible theory concerning Medora Leigh, the fact is established that Byron did not go to see her, and during the stay at Newstead with Augusta in January and February, 1814, made no response

of Mithridates, who by using himself gradually to poison of the strongest kind, at last rendered all others ineffectual when he sought them as a remedy for all evils, and a release from existence'.

Nothing could be more explicit than such a document. 'The strongest poison'—yes, incest was indeed to be that henceforth for Byron; and that is why he is possessed by it. So, until his marriage—the last great *event* of his life (if we except the Greek adventure; but then, the *event* was death), I shall confine myself, in the order of facts, to indicating the essential phases. On November 22, 1813, Byron opens a letter to Lady Melbourne with these words: 'Caroline has at last done a very good-natured thing; she sent me Holmes's picture for a *friend leaving England*, to which friend it is now making the best of its way'.[1] The friend in question was no other than Augusta who, so far from leaving England, was two months later to pay him the visit at Newstead which had earlier been talked of. This is proved by a fragment from the Journal for November 27: '. . . has received the portrait safe; and in answer, the only remark she makes upon it is, "indeed it is like" and again, "indeed it is like". With her the likeness "covered a multitude of sins"; for I happen to know that this portrait was not a flatterer, but dark and stern,—even black as the mood in which my mind was scorching last July, when I sat for it. All the others of me, like most portraits whatsoever, are, of course, more agreeable than nature'.[2] While again saluting in Augusta an adept of the *bis repetita placent*, we must be particularly careful not to forget that the Byronic 'scorching' is not here in any sense the outcome of the weather: July, 1813, is the month of the incest. And Augusta herself seems to have

to Mary's appeal for a visit to Annesley Hall. Was it, as Byron says, by Augusta's advice that he refrained? At this date—which is that of the resumption, more passionate than ever, of the incestuous intercourse—he did not need any advice to make him refrain. Besides, the text of his letter leaves no room for doubt; and though Mary had been for her hour important, she was entirely negligible at that with which we are now concerned.

[1]*Corr*. i. pp. 214-215.　　　　　　[2]*Letters and Journals*, ii. p. 350.

thought her acknowledgment of the miniature inadequate, for two days later, on November 29, she addressed to Byron the most revealing of all the documents published by Lord Lovelace—one which, like him, I must here display exactly as it stands:

> Partager tous vos sentimens
> ne voir que par vos yeux
> n'agir que par vos conseils, ne
> vivre que pour vous, voilà mes
> vœux, mes projets, et le seul
> destin qui peut me rendre
> heureuse. . . .

The note was accompanied by a little packet containing a lock of dark brown hair tied with a white silk ribbon. Under the lock was written on a sheet of paper the name:

AUGUSTA.

Byron added with his own hand:

> La Chevelure of
> the *one* whom I
> most *loved**.[1]

Byron kept his journal regularly until December 18, when he abandoned it for the composition of *The Corsair*—of which he was to say, two months later, in the same journal: 'It was written *con amore*, and much from *existence*'. A single entry, that of January 16, 1814, in which Byron announces his departure next day; then complete silence until his return to London on February 18. Now, in the interval Byron had been alone with Augusta at Newstead—a tête-à-tête accentuated by a severe frost and such a snow-fall as made it impossible to take any outdoor exercise. Yet not only did he never feel the least desire to resume his diary, but he did not return to London to enjoy *The Corsair* triumph—it was published during his absence, and Murray wrote to say that he had sold on the day of publication ('A thing perfectly unprecedented') ten thousand copies. But in the letter thanking

[1]The asterisk was used by him to designate Augusta (*Astarte*, p. 263).

Murray for this news, Byron wrote: 'Since I left London, though shut up, *snow*-bound, *thaw*-bound, and tempted with all kinds of paper, the dirtiest of ink, and the bluntest of pens, I have not even been haunted by a wish to put them to their combined uses, except in letters of business—my rhyming propensity is quite gone. . . . I have been sauntering and dozing here very quietly, and not unhappily'.[1] Finally, and perhaps most significant of all, from Newstead he wrote only twice to Lady Melbourne. The earlier letter, of which he says elsewhere that it was only on business, has disappeared—perhaps it was lost in the snow-drifts; in the second, of January 29, he confines himself to summing up the matrimonial situation of Mrs. Musters (whom one perceives to be now a useful smoke-screen), and only at the end does he mention Augusta, this time in the tone that one adopts towards a correspondent with whom one has no intention of going deeply into a subject: 'I mentioned yesterday that Augusta was here, which renders it much more pleasant, as we never yawn or disagree, and laugh much more than is suitable to so stolid a mansion; and the family shyness makes us more amusing companions to each other than we could be to anyone else'.[2] But Lady Melbourne's clairvoyance was not to be deceived. In Byron's next letter, written when he had left Newstead, after excusing himself for his neglect to visit Mary Musters, as he had promised Lady Melbourne to do, and having even —to prove Augusta guiltless in the matter—added that she had urged him to go (though elsewhere he had said the exact reverse) the postscript confronts us with this: 'You seem to think that I am in some scrape at present by my unequal spirits. Perhaps I am, but you shan't be shocked, so you shan't. I won't draw further on you for sympathy.'[3] That passage permits us to be practically certain that incest had been resumed, when we recall the letters of September, 1813, in which Byron says that if those relations are resumed he will consider that he has no longer any right to mention the sub-

[1] *Letters and Journals*, iii. pp. 22-24.   [2] *Corr.* i. p. 241.   [3] *Corr.* i. p. 242.

ject to Lady Melbourne. At the point we have now reached, he intends, and perhaps even wills, to go on with the incest; and so he resorts to silence. The second phase is that of April, 1814, marked by the birth of Medora Leigh. On April 25, having announced the event to Lady Melbourne in words that we have already seen, he concludes: 'But positively she and I will grow good and all that, and so we are *now*, and shall be these three weeks and more too'.[1] Did 'goodness and all that' last much longer than the three weeks of convalescence, when *virtue* was in fact a matter of necessity? In the domain of action, we know nothing; but it is certain that even a little while before Medora's birth, from the end of March, 1814, and in full agreement with Augusta, he was again tending towards the solution of marriage, sought at first by preference among Augusta's friends, from whose hands he evidently wished to receive his bride. (I shall presently return to this.) But that his feeling was, at heart, quite unchanged, we know beyond doubt from the symbolic fact that on the trunk of a tree at Newstead Byron, carving his own name and Augusta's, added this date: 'September 20, 1814.' On September 18 he had received Miss Milbanke's acceptance of the offer of marriage which, for the second time, he had just made to her.

*   *   *

But now we leave the domain of facts. What concerns us here is the reaction on Byron's genius, the reverberation set up by these events; and those were such that one may say it was they which put him in possession of that genius itself. 'Two-dimensional, lacking in that plastic depth which only an experience lived and realised to the full can supply'—so I characterized Byron's treatment of his theme in the two first cantos of *Childe Harold*. Now, if the central event of his life put Byron in possession of his genius, it was precisely because incest endowed that genius with the *third dimension* which until then it had lacked; and the genius burst forth on

[1] *Corr*. i. p. 251.

that fourteenth of November, 1813, which saw the Journal begun. Everything that was undifferentiated, anonymous, has disappeared; thenceforth, into every utterance of Byron's his whole personality passes—and even 'passes' is now the wrong word: concentrated, gathered, massed, every bit of it, the personality is projected as an indivisible whole, and for ever imprinted on the memory.[1]

Energy of expression—that is in my view the dominating factor in Byron's genius, and nowhere does it so sovereignly assert itself as in his Journals, which I hold to be, *par excellence*, his masterpieces. 'I like energy—even animal energy—of all kinds; and I have need of both mental and corporeal.' Animalism—human animalism in the grand style—is here at the root, not only of the nature, but of the expression itself; and when, as is the way with journals, the faculty works without any sort of limitation, with no purpose but to liberate its forces, the act of writing seems by virtue of that animalism to proceed from an energy both mental and corporeal which thus finds mutual satisfaction. This explains the importance and the prestige of the Byronic Journals, in which *something is*

[1] I have said that, in the order of poetry, the phenomenon did not make its appearance until May, 1814, with *Lara*; but I must go much farther and emphasize the fact that the phenomenon itself is as intermittent in the poetry as it is constant in the prose—the Journals and the Letters. Among the men of genius who have used both registers, there is perhaps none with whom prose and poetry are to such a degree incommensurable, impossible to bring into relation. As a prose-writer—and a prose-writer in spite of himself, since he never wrote what he called 'works' in anything but verse—Byron is the equal of anyone; as a poet (except for *Don Juan*, which must always be considered apart) there is scarcely any comparison with the work of an authentic poet, even a minor one, from which Byron's poetry would not suffer. This is because his prose, entirely spontaneous in its upspringing, goes its triumphant way in a zone which might be called *a-formal*; for (except towards the end of his life, when he found it in *Don Juan*) Byron is without any sense of form, whence the lapses, the inadequacies, the irredeemable blots on his poetry; whence also the complete antithesis between his defects as a poet and his qualities as a prose-writer—the blunders, the vaguenesses, the futile abundance, the inflated insistance are all things in whose very existence it is scarcely possible to believe after just rising from the Journals and Letters. But I am here concerned to point out an *intermittent* only as it contrasts with a *constant*; fortunately for me, Byron's poetry is not my subject.

always happening, even (and almost one should say, above all) when *nothing is happening*; for, in the latter instance, one sees still more nakedly, experiences still more directly, the extent of the power that can belong to the *statement*. As I said in our preamble: 'That the context should turn out to be quite neg-ligible in regard to the effect produced—there lies the very core of personal prestige'; and it is precisely because in the Byron of the Journals and Letters personality and expression are one, that something is always happening. I added that in the Journal the statement, the *It is so* of Byron, has 'the noble brevity of an epitaph', and we are now able to perceive the reason. There are journals—those of Stendhal in his youth, for example—which look towards the future, are wholly orientated by it, and whose sinuosities prepare and almost model the still multifarious aspects of the *possible*. In Byron's case, on the contrary, the Journals (and indeed all of his work that matters) have the *event behind* them—whatever their nature, the new facts which are penetrating his consciousness encounter in the background the ever-present memory, im-mutable and secretly cherished, of the event itself; it is from the memory that they rebound when they project themselves into expression, and that is why in every fact registered, there is *more* than the fact itself—there is, doubling it and aggravating its importance, the ground-bass of the incest. And the ground-bass here is that of remorse—and remorse is what provides Byron with exactly the emotional substance that his genius requires. Sombre and yet heady,[1] murky to the core, stirred, enriched, and as it were incubated in memory, the Byronic remorse gives rein to, indulges, decuples that vein of voluptuously guilty reminiscence in which for my part I am

[1] In the note-book to which, from time to time, I confide in passing the kind of comments which of their nature take an aphoristic form, I find this, in July, 1922: 'There is no perfume that goes to the head as remorse does'. When I wrote it, Byron was as far from my mind as could be; I give it here because—especially on account of 'goes to the head', which happens to be very applicable to the Byronic remorse—it seems to elucidate my immediate meaning.

inclined to see the mainspring of what, in spite of all, is still
poetic in Byron's genius. Suffocating under its onward flow,
Byron the poet, in hours like these, resembles a man who,
feeling as if he were stifling, throws the window open and
takes a long deep breath. Byron's verses, when they persuade
us, nearly always follow the rhythm of breathing itself; spontaneous as the elements, their effect resides in the animal heat
they liberate. With the exception of *Don Juan*, they owe
nothing to art; and if *Manfred* seems to me the most Byronic
of any of his works, this is because not only yielding, but on
that occasion wanting to yield, to the vein of voluptuously
guilty reminiscence, Byron there, more than anywhere else,
breathes to the full.

Le Bonheur dans le Crime—impossible to help invoking
here both the title of Barbey d'Aurevilly's story, and the
amazing stand of that couple, so well-matched, before the
menagerie in the Jardin des Plantes. Certainly, Byron would
not have admitted that the word *bonheur* could be applied to
him—in the first place because it does not belong to the
vocabulary of the Fatal Being, and then because the human
animal of the higher species (and it is one of his numerous
limitations) never regards happiness as anything but the *weak
beat* of existence itself. And yet, if not for the man, at all
events for his genius, there is a kind of happiness in being
carried in the direction that is one's own. In the incest Byron
had encountered 'his' fatality, which now lacked only the seal
of catastrophe. How that came to pass, we shall examine in
the final chapter, where, affronting the dense piled-up darkness, a light at last appears, where enters the woman whose
irreproachable greatness soars so high above all this story—
Annabella Milbanke, Lady Byron.

CHAPTER VI

. . . There was that in my spirit ever
Which shaped out for itself some great reverse.

IN his historical tragedy, *Marino Faliero*, Byron lends this speech to his hero—I say 'lends', because there is hardly any that issues more directly from Byron himself. The need of the 'great reverse' is inherent in him who carries the need of fatality, and indeed the two are one. Some time ago, when Nietzsche was my theme, in commenting on the lines in *Zarathustra* where Nietzsche proclaims his love for 'him who wills to founder', I said: 'That is just what Nietzsche wills: he wills to founder. Something in the subsoil of his nature needs to be confronted with disaster; only at that price can he in his own eyes become the incomparable, the sovereign spectacle ever implicit for him in the word *Untergang*; he can never be quite content unless he is to himself as a sun about to plunge into the gulf in which it will be reabsorbed. For him, all tragic value is incomplete that is not crowned by the ultimate catastrophe'. It is because with Nietzsche the fatality is wholly internal, because all things—even to the spectacle that he gives himself—are projected from within, utterly unalloyed, that Nietzsche is the supreme type of modern fatality. But it is none the less true that the need for the 'great reverse' is in the line of all tragic natures, even the low-voiced ones, those who are of a modesty so exquisite that they feel as though invaded by chaste alarm at the mere emergence of tragedy in their lives—let me recall the plaintive violin-tone of that lovable François who is the hero of Jacques Rivière's *Aimée*: 'Was it she on whom I was at last to be broken, on whom I was at last to founder? I steered for her like a madman—I sought the reef'.

The reef—the pride of a Byron does not even admit that it may have to be sought; he regards it as his by right, and should it fail to appear, he is quick to raise up, to create it. The Byronic pride is basaltic, impervious, set before us as an object—we might think to touch its massive stillness. In *Julian and Maddalo*, that poem in which Shelley's usual liquidity is accompanied by an ineffable and adorable pedestrian grace, and where, depicting Byron as Maddalo and himself as Julian (the Julian of whom, in his brief preface, he tells us no more than that 'he was rather serious') he lets us share in their rides on the Lido . . . in this poem, Shelley has understood and rendered better than anyone the Byronic pride, and has revealed its cause: there is nothing that invincible gentleness does not know about its contrary.

> . . . Pride
> Made my companion take the darker side.
> The sense that he was greater than his kind
> Had struck, methinks, his eagle spirit blind
> By gazing on its own exceeding light.

No one like an angelic nature for hitting the centre of the target. One does encounter in Byron the peculiar blindness engendered by the impossibility of being humble; and that his was a case of that impossibility Byron himself well knew. He expressly says so in the passage in *Manfred* where he draws the portrait of Astarte—a passage of such delicate beauty, so like the 'fresh breaking day' on the mountain-peaks which in his invocation Manfred salutes, that I can never read it without feeling that the sombre story of that incest is transmuted into crystal:

> She was like me in lineaments—her eyes—
> Her hair—her features—all, to the very tone
> Even of her voice, they said were like to mine;
> But softened all, and tempered into beauty:
> She had the same lone thoughts and wanderings,
> The quest of hidden knowledge, and a mind
> To comprehend the Universe: not these
> Alone, but with them gentler powers than mine,

Pity, and smiles, and tears—which I had not;
And tenderness—but that I had for her;
Humility—and that I never had.
Her faults were mine—her virtues were her own—
I loved her, and destroyed her!

WITCH

With thy hand?

MANFRED

Not with my hand, but heart, which broke her heart;
It gazed on mine, and withered. . . .

'Humility—and that I never had.' Let me add that Byron's
massive pride made him opaque, impenetrable to and by
others; I mean that between him and others was not formed,
could not move, not circulate, the atmosphere which alone is
propitious to—I will not even say exchanges (in Byron's case
we have seen that they were excluded), but mere communications, any communication but that which the line from
Manfred defines with tragic simplicity, 'the other's heart'. That
heart, whatever woman might be in question, 'gazed on his,
and withered'. Like all those who are greatly proud, Byron
destroys; but in addition he belongs to that race of the proud
in the second degree with whom pride—at once a need and a
passion—never knows its ultimate throb until they have destroyed themselves. For my own part, I am persuaded that the
bent, or more plainly the love, for self-destruction may sometimes be associated with real greatness, may even bear some
mysterious relation to it; and I am persuaded, too, that then
the sensibility may expend itself wholly—and, so doing, have
a sense of strange but intense vitality—on the mere act of
self-destruction, an act the stranger for being passive, looked
on at rather than performed. But this theme is of such complex and subtle richness that it would lead us too far afield.
'He always wanted to ruin himself, this Byron'—so Barrès in
his *La Mort de Venise* closes his evocation of the Byronic
shade among those which 'float on the Adriatic sunsets'; and

because at certain hours in his life Barrès had been himself so sensible of the throb that lies in self-destruction, no one was better qualified here to pronounce on Byron.

The portrait of Astarte is contemporary with the Journal kept by Byron for Augusta during his tour of the Bernese Alps (September 18-29, 1816), and sent her immediately, so that she might share his emotions. Less than twenty pages, but it is sublime; never perhaps has the grandiose in nature —as seen among mountain-peaks—been so perceived and rendered, under the aspect, ever-present, of the Creation in travail. I cannot resist giving one or two specimens: 'The torrent is in shape curving over the rock, like the *tail* of a white horse streaming in the wind, such as it might be conceived would be that of the '*pale* horse' on which *Death* is mounted in the Apocalypse. It is neither mist nor water, but a something between both; its immense height . . . gives it a wave, a curve, a spreading here, a condensation there, wonderful and indescribable. . . . Heard the Avalanches falling every five minutes nearly—as if God was pelting the Devil down from Heaven with snow balls. . . . A very fine Glacier, like *a frozen hurricane.* . . . Passed *whole woods of withered pines, all withered*; trunks stripped and barkless, branches lifeless; done by a single winter,—their appearance reminded me of me and my family'.[1] Not only were the Bernese Alps the setting and the atmosphere for *Manfred* ('I have lately repeopled my mind with Nature', says the Journal), but they seem to have moulded the figures themselves— Astarte, in the Byronic delineation, gleams glacier-like, illumined, translucid. We are here at the very heart of the Augusta myth, and more generally, of Byron's faculty for *myth-making.* The more his case is studied, the more Byron appears as the man whose work, and life no less, proceed on two planes so remote from one another that they function in

[1] *Letters and Journals*, iii. pp. 358-360.

water-tight compartments, and cannot possibly be unified; and it is to this wide separation between the two planes that we must assign the fact that some have doubted the Byronic sincerity, which nevertheless is among the most incontestable there are. On the one hand he is the piercing, the concise observer—and quite involuntarily, with that lordly negligence of his to which I have alluded; nothing escapes him, and he never emits that secretion of commentaries, explanations which tenderly mitigate the crude results by filtering them through a protective veil. But on the other hand, and above all when concerned with the women who gravitate round his star, Byron, once he has entered the phase of poetic creation, becomes a prodigious myth-maker.[1] It is by virtue of these two planes that in Byron's eyes, and with equal sincerity, Augusta can be 'a fool', and the model for the portrait of Astarte.

True, the portrait of Astarte was written in exile, at a time when, though he would not yet admit it, something in Byron already felt and knew that Augusta was lost to him, and lost by his own fault; but his myth-making faculty needed, for its full functioning, the theme of *absence*—an irremediable, avenging absence, which yet had also its own intoxicating power; and that theme had to make itself heard in, had to colour insistently, the poetic discharge. Here we can apprehend, in the second degree, the impossibility of bringing the two planes into relation; for if on the one hand (as he himself said twenty times over)[2] Byron could not love anyone unless the person was there, if for him, in actual life, the

[1]Here we are in possession of the psychic reason for the impossibility of bringing Byron's prose into relation with his poetry. In prose, it is the piercing and concise observer who speaks; in poetry, on the contrary (*Don Juan* always excepted), it is the myth-maker.

[2]'This I must say for myself, that my attachment always increases in due proportion to the return it meets with, and never changes in the presence of its object' (*Corr*. i. p. 288).

absent were always wrong, on the other hand, in the mythical sphere and no less in the amorous sentiment induced by the mythical activity (I may recall Mary Chaworth, and even, at her propitious moment, Lady Caroline), the absent were always right. Perhaps we may see in this both the proof and the ultimate reason for Augusta's unique place in Byron's destiny: he never loved any woman but Augusta, for she was the only one whom he loved both in *presence* and in *absence*, the only one in whose favour was achieved that unification which everywhere else was impossible to him—and that because his tragedy consisted in having been born, so to say, in two halves.

And here, before proceeding, I feel an urgent need to make a *mea culpa*. Though it is possible that at the beginning of their relations the incest was what Byron principally loved in Augusta,[1] from the January of 1814 (thus two years and a half before the rending farewell-evening on which I wrongly declared that love, strictly speaking, was first born) he did love Augusta for herself, independently of the fact that she was his sister; and my *mea culpa* is made the more imperative by my sense that, for him to have loved her thus, she must have been *lovable*.[2] If further proof of Byron's love for her were needed, it might be found in the passionate eagerness with which he always defended her, and took upon himself the entire responsibility for the incest. In this very January of 1814, replying to the letter in which he compared his state to that of Mithridates and obeying a very feminine impulse, Lady Melbourne had tried to throw all the blame on Augusta; and here is Byron's instant reaction: 'You are quite mistaken, however, as to *her*, and it must be from some misrepresenta-

---

[1] In this view I am inclined to persevere on account of the sincerity of Byron's love for Lady Frances in October, 1813; for let us remember that at that time he did not answer Augusta's letter, and that not only was he prepared to run away with Lady Frances, but he wished to join his life with hers definitely.

[2] 'Now grant me this, that she is in truth a very *lovable* woman and I will try and not love any longer' (*Corr.* i. p. 256; from a letter to Lady Melbourne of May 1, 1814).

tion of mine that you throw the blame so completely on the side least deserving, and least able to bear it. I daresay I made the best of my own story, as one always does from natural selfishness without intending it, but it was not her fault, but my own *folly* (give it what name may suit it better) and her weakness, for the intentions of both were very different, and for some time adhered to, and when not, it was entirely my own—in short, I know no name for my conduct. Pray do not speak so harshly of her to me—the cause of all'.[1]

Most likely it is the exasperation that Augusta's personality arouses in me—I mean, from the ignorance that we are kept in, by the way she expresses herself, about her feelings, and the type of being she represents—which makes me, when she is concerned, as blind as Byron's pride made him. I was anxious to make these amends to a memory that, in spite of myself, I ill-treat.

And indeed, at the point we have reached, Augusta was quite sincerely urging Byron to marry, and for the best of motives. In a letter written a fortnight after his engagement, Byron expressly tells Lady Melbourne: 'She wished me much to marry, because it was the only chance of redemption for *two* persons'.[2] Truly, it was in those terms that the problem of Byron's marriage not only was, but *had to be* stated; and yet even though correctly stated, even though morality was so vitally interested in its solution, the problem remained insoluble, could not but lead to the 'great reverse', and Byron himself supplies us beforehand with the reason. 'I have no heart to spare and expect none in return.' The phrase occurs in a letter of January 16, 1814, to Lady Melbourne; I add so much of the context as here concerns us: 'A wife, you say, would be my salvation. . . . I do believe that to marry would be my wisest step—but whom? . . . All wives would be much the same. I have no heart to spare and expect none in return; but, as Moore says, "A pretty wife is something for the fastidious vanity of a *roué* to *retire* upon". And mine might do as

[1]*Corr.* i. pp. 231-232.　　　　[2]*Corr.* i. pp. 273-274.

she pleased, so that she had a fair temper, and a quiet way of conducting herself, leaving me the same liberty of conscience. What I want is a companion—a friend rather than a sentimentalist. I have seen enough of love matches—and of all matches—to make up my mind to the common lot of happy couples. The only misery would be if I fell in love afterwards—which is not unlikely, for habit has a strange power over my affections'.[1] In the passage immediately preceding this, Byron speaks of his fancy of the moment, the young sister of Lady Frances, Lady Catherine Annesley; but he admits that the chief attraction for him in that match would be the sort of revenge it would signify on Lady Frances, whom he can never quite forgive (and here we see a 'second thought' which was indeed the reverse of the medal) for his own good action. Now, in his diary of the same day, we find, in connection with Lady Catherine, certain reflections which fully enlighten us on the Byronic view of marriage: 'A wife would be my salvation. I am sure the wives of my acquaintances have hitherto done me little good. Catherine is beautiful, but very young, and, I think, a fool. But I have not seen enough to judge; besides, I hate an *esprit* in petticoats. That she won't love me is very probable, nor shall I love her. But, on my system, and the modern system in general, that don't signify. The business (if it came to business) would probably be arranged between papa and me. She would have her own way; I am good-humoured to women, and docile; and, if I did not fall in love with her, which I should try to prevent, we should be a very comfortable couple. As to conduct, *that* she must look to. But *if* I love, I shall be jealous;— and for that reason I will not be in love. Though, after all, I doubt my temper, and fear I should not be so patient as becomes the *bienséance* of a married man in my station. Divorce ruins the poor *femme*, and damages are a paltry compensation. I do fear my temper would lead me into some of our oriental tricks of vengeance. . . . So "I'll none on't", but

[1] *Corr.* i. p. 237.

163

e'en remain single and solitary;—though I should like to have somebody now and then to yawn with one'.[1] It is worth recalling that both letter and diary were written the day before he left London for the tête-à-tête with Augusta at Newstead; for the fact shows that, even when most absorbed by incest, Byron never wholly lost sight of the idea of marriage, regarded as the sole means of salvation.

'I have no heart to spare and expect none in return.' We need not dwell upon 'and expect none in return', which Byron—with the *naïveté* of those who have overdone experience—believed to represent a restoring of the balance. To 'have no heart to spare' means either that that organ has been omitted from a person's composition, or that it exists but has already been disposed of. On the first hypothesis, if by virtue of a fortunate and not infrequent dispensation, the organ has on both sides been omitted, the couple run no worse risk than do performers on the parallel bars that one sees in gymnasiums; but once there comes from either side no matter how faint a pulsation, things get more complicated. Now, in the case we are considering, Byron had a heart, but it functioned for Augusta only; and that is why Annabella, who brought him, centupled, that which he 'did not expect', never could find the clue to that heart. But I must not anticipate; let us return to the facts.

Though with Byron, as he once said to Lady Melbourne, we must always take into account his epistolary levity, and (even in the Journal) that La Rochefoucauld vein of self-depreciation, it is no less true that—again to use his own word —the Byronic 'system' of married life shows a remarkable consistency. It is only fair to add that before the incest, the system (an edifice so well constructed that it comprised every one of the commonplaces relating to the conjugal state) included yet another detail of the kind, and that the oldest and most venerated—namely, the question of money. In 1811, as we remember, Byron had written to Augusta: 'By-the-bye, *I*

[1] *Letters and Journals*, ii. pp. 380-381.

shall marry, if I can find any thing inclined to barter money for rank within six months'. From the time of the incest, that brick fell out;[1] but only to be replaced by another which, when we know Byron, we see to be of cardinal importance—aristocracy of birth. In a letter to Lady Melbourne he mentions among his reasons for admiring Miss Milbanke that she is 'of high blood, a score on which I have still a few Norman and Scotch prejudices, were I to marry'; and to complete the cycle of our impressions, it will be worth seeing how Byron expounded the system to a male friend so intimate as was Moore. This letter is of August 28, 1813, six weeks after the incest: 'After all, we must end in marriage; and I can conceive nothing more delightful than such a state in the country, reading the county newspaper, etc., and kissing one's wife's maid. Seriously, I would incorporate with any woman of decent demeanour to-morrow—that is, I would a month ago, but at present, . . .'[2] Byron breaks off abruptly because he remembers the actual situation and the fact that he has confided it to Moore; but the persistence and, despite the tone, the sincerity with which he continues to play with the idea of marriage, are only the more striking for that. And now that—like a vessel self-prepared, equipped and armed for its destination, the 'great reverse'—Byron is ready to set sail, let us begin at the beginning of his relations with Annabella Milbanke.

* * *

On the first of May, 1812, here is what Byron wrote to Caroline Lamb: 'My dear Lady Caroline—I have read over the few poems of Miss Milbank (*sic*) with attention. They display fancy, feeling, and a little practice would very soon induce facility of expression. Though I have an abhorrence of Blank

[1] I want to lay stress on the fact that in money-matters Byron always showed as not only disinterested but liberal; and though at the end of his life he said that he had 'taken up with avarice, which is the only vice I have not yet tried, and a good old-gentlemanly one it is', this must be regarded simply as a pose, for it influenced his practice in no wise.

[2] *Letters and Journals*, ii. p. 253.

Verse, I like the lines on Dermody so much that I wish they were in rhyme. The lines in the Cave at Seaham have a turn of thought which I cannot sufficiently commend, and here I am at least candid as my own opinions differ upon such subjects. The first stanza is very good indeed, and the others, with a few slight alterations, might be rendered equally excellent. The last are smooth and pretty. But these are all, has she no others? She certainly is a very extraordinary girl; who would imagine so much strength and variety of thought under that placid Countenance? It is not necessary for Miss M. to be an authoress, indeed I do not think publishing at all creditable either to men or women, and (though you will not believe me) very often feel ashamed of it myself; but I have no hesitation in saying that she has talents which, were it proper or requisite to indulge, would have led to distinction. A friend of mine (fifty years old, and an author, but not *Rogers*) has just been here. As there is no name to the MSS. I shewed them to him, and he was much more enthusiastic in his praises than I have been. He thinks them beautiful; I shall content myself with observing that they are better, much better, than anything of Miss M.'s protégée [*sic*] Blacket. You will say as much of this to Miss M. as you think proper. I say all this very sincerely. I have no desire to be better acquainted with Miss Milbank; she is too good for a fallen spirit to know, and I should like her more if she were less perfect'.[1] The concluding phrase is on a plane which at every point transcends the personalities in question, a plane truly universal, and raising the most attractive but the most mysterious of problems; and though it is not yet the time to dwell upon this, we already have the key to, and the symbol of, all the future relations between these two. Let us keep it in mind, and once more admire the infallible observer in Byron. Strength and variety of thought, placid countenance, kindness, perfection—all central features in the portrait of Annabella, almost indeed those which compose it; and if

[1]*Letters and Journals*, ii. pp. 118-121.

in her letters (which we now possess) variety of thought seems less perceptible than strength, that is because we are unconsciously inclined to postulate a necessary relation between variety of *thought* and variety of *expression*. It is true that experience for the most part confirms this, but not always. Until life gripped Annabella, she is devoid, strictly speaking, of any gift of expression: all her writings are stereotyped, monotonous, and, as Ethel Colburn Mayne says, 'heavy-handed'; but when we study the content underlying this monotony, we see that there is much variety of thought— only it too is distributed so uniformly that it leads us still farther astray. From the moment that, in this respect as in all others, sorrow unlocked Annabella, the variety of her thought is no less perceptible than its strength.

Her 'placid countenance' was of course the mask of placidity's very opposite; and Ethel Colburn Mayne, imagining Annabella's feelings on hearing this letter of Byron's read to her by Caroline Lamb, is quite right when she says: 'Her own "placid countenance" . . . So placid, was it? Had one not, when unjustly accused, felt "the madness of pride to such a degree that I have struck my head till I staggered back?" Had one not had "great difficulties to surmount from the impetuosity and sensitiveness of my character?" How little Lord Byron knew about one!'[1] And yet this does not contravene Byron's diagnosis, for in Annabella the placid countenance is as important as 'the impetuosity and sensitiveness' of character; it represents the other pole, that of self-control, and what rounds off the greatness of her character is precisely the alliance in it of the two extremes—passionate feeling and self-control.

Born in May,[2] 1792, and thus four years and five months younger than Byron, Anne Isabella (for her friends, Anna-

[1] *Life of Lady Byron*, pp. 42-43.

[2] Her birthday was the 17th, Ascension Thursday. An English proverb says: 'Thursday's child has far to go'; on which Ethel Colburn Mayne comments: 'Like other oracles, it was ambiguous' (*Life of Lady Byron*, p. 1).

bella) was the only child of Sir Ralph Milbanke and the Hon.
Judith Noel. Through her father, who was Lady Melbourne's
brother, she was the niece of Byron's dearest and unique confidante; and I am persuaded that the pleasure (in which he
indulged even before his engagement) of calling Lady Melbourne *ma tante* played an important part in his final choice.
It may be added—since, in Byron's case, to 'keep things in
the family' applied to satellites no less than to the star himself—that Annabella was cousin by marriage to Caroline
Lamb.

The frontispiece to *Astarte* shows us Hoppner's fine portrait of Annabella as a child—a picture scarcely less velvety
in its beauty than that of the too succulent Lady Oxford; but
this time the fresh radiance in the round face of a little girl
of ten confronts us, looking straight before her with that
childish eagerness which frequently inspires us with a respect
that is full of compunction. When she was six years old her
mother wrote of her: 'She is excessively talkative and entertaining *if she likes people*, and very coaxing to her favourites;
and she will judge *for herself* and cannot be *made* to like anybody'. Her aunt Mary Noel tells us that 'Annabella was never
fond of a doll', upon which Ethel Colburn Mayne observes:
'We need not interpret this exclusively as lack of the maternal
instinct—too simplified explanation of what in her was a
complex trait. Like all children, she loved make-believe, and
her make-believe always implied self-devotion; but it implied
as well a struggle against adverse destiny from which *she* was
to be the rescuer. "Like a boy"—and just as much like a girl,
if the girl is one with an impulse to protect the conscious, not
the merely helpless, struggler. That impulse was strong in
Annabella Milbanke; in Annabella Byron it became supreme,
excessive—the expression of an almost fanatical ideal. The
helplessness of infancy and childhood did not awaken it; she
had too much of intellectual pride for that. The mind must
take part before she could feel devotion'. I shall presently define my view of the expression 'intellectual pride' as applied

to Annabella; but in this penetrating analysis, the last phrase
is that which I think particularly admirable. Annabella is the
pure type of those natures which need that the mind should
set the feeling in movement, but with whom—once the
movement has been set up—there is no limit to the powers of
feeling and self-devotion; and Ethel Colburn Mayne immediately adds: 'Magnanimity—that was the spur. But not blind
magnanimity! Part of her formidable incorruptibility, this
was. Devotion was not to be a reason for denying the weaknesses of its objects. So early as her seventh year she sounded
that note. Someone asked her if her father were not always
right. She answered: "Probably not. Sometimes right, sometimes wrong, as we all are" '. Need that the mind should
encourage the feeling, that reflection should accompany
love, and, in the very heart of that love, that impartiality and
objectivity should not be out of court—all this is truly fundamental in Annabella. When in 1812 we come to know her
better (she was then just twenty), we have a further repre-
sentation of her in the shape of a miniature by the same
Hayter who, by a coincidence that events were to load with
significance, had done in the same 1812 that drawing of
Augusta prior to the incest. The manner imposed on the
artist by the difference in his two sitters makes the comparison
between these two human types a revelation in itself—for
while, in the drawing, his pencil abandons itself to the charm
of what I have called 'a beauty at once regular and languorous', the miniature presents a strikingly sculptural aspect,
reminding us both in treatment and attitude, somewhat
constrained and affected as they are, of the over-polished
marbles of Canova or Chinard. Augusta's face yields; Annabella's, despite its roundness,[1] and even under the mask of
its smiling amenity, resists. She declared that Hayter had
never seen *her* countenance, 'because it is under the de-

[1]This roundness made Byron give her the nickname of Pippin, of which,
doubtless because it belonged to the too rare halcyon moments, she was
fond, sometimes using it herself in her letters to him.

pressing influence of shyness in his presence'; and Ethel Colburn Mayne adds: 'It was a self-conscious countenance that Hayter saw, or at any rate rendered—the countenance of a young lady unmistakably sitting for her portrait'. But she and I are at one as to the general impression given by the portrait, for she says: 'Even if we knew nothing about her, this picture would speak to us of a girl who was going to take things hard'. And this is how Byron himself, in November, 1821, described the Miss Milbanke of 1812 to Medwin: 'There was something piquant and what we term pretty in Miss Milbanke. Her features were small and feminine, though not regular. She had the fairest skin imaginable. Her figure was perfect for her height; and there was a simplicity, a retired modesty, about her which was very characteristic, and formed a happy contrast to the cold, artificial formality and studied stiffness, which is called fashion'.[1]

Simplicity, modesty, discretion are sometimes signs of the quality which is of all perhaps most rarely met with in human beings—I mean *solidity*; and (it is a case for use of the cliché, which in this instance is for once literally and tragically true) Annabella was of a solidity that was proof against anything. In her, not only was the mind solid in all that it approached or attempted, but it had besides that much rarer solidity which consists in never losing one's head over the results of one's own activities; and, on the purely intellectual plane, it is a signal merit to have no pretensions, not *in spite* of but *because* of one's right to have many. No one knew that better than Byron, for in his Journal for November 26, 1813, he wrote of Annabella: 'She is a very superior woman, and very little spoiled, which is strange in an heiress—a girl of twenty —a peeress that is to be, in her own right—an only child, and a *savante*, who has always had her own way. She is a poetess —a mathematician, a metaphysician, and yet, withal, very kind, generous, and gentle, with very little pretension. Any other head would be turned with half her acquisitions, and a

[1]Medwin, *Conversations with Lord Byron*, pp. 44-45.

tenth of her advantages'.[1] Here is the place to define my view
of the expression 'intellectual pride' as applied to Annabella.
I agree in the main with what Byron's Journal says of her,
but I can understand the accusation of intellectual pride.
Indeed, we are now considering a problem which, as I think,
gives birth to a serious misconception. Beings of Annabella's
type are modesty itself in presence of any real superiority
which they can recognize for such; only, as they seldom encounter it in their immediate surroundings, and in what is
called 'the world', what comes to pass is, that their own
superiority intensifying and deepening their sense of isola-
tion in daily life, they give, in spite of themselves, the impression of pride. Nothing is more resented than intellect by
those to whom it is denied, and who of course are convinced
that they possess it. It is true that from Annabella we have
an avowal oddly resembling that of Byron in *Manfred*: 'About
one of her new acquaintances she had this to say: "She has
more humility than I have" ';[2] and it is certain that of all
virtues, humility is the one that came hardest to her, for it
was not in the line of her nature. But one may—and, to my
thinking, it was so with her—be modest without being
humble; for modesty, though it implies finding one's level
among superiors, does not prevent one from remembering
one's own value as compared with others; and moreover, in
any case to be not humble is not *ipso facto* to be the prey of
'intellectual pride', for the other consciousness, ever present,
of those who surpass one is sure to re-establish the balance.
On the other hand, when Ethel Colburn Mayne writes:
'There was a vein of spiritual pride in Annabella Milbanke,
always to be reckoned with despite the efforts at subdual',[3]
it would be dangerous to dispute the point. Though she
tried to subdue it, there *was* in her a vein of spiritual pride;
and this is explained by the fact that, rare as it is, intelligence
is yet not so rare as virtue, and that spiritual pride is the

[1]*Letters and Journals*, ii. p. 357.   [2]*Life of Lady Byron*, p. 16.
[3]*Life of Lady Byron*, p. 16.

obstacle that virtue is peculiarly called on to surmount. I shall not dispute Byron's verdict as to her poetic dispositions or gifts; with regard to her mathematical powers,[1] I shall permit myself to shelter my incompetence under a like 'discretion' to her own. Before calling her, in the frantic imprecations from his exile, his 'mathematical Medea', Byron was fond of the nickname 'Princess of Parallelograms', as we see in this passage from a letter to Lady Melbourne of October 18, 1812: 'I thank you again for your efforts with my Princess of Parallelograms, who has puzzled you more than the Hypothenuse; in her Character she has not forgotten "Mathematics", wherein I used to praise her cunning. Her processes are quite rectangular, or rather we are two parallel lines prolonged to infinity side by side, but destined never to meet'.[2] It is a pity that the parallelism was not prolonged to infinity, for here there was a line of heart as well, and whatever Byron might say about rectangular processes, that was the 'mathematician's' line. What did he mean when he called her a metaphysician? Judging by the extensive extracts from their correspondence which we now possess,[3] it is clear that she did not pretend to be a metaphysician in the technical sense of the word. Probably, when using the term 'metaphysical', Byron, like almost everyone, had in view any lofty effort of the mind—praiseworthy no doubt, but in his eyes abstruse and divorced from any reality whatever. It is the attitude of those —whether geniuses or not—who refuse, and mostly without being aware of their refusal, to set or to set themselves or even to let others set in its entirety the problem raised by the mere fact of existence. Far from being a 'rectangular process', this is the very reverse: an insidious, a convenient one, though it is also extremely adroit and too often efficacious, for it tends to nothing less than to relegating to the unreal that which is the very centre of all reality. Now Annabella was a

[1]The daughter of Byron and Annabella, Ada, Countess of Lovelace (mother of the author of *Astarte*), was still more gifted in this respect.

[2]*Corr.* i. p. 94.   [3]*Life of Lady Byron*, pp. 57-80.

metaphysician in the very simple acceptation—though every day becoming rarer—in which anyone must be who does set himself the problem in its entirety; and whether a solution be reached or not, the fact of setting the problem is, in the last analysis, the sole valid test of a person's *solidity*. Annabella had not only set herself the problem, but for herself had solved it; and to this solution had respectively contributed the convergent activities of her intellectual, moral, and religious faculties. Leaving aside *applications*, which from the absolute standpoint (by which I here mean no more than in relation to the mind from which they proceed) remain after all, unless creative genius is in question, sub-products,[1] and scrutinizing Annabella's intellectual nature, we find that behind all its manifestations, and whatever the sorrowful, the atrocious intensity of the personal feelings involved, there is the invariant of an unflinching reflection which issues in judgments so objective, so impartial that to this day, those who understand her—and who love her because, imagining themselves more fortunate than she was with Byron, they imagine that they have found the way to her heart—can personally suffer in representing to themselves the redoubled anguish doubtless inflicted upon her, in that interior crypt which she withholds from sight, by the recoil of thought upon itself. About Byron, about Augusta, and about others too, everything she has said is final, with the finality belonging to those who take each human being into consideration, esteem him in advance, open the most extensive credit to him, pronounce upon him only when every alternative is exhausted—and then say the last word. Annabella never gives in to intuition; on the contrary, for the moral reasons to which we are coming, she distrusts intuition, guards herself against it, and even discounts it; but reflection gives her back, in an enhanced measure, what elsewhere intuition runs away with—or fails

[1]Especially in the case of women, whose relative lack of creative power is in this respect compensated for by the marvellous flexibility, resourcefulness, and resilience of feminine intelligence as a whole.

to carry off. Hence she is of the restricted, the admirable company of what I must call psychologists in spite of themselves —those in whom, held in hand with a slightly disdainful austerity, the psychological gift as such enters into action only under the pressure of events, when imperatively urged thereto by respect for the truth transgressed against. And then they are very far from feeling any complacent satisfaction in the results to which that exercise has led them (or rather, which it has imposed on their obedience); they would fain recoil, but dare not—humanly, they long to recoil, and dare not because of the reverence due to truth. Their only hope is that they may have been mistaken, but consternation mingles with that very hope, for the possibility of such error is at once construed by them as the sign of an imagination monstrous, impure, radically depraved—and here we are already in presence of the picture of what was one day to be Annabella's situation, incessantly fighting as she was against her indwelling suspicions. That, in its essence, is a situation to which are subject those who before and above all belong by birth to the moral life, for whom psychology is no more than a means towards elucidation of that life, and from whom psychologists in spite of themselves are principally recruited. Now, apart altogether from circumstance, to such a situation Annabella was so much the more predestined that she had a vocation (in the precise and exclusive sense of the word), and that this was the *moral vocation*: to that she was called, to that she responded, to that she so dedicated herself that, as her life unrolls itself, there moves, is carved before our eyes, with the sobriety of ideal appropriateness, the very frieze of Duty —and Duty in the Kantian sense, with its impersonal, disinterested, universally valid attributes. When a virtue attains complete fulfilment, it always happens that a ray from the virtue that transcends comes down to rest upon it; and Annabella's moral being is irradiated by a religious light, deserves to be given the beautiful name of *mystic morality*, which Henri Bremond felt to be the only one applicable to some of his saintly heroes. In fact, we are in the zone where in Annabella morality and religion are indissolubly united. It already appeared clearly, from Chapter VIII of *Astarte*, and since the publication of *The Life of Lady Byron* has become evident, that with Annabella faith was fundamental, and from certain expressions in Byron's letters, acknowledging that he prefers to 'avoid controversy with so expert a casuist', we had guessed that it was well thought out, well reasoned, that it had reaped all the benefits of her intellectual solidity. Whether emanating from, or on the contrary issuing in, religion, her morality had the virtue of religion, in the etymological sense of the word, which is at once so simple and so strong; she felt and knew herself to be *related*, and knew that so were all others, whether they were conscious of it or not. Her conduct towards Augusta—which in the moral order is one of the most consummate of masterpieces in its combination of discretion, firmness and mercy—is from first to last a testimony to the fact that the central idea of the soul's salvation inspired and guided her slightest actions. In the closing years of her life, she had the consolation of at last meeting with a friendship worthy of her—that with the great preacher, the Rev. Frederick Robertson. When he inquired about her feelings for Augusta, she replied: 'I loved her—I love her still'.[1] One sees why Robertson said that 'she was the noblest woman he had ever known'.

Irreproachable—to that word we must always, and should always, come back with Annabella; it accounts for the 'great reverse' which she shared with Byron, and—in a still deeper sense—for the persistent antipathy felt for her memory

[1]In the Introduction to the second edition of *Astarte*, Lady Lovelace says: 'The letters I now for the first time publish will answer, I think finally, one of the principal objections to the argument of *Astarte*, made especially by women, that Lady Byron *could* not have continued to show affection, or even pity, for Augusta, if at the time she had really believed in her guilt. Many years later, questioned about these things by the friend of her old age, Frederick Robertson, the great preacher, Lady Byron said: "I loved her, and I love her still!" ' . . . One understands that most women might have their doubts, for in such circumstances very few would have been capable of feeling affection or even pity.

throughout three-quarters of a century, and until the publication of *Astarte*, by many people, often those to whom
Byron's personality offered no particular attraction. For it is
with an instinctive hatred, complex, indestructible, that the
world pursues irreproachable beings. 'Simplicity, modesty,
discretion' are here of no avail; what the world cannot forgive them is the mere fact of their existence, because that fact
is to it a living reproach; and so, with the base but effectual
adroitness born of exasperation, the world transforms into a
defect the very absence of defects, and denies the humanness
of those who are guilty of realizing its loftiest ideal. Of this
we possess a proof, almost too arresting, in the letter written
to her by her own mother at the most poignant hour of her
destiny, that of the separation: 'I neither do, or can expect
that you should not *feel* and *deeply feel*—but I have sometimes thought (and that not *only lately*) that Your mind is too
high wrought—too much so for *this* World—only the *grander*
objects engage your thoughts, Your character is like *Proof
Spirits*—not fit for common use—I could almost wish the
Tone of it *lowered* nearer to the level of *us every day people*,
and that You would *endeavor* to take *some interest* in *every
day concerns*—believe me, *by degrees*, You will find the
benefit of it—I have not slept on a Bed of Roses thro' my
life—I have had afflictions and *serious ones*, tho' none *so
Severe* as the *present*—Yet in my sixty-fifth Year, I have en-
deavored to *rally*, and *shall rally*, if *You do* so—Now my
Love here is a Sundays Sermon for You—and here it shall
end—'.[1]

Assuredly, Lady Noel loved Annabella; assuredly, in the
words of the terrible, the tragic commonplace, she said these
things to her 'only for her good'—and how many mothers
have said, have thought it their duty to say, like things to
their daughters! Doubtless, for creatures of Annabella's race,
to hear those words, accept them without a murmur, even

---

[1] *Astarte*, pp. 55-56. The letter is dated March 3, 1816. Lady Byron had
come back to her parents on January 15; the deed of amicable separation
was signed on April 21.

heed the admonition in the degree wherein to heed it may be a stepping-stone towards the further perfectioning of their natures, constitutes the appointed ordeal,—but how severe an ordeal it is, and how deeply they must feel it to be addressed to what is best in them, to be expressly directed against that very best!

Despite the disadvantage of thus anticipating the narrative of events, it was indispensable to draw a cartoon of Annabella if only for the purpose of measuring the effects of the events themselves; and as that cartoon is of her nature and general line of conduct, and does not attempt to delineate this or that detail or particular phase, I see nothing to change in it even to-day. When we come to the part played by her letters in Byron's second offer of marriage, I shall have something to say concerning her irreproachability.

At present we are about to follow all the revulsions incident upon the encounter of a character 'like proof spirits' with that other alcohol, the very reverse of proof spirits, with which we are already acquainted as one that could not feel itself to be alive unless auto-poisoned by its numerous dense vapours.

*　*　*

Three days after Byron's letter to Caroline Lamb, circumstances give us our first complementary piece of information, and very instructive it is. Though at this time Annabella was not yet twenty, she had already had more than one suitor; but she had rejected them all, and for the reason, as we cannot doubt, which is mentioned in this passage from what she called an Auto-Description, written when she was thirty-nine: 'I met with one or two who, like myself, did not appear absorbed in the present scene—and who interested me in a degree. I had a wish to find amongst men the character I had often imagined—but I found only parts of it. One gave proofs of worth, but had no sympathy for high aspirations—another

seemed full of affection towards his family, and yet he valued
the world. I was clear-sighted in these cases—but I was to
become blind!'[1] One of these rejected suitors was Augustus
Foster, the same young man whom we have seen upset by
Caroline's marriage and reassured about it by his mother.
That mother—Lady Elizabeth Foster, afterwards Duchess of
Devonshire—had, this time, a much more urgent motive for
wishing to reassure her son, since the question was of his
own marriage. She had written to him at Washington, telling
him that Mrs. George Lamb would sound Miss Milbanke as
to her feelings: 'Caro[2] means to see *la bella* Annabella before
writing to you. . . . I shall go very near hating her if she seems
blind to the merits of one who would make her so happy'.
And on May 4 here is what the mother had to tell her son:
'She persists in saying that she never suspected your attachment to her; but she is so odd a girl that, though she has for
some time rather liked another, she has decidedly refused
them, because she thinks she ought to marry a person with a
good fortune; and this is partly, I believe, from generosity to
her parents, and partly owning that fortune is an object to herself for happiness. In short, she is good, amiable, and sensible,
but cold, prudent, and reflecting. Lord Byron makes up to
her a little; but she don't seem to admire him except as a poet,
nor he her except for a wife'; adding in another letter of June
2: 'Your Annabella is a mystery; liking, not liking; generous-
minded, yet afraid of poverty; there is no making her out. I
hope you don't make yourself unhappy about her; she is
really an icicle'.[3] Let us condole with the feelings of a mother
whose son has just been rejected; moreover, we owe her some
gratitude, for mistakes which are conducive of truths sometimes turn out to be the most useful of things. That Annabella
should prove indecipherable to an accomplished woman of

[1] *Life of Lady Byron*, p. 15.

[2] Mrs. George Lamb was also named Caroline; in the family the two
were called respectively 'Caro George' and 'Caro William'.

[3] *Letters and Journals*, ii. pp. 119-120.

the world, is only what might have been expected with the Duchess of Devonshire-to-be. Besides, it is but fair to recognize that in attributing (be it but in part) Annabella's taking fortune into account to her 'generosity towards her parents', her ladyship hits the mark. It is almost impossible for us to-day—and perhaps especially for the young girls of to-day—to imagine in that respect the then situation of a young girl belonging to the landed aristocracy, to say nothing of the fact that frequently the money question is brought forward, so as politely to evade certain proposals and conceal repugnances which can only inflict useless mortifications. 'Cold, prudent, and reflecting'—a hackneyed triad of adjectives, very serviceable to those who resort to it. Let us retain for Annabella, without further insisting on it, the adjective 'reflecting'; nor do I forget that when 'prudent' is used in a disparaging sense, it is often to avert suspicion by denouncing abroad what might else be discovered at home. There would indeed be matter for a fine debate—but this is not the place for it—on the idea of prudence, which includes things as disparate as the entirely human prudence on which the Duchess of Devonshire was so obviously an expert—the kind called 'of the serpent'—and that which derives from the Holy Spirit. It is not for me to claim the latter for Annabella; I content myself with pointing out that her species of prudence was that which always gravitates towards issues good in themselves, the species which La Bruyère defines by contrast when, speaking of the 'bad man', he says: 'If his ends are evil, prudence has no part in them'; and he goes so far as to conclude his paragraph with these words: 'and where prudence lacks, find greatness if you can'.[1] We have become so inured to finding greatness *elsewhere* that for us the problem is almost inverted, and consists in knowing how to find great-

[1]'In a bad man there is not the stuff of a great man. Praise his views and his plans, admire his conduct, exaggerate his skill in making use of the fittest and quickest means to his ends, if his ends are evil, prudence has no part in them, and where prudence lacks, find greatness if you can' (*Des Jugements*).

ness where that very prudence prevails. However it may be in other categories—and by its generality La Bruyère's saying reminds us that, from the classic standpoint, the disjunction was nowhere admitted—there is no question that in the two which Annabella's case imports, those of *morality* and *religion*, real greatness cannot exist without its adjunct in the virtue of prudence.

But now we come to the disparagement felt to be so essential that the Duchess of Devonshire had to state it twice. Annabella is 'cold'—so cold that in truth 'she is an icicle'. And with this, we are at the heart of the offensive conducted by the world against irreproachable beings, and let us bow before the skill with which the ground has been chosen; for once establish the fact that they are cold, and the battle is not only won at a blow, but perhaps deserved to be won. But yes, to be sure, this explains everything: people are irreproachable only because they are cold, and it is by *default* of heart that they seem to have no faults; Annabella sufficiently proves it; did not everyone—even to Byron himself—agree about her 'placid countenance'?

Let us beware of intervening in this contention, leaving to events a reply quite differently effective from any that we could produce. I shall confine myself to saying that Byron, having read the poems (whose transmission to him constituted perhaps one of those minor passages in which the theme of fatality makes a tentative appearance before declaring itself), shared in no wise the common error—he knew that there was 'strength and variety of thought' behind that 'placid countenance', and I even think he was slandering himself when he said that he could not have 'imagined' it to be so. And I incline the more to this view because the unerring observer that Byron was would scarcely be taken in by the myth of 'the cold woman', a myth so convenient for evading, in these spheres, the solving of any perplexity. Though he did write to Lady Melbourne of Lady Frances: 'I should think she is of a *cold* temperament', he at once added: 'yet I have my doubts on that point, too'. Knowing as he did that Annabella's mind was warmly responsive, Byron had from the first perceived in her not only the existence of a heart but the kindness of that organ—if not until his engagement to her was he in a position to decide upon her supposed coldness of temperament. But the mere fact of doubting a woman's real coldness can give to the appearance of it a piquancy which is no negligible attraction; and when to Miss Milbanke's 'simplicity, modesty, and discretion' was added her 'coldness', it probably had in Byron's eyes a charm[1] which formed an agreeable contrast with the excessive manifestations that Caroline Lamb was then showering on him.

And yet, for all these varying indications, we are very far from being clear as to the exact nature of Byron's feeling for Annabella in the autumn of 1812 when, slightly exceeding her mission, Lady Melbourne made in his name that first offer of marriage which Miss Milbanke declined. On September 13, 1812, in Byron's second letter to Lady Melbourne, here is what he wrote: 'Now, my dear Lady M., you are all out as to my real sentiments. I was, am, and shall be, I fear, attached to another, one to whom I have never said much, but have never lost sight of, and the whole of this interlude has been the result of circumstances which it may be too late to regret. . . . As I have said so much, I may as well say all. The woman I mean is Miss Milbanke; I know nothing of her fortune, and I am told that her father is ruined, but my own will, when my Rochdale arrangements are closed, be sufficient for both. . . . I know little of her, and have not the most distant reason to suppose that I am at all a favourite in that quarter. But I never saw a woman whom I *esteemed* so much. But that chance is gone, and there's an end'.[2] 'The whole of this interlude' refers to the so perturbing relations

[1]This is also the impression of the editor of *Letters and Journals*, who says: 'Miss Milbanke's unaffected simplicity attracted Byron; even her coldness was a charm' (*Letters and Journals*, ii. p. 120).

[2]*Corr.* i. pp. 74-75.

with Caroline in which, at this date, Byron was still involved. True, Caroline had just left for Ireland; but if she did not get over it, if she persisted in what Byron called her infatuation, he was still prepared to act up to the point of honour by linking his life to hers. When he said that Caroline's passion had frustrated his attachment to Miss Milbanke—was that true? (by which I do not mean, was it sincere? for sincere, with Lady Melbourne, Byron nearly always was), but was it clear-sighted? did it correspond to his real feelings? On that point, which is such a very important one, until the publication of the *Life of Lady Byron*, as far as facts went we were quite in the dark. Now, thanks to Ethel Colburn Mayne, we are in possession of a clue, which moreover she has interpreted. Let us first transcribe the passage: 'He had spoken of Miss Milbanke to Caroline, saying how much he admired her, how superior she seemed to all the rest; and Caroline had been 'all acquiescence and approbation', until the 'temporary satisfaction' became evident. Then, getting frightened, she had remembered George Eden.[1] What had become of his suit to Miss Milbanke? No one had ever been told. Annabella was much with him—perhaps she was only waiting to be asked? This kind of Perhaps can easily be turned into Certainly, and that was what Caroline had done with it. She had told Byron that the attachment was mutual, salving her conscience by the knowledge that her sister-in-law, Mrs. George Lamb, had told him the same thing. . . . But Caroline Lamb was Caroline Lamb—a creature of generous impulse, if a creature torn by jealous fear. She fell ill between her jealousy and her remorse; and (always histrionic) could not rest until both had been acknowledged. The most dramatic confession —to whom could that be made? To whom but Annabella? Annabella was accordingly summoned, and on the 2nd of May she came. Her diary says merely: 'Went in morning to Lady Caroline Lamb, and undeceived her by a painful acknow-

[1] This was the earliest of Annabella's many suitors, and a friend of her childhood: heir to his father, Lord Auckland.

ledgment. . . . Received Lord Byron's opinion of my verses'.
The painful acknowledgment we must suppose to have been
that she had refused George Eden. . . . The interview altered
her intercourse with Byron. . . . Both had been made self-
conscious; Byron, moreover, had been told that she was
engaged, or as good as engaged, to George Eden. . . . The
triumphant season was spoilt for Miss Milbanke'.[1] Putting
all these facts together, I willingly admit that Byron may have
been justified in saying that Caroline's passion had frustrated
the sentiment he had long felt for Miss Milbanke; but the
problem for me here is not at all a problem of justification: it
centres wholly on the nature of Byron's sentiment, and there
nothing brought to light alters my previous conviction as to a
feeling of which I am persuaded that, even had there been no
such person as Caroline, it would have remained substanti-
ally the same. In the letter to Lady Melbourne above quoted,
the greatest possible stress should be laid, the greatest possible weight attached, to Byron's use of the word 'esteemed'
—which, moreover, he is careful to italicise. (Of course he
uses the past tense only because he considers that the existing
situation with Caroline obliges him to regard that opportunity as a forfeited one). On one side, Byron was the very
man for a marriage of esteem; with him esteem was not at all,
as it is with others, the *weak beat*, but on the contrary the
strong beat, of marriage; and on the other hand (and there is
much more of identity than of antithesis between the two
things) Byron belongs to that queer race of men—much more
numerous, though, than is commonly supposed—who lay
down the law that to encounter a woman really worthy of
esteem is well-nigh impossible, and yet who lay it down with
the proviso that such an encounter is the only kind worth
having, and who put to the credit of esteem all that they have
withdrawn from love that they scorn. And then, if the en-

---

[1] *Life of Lady Byron*, pp. 41-43. In the comment of mine that follows,
I am concerned only with Byron's feelings, and will shortly return
to those of Annabella.

counter does take place in circumstances which indisputably
compel esteem, the novel element thus introduced into their
sentimental experience is such that it may very well lead them
to take themselves in as to the true nature of their feelings.
I am persuaded that at no moment did Byron, in the strict
sense of the word, *love* Annabella, but I am equally persuaded
that at more than one he had no doubt that he did love her,
simply because at no moment (even when he would so much
have wished to) could he cease to esteem her.

Now, exceptional as Lady Melbourne was, she would have
been self-excluded from the feminine community if she had
been able to resist match-making; and especially for Byron
whom, had circumstances been otherwise, she would—doubtless not herself have married, but loved, and might even if
necessary have given him in marriage to another so as to love
him in perfect peace of mind; and whom, as things were, it
would be very pleasant to have for a nephew and constant
interlocutor, highly diverting to observe while her irreproachable niece was leading him back into the paths of duty—to
say nothing of the fact that such a solution, which would have
put a definite end to the situation with Caroline, could not
but have been welcome to Lady Melbourne. Nevertheless, as
we saw, Lady Melbourne is 'straight', in the same way as a
man is straight; ready to take action, she first puts a question:
'Are you sure of yourself?' In his letter of September 18 Byron
answers by that delegation of authority in which we know
that he delights when she is concerned: 'You ask, "Am I sure
of myself?" and I answer no, but *you* are, which I take to be
a much better thing. Miss M(ilbanke) I admire because she
is a clever woman, an amiable woman, and of high blood, for
I have still a few Norman and Scotch inherited prejudices on
the last score, were I to marry. As to *love*, that is done in a
week (provided the lady has a reasonable share); besides,
marriage goes on better with esteem and confidence than

184

romance, and she is quite pretty enough to be loved by her husband, without being so glaringly beautiful as to attract too many rivals'.[1] We must here pay tribute to the honesty of Byron who, before delegating authority, answers 'No' to Lady Melbourne's question. Byron, for that matter, never claims to be sure of himself; but we must also notice how the tone of this letter degenerates by comparison with that of the one before, and in those which follow we see it degenerate more and more. 'Before I become candidate for the distinguished honour of nepotism to your Ladyship, it will be as well for me to know that your niece is not already disposed of to a better bidder; if not, I should like it of all things, were it only for the pleasure of calling you *aunt*! and soliciting your benediction.'[2]—'As to Annabella, she requires time and all the cardinal virtues, and in the interim I am a little verging towards one who demands neither, and saves me besides the trouble of marrying, by being married already.'[3] Here intervenes an episode which was not without its influence on the course of events. The passage in Byron's letter to Lady Melbourne, which is our only source of information, leaves us in the dark as to its precise significance, but very evidently it was one of those bits of tittle-tattle which, in society, sometimes delay and sometimes precipitate action: 'I never heard of the report Lady M(ilbanke) *starts* from, and I am sure you will do me the justice to believe I never dreamed of such a thing, and, had I heard it, should have disbelieved such nonsense, as I do now. I am not at all ashamed of my own bias towards your niece, nor should have the least objection to its being posted up at Charing Cross, though I should never wish to hazard a refusal. I certainly did wish to cultivate her acquaintance, but Caroline told me she was engaged to Eden, so did several others; Mrs. L. (Mrs. George Lamb), *her* great friend, was of opinion (and upon my honour I believe her) that she neither did, could, nor ought to *like* me; and was,

[1]*Corr.* i. p. 79.   [2]*Corr.* i. p. 82. The letter is dated September 21.
[3]*Corr.* i. p. 84. The letter is dated September 25.

moreover, certain that E. would be the *best husband* in the
world and I its *antithesis*; and certainly her word deserved
to be taken for *one* of *us*. Under all circumstances, and others
I need not recapitulate, was I to hazard my heart with a
woman I was very much inclined to like, but at the same time
sure could be nothing to me? And then you know my unfortunate manner, which always leads me to talk too much
to some particular person, or not at all'.[1] The concluding
words enable us, I think, to reconstruct the gossip. After
having for several months shown Annabella the somewhat
marked attention to which Lady Elizabeth Foster refers,
Byron (for reasons pointed out by himself) had suddenly held
aloof. Society at once drew the conclusion that he had lost
interest in her, and had compromised a young girl without
proceeding to a proposal of marriage—which was doubly
affronting to her family circle, and of course to her mother
more than anyone. Byron, who was always extremely punc-
tilious in social matters, understood and even sympathized
with this; and that is why at the end of his letter, after having told Lady Melbourne, in his most authentic vein, of a
budding love affair with a singer 'very much in the style I like',
he recurs to Annabella thus: 'Does Annabella *waltz*? It is an
odd question, but a very important point with me. I wish
somebody could say at once that I wish to propose to her;
but I have great doubt of *her*—it rests with herself entirely'.[2]
In this letter we see Byron almost divided between two
wishes so incompatible that they tend to annul one another—
on the one hand, the wish to offer Annabella, and that as soon
as possible, a reparation for the affront he is supposed to have
put upon her; but, on the other hand, the no less lively wish
not to expose himself to a refusal. From the moment he
showed his desire that she should be informed of his intended
proposal, Lady Melbourne is excusable enough for having
turned the *intention* into a formal offer of his hand; but she is
less so (there failing for once in the *tactique* which Byron's

[1]*Corr.* i. pp. 86-87.   [2]*Corr.* i. p. 88.

Journal praises) for not having taken some soundings before exposing him to the very refusal that he dreaded. That was what came to pass: Lady Melbourne made the offer at the beginning of October, and Annabella declined it in a letter to her of the 12th. I shall presently return to Annabella; let us now follow Byron's reactions. Lady Melbourne, feeling slightly to blame, was not quite easy in her mind as to his probable attitude; and so, when transmitting the refusal, she begged him not to show any resentment. He quickly reassured her on that point, and we shall see that no more than three days sufficed to set Lady Oxford's star in the ascendant, to the complete eclipse of Annabella's. 'October 17. "Cut her!" my dear Lady M. Marry—Mahomet forbid! I am sure we shall be better friends than before, and if I am not embarrassed by all this, I cannot see for the soul of me why *she* should. Assure *her*, con tutto rispetto, that the subject shall never be renewed in any shape whatever, and assure yourself, my carissima (not *Zia*; what then shall it be? Choose your *own* name) that were it not for this *embarras* with Caroline I would much rather remain as I am. I have had so very little intercourse with the fair philosopher, that if when we meet, I should endeavour to improve our acquaintance, she must not *mistake* me, and assure her I shall never mistake her.... Finding I must marry, however, on *that* score I should have preferred a woman of birth and talents; but such a woman was not at all to blame for not preferring me; my *heart* never had an opportunity of being much interested in the business, further than that I should have very much liked to be *your relation.* . . . You talk of my "religion"; *that* rests between man and his Maker, and to him only can my feelings be known; for A(nnabella), it had been sufficient not to find me an "infidel" in anything else.'[1] 'October 18. Of A(nnabella) I have little to add, but I do not regret what has passed; the report alluded to had hurt her feelings, and she has now regained her tranquillity by the refutation to her own satis-

[1]*Corr.* i. pp. 90-91.

faction without disturbing mine. This was but fair, and was not unexpected by me; all things considered, perhaps it could not have been better. I think of her nearly as I did. The specimen you send me is more favourable to her talents than her discernment, and much too *indulgent* to the subject she has chosen; in some points the resemblance is very exact, but you have not sent me the whole (I imagine) by the abruptness of both beginning and end.[1] I am glad that your opinion coincides with mine on the subject of her abilities and her excellent qualities; in both these points she is singularly fortunate. Still there is something of the *woman* about her; her *preferring* that the letter to you should be sent forward to me, per esémpio, appears as if, though she would not encourage, she was not disgusted with being admired. I also may hazard a conjecture that an *answer* addressed to *herself* might not have been displeasing, but of this you are the best judge from actual observation. I cannot, however, see the necessity of its being forwarded, unless I was either to admire the composition, or reply to ye contents. *One* I certainly do, the other would merely lead to mutual compliments, very sincere but somewhat *tedious*.'[2]—'October 20. Tell A(nnabella) that I am more proud of her *rejection* than I can ever be of *another's acceptance*; this sounds rather *equivocal*, but if she takes it in the sense I mean it, and *you* don't blunder it in the delivery, with one of your *wicked laughs*, it will do for want of something better. It merely means that the *hope* of obtaining *her* (or *anybody else*—but skip this parenthesis) was more pleasing than the possession of St. Ursula and the 11,000 virgins (being a greater number than have ever *since* existed at the *same time* in that capacity) could possibly have been to her "disconsolate and unmathematical admirer, X. Y. Z.".'[3] Then, abandoning once for all the subject of Annabella, which we can easily imagine to have been getting as 'tedious'

[1] This refers to the 'Character of Lord Byron' which Annabella composed before writing the letter of refusal to Lady Melbourne; the two documents are reproduced farther on.

[2] *Corr*. i. p. 92.   [3] *Corr*. i. pp. 94-95.

as the letter he had been so careful not to write her, and returning to that of the everlasting Caroline, this is what he adds: 'I mean (*entre nous*, my dear Machiavel) to play off Lady O. against her', which shows him preparing a fortnight in advance for the unspeakable Glenarvon letter, and ensuring, by the confession, his 'Machiavel's' complicity.

Truly, Byron's methods of reassuring an anxious friend were all his own, and thenceforward Lady Melbourne had every reason to be easy in her mind about his reception of her niece's refusal. For myself, I am persuaded that the dazzling cynicism of these letters represents the truth of the situation. At that moment, Byron's principal fear was that Caroline would land on him from Ireland and, relying on the offer to fly that honour had dictated to him, would oblige him to abduct her. Now it is clear that no better way of avoiding marriage with one woman has yet been devised than that of marrying another; personally (as he has just told us), 'were it not for the *embarras* with C.' he 'would much rather remain as I am'. But since he has no choice. . . . there is no woman he esteems so much as Miss Milbanke, and behold the point of honour coming into play with her too! That affront at any rate can be made good. Miss Milbanke refuses. What a relief! He has behaved like a man of honour, and kept his liberty into the bargain; he can see that, thanks to Lady Oxford (an ally doubtless less intellectually accomplished than Lady Melbourne, but otherwise still so agreeably on active service), the *embarras* with C. can be disposed of—yes, indeed, 'all is for the best', and so much the more for the best that 'my *heart* never had an opportunity of being much interested in the business'. Do not mistake me. I do not mean to say that *afterwards* (but a very long time afterwards), Miss Milbanke's refusal did not entail certain results that we shall examine when the time comes. I merely say that at the time it happened, her refusal leaves Byron indifferent, even suits him, is a relief to him; and the best proof of this is that Miss Milbanke completely disappears from Byron's life and thoughts until August 22, 1813, when, by initiating a correspondence with him, she elects to re-enter both.

But Annabella? There are a few cases in which to be refused is nothing to having made the refusal, and this one seems to me an extreme instance in the kind. I sum up my ideas as follows. Though the refusal, at its actual moment, left Byron indifferent and eliminated Annabella from his horizon, on the contrary the fact of having refused Byron obliged Annabella to become conscious of her love for him. Since the publication of the *Life of Lady Byron*, the sequence of events is clear. Though she was unwilling to admit it to herself, Annabella was already in love with Byron during the season of 1812; then had intervened the Caroline manipulation—both had been made self-conscious, both had avoided one another, and yet now the proposal had come. But here I must let Ethel Colburn Mayne speak: 'She was at Richmond with her parents. It was on a Thursday (October 8) that Thursday's Child sat down to compose her Character of Lord Byron. The proposal-by-proxy had reached her then, for she took some days before she answered it. Strangest of reactions —to vivisect the man who had now confessed (however unsatisfyingly) to her instinctive sense of attraction between them! That she had felt this we have seen; then came the blazing publicity of the Caroline affair, her interview with Caroline, Byron's subsequent aloofness—and she had put it all away from her: "Look on't again I dare not".

'Now she was forced to look on it again. He *had* found that satisfaction, and wanted it to be more than temporary. Her heart had leaped as she read, but there was a monitor to be obeyed before she listened to a mere heart. Aware (as she afterwards told him) that he could "excite affection", she was still uncertain whether he could "inspire esteem". That spectre had always haunted her; now it appeared in all its dismal majesty, and she gazed loyally into its leaden eyes. Affection, disgusted by the dowdy rival, withdrew; but Annabella could not quite forget that it was there. To which mute presence should she—ought she to—give her allegiance? Suppose one wrote a Character of Lord Byron? That might clarify one's feelings.

'"The passions have been his guide from childhood, and have exercised a tyrannical power over his very superior intellect. Yet amongst his dispositions are many which deserve to be associated with Christian principles—his love of goodness in its chastest form, and his abhorrence of all that degrades human nature, prove the uncorrupted purity of his moral sense. In one of his juvenile poems he says:

> I love the virtues that I cannot claim.

There is a chivalrous generosity in his ideas of love and friendship, and selfishness is totally absent from his character. In secret he is the zealous friend of all the human feelings: but from the strangest perversion that pride ever created, he endeavours to disguise the best points of his character. He has felt himself wronged, and he scorns to show regard to illiberality of opinion by condescending to a justification. . . . When indignation takes possession of his mind—and it is easily excited—his disposition becomes malevolent. He hates with the bitterest contempt; but as soon as he has indulged those feelings, he regains the humanity which he had lost— from the immediate impulse of provocation—and repents deeply. So that his mind is continually making the most sudden transitions—from good to evil—from evil to good. . . . He laments his want of tranquillity and speaks of the power of application to composing studies, as a blessing placed beyond his attainment, which he regrets.

'"He is inclined to open his heart unreservedly to those whom he believes *good*, even without the preparation of much acquaintance. He is extremely humble towards persons whose character he respects, and to them he would probably confess his errors—"

'There she broke off.

'But she had clarified her feelings. The enigma of Byron unravelled or not, the enigma of *them* was. And she wrote to her aunt.' . . . Ethel Colburn Mayne quotes only the few sentences which contain the gist of the answer, but the letter is so characteristic as to the whole of the future relations that it must stand here in full: 'I do not give my answer without that serious deliberation which is due to the honourable and disinterested nature of Lord Byron's sentiments. I am convinced that he considers my happiness not less than his own, in the wishes which he has expressed to you, and I think of them with the sincerest gratitude.

'I endeavour not to yield to any decided preference till my judgment has been strengthened by longer observation, but I will not assign this as my only motive for declining the estimable and very uncommon advantages now offered. I should be totally unworthy of Lord Byron's esteem if I were not to speak the truth without equivocation. Believing that he never will be the object of that strong affection which would make me happy in domestic life, I should wrong him by any measure that might, even indirectly, confirm his present impressions. From my limited observations of his conduct, I was predisposed to believe your strong testimony in his favour, and I willingly attribute it more to the defect of my own feelings than of his character that I am not inclined to return his attachment. After this statement that I make with real sorrow from the idea of its giving pain, I must leave our future intercourse to his judgment. I can have no reason for withdrawing from an acquaintance that does me honour and is capable of imparting so much rational pleasure, except the fear of involuntarily deceiving him. I cannot appear insensible to kindness, and its influence on my manner might lead him erroneously to suppose that I had a stronger interest. Whatever may be his determination from a full consideration of these circumstances, I shall acquiesce in it with an anxious wish that it may prove for his happiness.

'Perhaps the most satisfactory method of acquainting him with the contents of this letter would be to let him have it. I have too much confidence in his liberality, to think reserve or caution necessary in communicating my feelings. The generous delicacy of his whole conduct towards me, particularly when he acted from the false information of my engagement to another person, is one of many proofs that his principles of Honor deserve my entire reliance. I assure him of my perfect silence on this subject.

'Richmond, October 12.'[1]

Now, so long ago as the April of this 1812, Annabella had written to her parents: 'He has no comfort but in *confidence*, to soothe his deeply wounded mind. I consider it an act of humanity and a Christian duty not to deny him any temporary satisfaction he can derive from my acquaintance— though I shall not seek to encrease it'. And, blind to what we can so easily read between those lines, she had added: 'He is not a dangerous person to me'.[2]

In October, for all the dispassionateness which she thought to display in her Character of Lord Byron, we may question whether Annabella could sincerely have repeated that concluding phrase: 'He is not a dangerous person to me'. The truth seems to me that the Character shows her, though still unconscious of the fact, to be far beyond that phase of feeling where we still think of those we love as 'dangerous persons to know'; there is then no other danger, and that an inconceivable one, but the danger of having never known them. Of course, when mistaken, clear consciousness is not righted in a day, it goes on for some time doing its usual work, and here carries off in fact its last trophy: the achievement of the refusal. But it is its last; and how complex, how moving are the reactions that the refusal engenders in Annabella! One after the other, we shall see them at work, but here it

---

[1]Mabell, Countess of Airlie, *In Whig Society*, 1921, pp. 141-142.

[2]*Life of Lady Byron*, p. 41.

should be stated that, as regards her, the extreme importance
of the refusal lies, not in giving birth to the feeling, but in
developing it to the utmost, and in enlisting thenceforward
in its favour the whole of her nature.

Inscrutable as Annabella was, essentially speaking, to the
Duchess of Devonshire, I think that that lady was partly
right when she said in May, 1812: 'She don't seem to admire
(Lord Byron) except as a poet', though doubtless she did
not give that kind of admiration all the force which in such
a case it possesses. For while Byron himself quite sincerely
thought little of the first *Harold*, and never could understand the fuss—source of so many complications for him!—
that people were making about it, it was impossible that a
cultivated young girl who put the productions of genius, by
definition, so high in her scale of values, who made attempts
of her own at poetry, should not have taken those two
cantos very seriously.[1] We now know, however, that the
Duchess's remark contains but a half-truth, and that the impression conveyed by Annabella must have been due to her
'placid countenance'. Having finished reading the two cantos
of *Harold* on March 24—the day before she was to see Byron
for the first time—she immediately sets down her opinion in
her diary: 'It contains many stanzas in the best style of poetry.
He is rather too much of a *mannerist*, that is, he wants variety
in the turns of his expression: he excels most in the delineation
of deep feeling, and in reflections relative to human nature'.[2]

---

[1] When Caroline Lamb read Byron's opinion of her poems to Annabella, there must have been, besides the natural pleasure in hearing it,
that of finding how seriously he had taken them; and this could not but
reinforce the conviction that his was a serious nature, and thus stimulate
her admiration. Moreover, as we shall see (and precisely because he
esteemed her more than anyone), Byron is always at his best, and his most
serious, when addressing himself to Annabella; the esteem he felt for her
has here for result (without our being obliged to attribute it to deliberate
design or any kind of interested motive in him) the confirming of her
views about him; it is indeed one of the most poignant aspects of the
misunderstanding between them that both always took one another as
seriously as possible.

[2] *Life of Lady Byron*, p. 35.

There can be no doubt that the 'beautiful pale face' of March 25 signified much more than these few tame sentences, and of course what counted most of all, what supremely counted, was the episode of a few weeks later, that which was kept for the Auto-Description, that which Annabella only ventured to write down when she was thirty-nine: ' "Do you think there is one person here who dares to look into himself?" was one of his abrupt questions at a party where— in the crowd—I felt that he was the most attractive person; but I was not *bound* to him by any strong feeling of sympathy till he uttered these words, not to me, but in my hearing—"I have not a friend in the world!" It is said that there is an instinct in the human heart which attaches us to the friend- less. I did not pause—there was my error—to inquire why he was friendless; but I vowed in secret to be a devoted friend to this lone being'.[1] Here we have the whole of her feeling, and, in many ways, *genius* does play an important part in it: genius is lonely, friendless, needs both 'confidence' and pro- tection, and in return would bring understanding, possibly the only understanding worth having, that which one always seeks for and never finds: a few days after having refused Byron's proposal, did not Annabella write to her friend M. G. (Lady Gosford): 'I did not think anything of Genius requisite for the man who would make me a good husband, but I am afraid that *some* genius is requisite to understand a fellow-creature, and a good heart is not the best proof of *penetration*. I think matrimonial unhappiness is often the consequence of one or both the persons having believed that they should be too easily contented'. And when summoned by Lady Melbourne to draw up an account of the qualities she did desire in a husband, Annabella reverts to the subject, and almost in the same terms: 'Genius is not in my opinion *necessary*, though desirable, *if united* with what I have just mentioned'.

We are here at the root of a frequent misunderstanding, in

[1] *Life of Lady Byron,* p. 39.

itself a grave one, and productive of many consequences—
that between a certain type of irresponsible genius and the
readers who most appreciate, and are most worthy to appreciate, it. Youthful, unversed in life's lessons (sometimes,
when learnt, so roughly awakening that they lead to an excessive attitude of dislike for literature itself)—such readers
assume as a principle that the act of composition is an act
which, for those who give themselves up to it, connotes more
responsibility than almost any other, and that the more
genius is displayed, the more responsible the writer feels.
Too often, unfortunately, the reverse is the truth: there is a
certain type of genius—and Byron is one of its most signal
examples—which not only cannot live, but (as genius) cannot
produce anything of value unless completely irresponsible.
In Byron's case, this irresponsibility is so complete that even
his vein of unerring observation is wholly instinctive; and on
this point Goethe has said the last word, as he always did on
Byron's character: '*Sobald er reflectirt, ist er ein Kind*' (As soon
as he reflects, he is a child). But Annabella does not know
that, and she loses every chance of ever learning it on the
day she receives Byron's proposal of marriage. For, from her
point of view, this is a step involving all that a human being
has of character, one which postulates in a supreme degree
the sense of responsibility; and so, countersigning her admiration for the poet, there awakens in her an admiration
for the man who has thus given her the only valid proof of
the sincerity, the seriousness, and the depth of his feelings.
We who are acquainted, through Byron himself, with the
motives inspiring his conduct, feel the contrast to be really
tragic between the half-worldly, half-cynical levity that rules
his offer, and the grave scruples of conscience it arouses in
her to whom it is addressed. True, she refuses him—she does
not feel that she really knows him, in the sense which a reflective mind attaches to that word; but it is with no light
heart that she writes her refusal; she is uneasy as to its effect
on Byron, and through her aunt (who has a mistake to atone

for, and is therefore all the more careful to discount not only the Byronic parentheses, but the Byronic comments), she learns that Byron is prouder of having been refused by her than he would have been of being accepted by anyone else. Now nothing was more certain than this to put the finishing touches to those reactions that the refusal itself had engendered: for Annabella, esteem—reciprocal esteem—is the core of every marriage, but for reasons the very reverse of Byron's, since for her reciprocal esteem is at the core of love itself. She cannot even conceive of love without esteem. From the moment when first, thanks to his proposal, then thanks to the message transmitted through Lady Melbourne concerning the light in which he views her refusal, Annabella is able to *esteem* Byron without reserve, her feeling for him is full to the brim, and it is in that sense that one can say that she loves Byron wholly from the moment she has refused him.[1]

Ten months elapsed between her refusal and the day in August, 1813, when she wrote to Byron in explanation of it. We must not forget, however, that he had assured her through Lady Melbourne that he would never re-open the subject in any way whatever, and that—this being understood—he was so far from wishing to 'cut' her that he desired to cultivate her acquaintance. They moved in the same circles, so we may assume that they would meet rather frequently, and under those at once favourable and perilous conditions where two people, having decided that there shall be nothing between them, unconsciously feel freer to establish a something. I say *two*: in reality I ought to say *one*; for Byron, from November 1812 to June 1813, is so satisfied with Lady Oxford that he goes so far as to be faithful to her,

[1]The proof of this is in a letter she wrote to a friend, five days after she had become engaged to Byron: 'It is no precipitate step. The attachment has been progressive for two years' (*Letters and Journals*, iii. p. 147). We know how scrupulous she was, and so can no longer doubt that her attachment had begun in October, 1812.

and from the end of June to the end of August he belongs to Augusta. And yet perhaps I am not wrong in saying *two* if, as I imagine, Annabella was beginning to be in that disposition when one asks and answers one's own questions. She arrived in London with her parents at the beginning of the season of 1813; she did in fact see Byron in society several times, at first without renewing acquaintance; then came the day marked out in this important passage from the Auto-Description: 'We met in the following spring in London. I was extremely agitated on seeing him—and offered my hand for the first time. He turned pale as he pressed it. Perhaps—unconscious as I was—the engagement was then formed on my part. We met frequently, but every time I felt more pain —and at last I shunned the occasions'.[1] Like almost everything in the Auto-Description, the retrospective view is faultless: unconscious as she was, it was not *perhaps*, but *certainly*, then that the engagement was formed on her part, and the fact explains that the initiative of opening a correspondence with Byron should have proved a few months later well-nigh irresistible.

Byron, who on principle always upheld Lady Melbourne, had not at the time felt inclined to reproach her in the least for the refusal to which she had exposed him; it was not until much later that he observed in course of conversation, and without insisting on it, that she had perhaps gone a little too far. Lady Melbourne mentioned this to Annabella; and she, moved both by the unconscious desire to be in direct written communication with Byron, and the other desire—this quite conscious—to give him her reasons for refusing him, wrote to him at the end of August, 1813. Indeed, she did not even wait for this pretext to be offered her; she created it, or at least opened the door to a correspondence when she wrote to Lady Melbourne on July 18, just before leaving London: 'I am sorry to find that a report very disadvantageous to Lord Byron is in circulation, and as I cannot believe it I wish it

[1] *Life of Lady Byron*, p. 55.

may be contradicted. It is said, and in a circle where it is likely to have credit, that he has behaved very unhandsomely to the young man who purchased Newstead—that the latter from the imprudent eagerness of youth bid much more for the property than it was worth and that, though almost ruined by the contract, Lord B. cruelly takes advantage of the Law to make him adhere to unfair terms. I should be very ungenerous if I did not put the most candid construction on all Lord Byron's actions, and if I did not wish that others should do the same. As I shall not have an opportunity of seeing him again, I should be glad if you would tell him that, however long his absence may be, I shall always have pleasure in hearing that he is happy, and if my esteem can afford him any satisfaction, he may rely on my not adopting the opinions of those who wrong him. Of the propriety of this communication you will judge, but I feel certain that it would not be misunderstood, and unless he is more changeable than I imagine, he may be gratified by my friendly dispositions, particularly at the moment he experiences such painful injustice'.[1] Lady Melbourne immediately gave Byron the message, for the same day, after having vindicated himself about the sale of Newstead, he added in a postscript: 'You will make my best acknowledgments to Miss M. and say what is most proper. I have not the skill—you are an adept; you may defend me if it amuses you, not else'.[2] We need not doubt that Lady Melbourne knew how to ' say what was most proper', that Annabella was delighted to be thus given her opportunity, and we may be certain that even to wait until August 22 to make use of it was an exercise of her patience.

In Chapters VI and VII of the *Life of Lady Byron* we now possess Annabella's letters, or at least all the essential passages from them, together with parts of Byron's letters hitherto unpublished. Nothing could replace the reading of these two chapters, from the double point of view of the texts themselves and the penetrating commentaries. They can come in

[1] *In Whig Society*, pp. 159-160. [2] *Corr.* i. p. 167.

here only so far as they supply a fact or help towards its interpretation. Annabella's letter, which opens the correspondence, is dated August 22: it is so long that Ethel Colburn
Mayne does not give it in full, but it is, as she says, so
'characteristic', conveying 'so much of the truth, or one aspect
of the truth' about her, that from this letter I too must
extract some passages: 'I have received from Lady Melbourne an assurance of the satisfaction you feel in being
remembered with interest by me. Let me then more fully
explain this interest, with the hope that the consciousness
of possessing a friend whom neither Time nor Absence can
estrange may impart some soothing feelings to your retrospective views. You have remarked the serenity of my countenance, but mine is not the serenity of one who is a stranger
to care, nor are the prospects of my future years untroubled.
It is my nature to feel long, deeply, and secretly, and the
strongest affections of my heart are without hope. I disclose
to you what I conceal even from those who have most claim
to my confidence, because it will be the surest basis of that un-
reserved friendship which I wish to establish between us—
because you will not reject my admonitions as the result of
cold calculation, when you know that I *can* suffer as you have
suffered. . . . In a letter to Ly. Melbournè (after I had informed
you of my sentiments) you expressed the determination to
render your conduct as conformable to my wishes, as if your
attachment had been returned. I now claim that promise, and
I do not fear that you will answer, 'You have no right'. I have
the right of a constant and considerate zeal for your happiness, and the right which you have given, and will not un-
reasonably withdraw. I entreat you then to observe more consistently the principles of unwearied benevolence. No longer
suffer yourself to be the slave of the moment, nor trust your
noble impulses to the chances of Life. . . . Do good. Feel
benevolence and you will inspire it—you *will* do good, for to
excite such dispositions is to bless. . . . Imperfect as my practice is, I *have* enjoyed the happiness of giving peace and awak-

ening virtue on occasions which only this habitual direction
of my thoughts could have enabled me to seize. Your powers
peculiarly qualify you for performing these duties with success. . . . Will you undertake this task, and will you lay aside
the seeming misanthropy which repels the affection of your
fellow-creatures? I have lately had very little information concerning you on which I could depend. . . . Need I say that
such information from yourself would be received with gratitude? I request your secrecy as to this communication and its
contents. Only my parents are aware of it. In particular I
would not have it known to Ly. Melbourne. I am indebted to
her kindness, but we have little sympathy, and she is perhaps
too much accustomed to look for design, to understand the
plainness of my intentions. I trust them to your candour. You
must be sensible of my great confidence in you, since I mention opinions which I should be very sorry to have repeated.
Believe in the sincerity of a regard, which, though it never can
change to love, deserves to be considered as more than worldly
friendship. Yours most faithfully, A. I. Milbanke.

'P.S.—I shall be obliged to you at least to acknowledge the
receipt of this letter, that I may not apprehend it has fallen
into other hands.'[1]

As I have already mentioned in the Introduction, we are
here face to face with that accentuation of Annabella's
departure from the truth which was to prove even more
momentous than the actual departure. For her, otherwise
truthfulness itself, it was already grave enough to have in
October, 1812, written to Lady Melbourne the reverse of the
truth, but still she had then the excuse of the indirect mode of
approach, always liable to disappoint or to hurt, the excuse
also that her personal sentiments for Lady Melbourne in no
vay induced her to make of her a confidante in the sense that
Byron delighted in. But now, in August, 1813, she addresses
Byron himself, insists upon addressing him, assumes until the
engagement the entire initiative: she can no longer entertain

[1]*Life of Lady Byron*, pp. 57-59.

the slightest doubt as to her own feelings: of course, having begun with the white lie, she is obliged to keep to it and even to underline it. I am too *Annabellian* not to leave her even here the benefit of that whiteness—all the more so that, owing to it, all the livid colours of the spectrum were later to turn against her; but the predicament seems to prove that the veritable lovers of truth are at the same time the most severely treated for any infraction of what is always due to the austere goddess. But let us listen to Byron's answer, dated from London on August 25: 'I am honored with your letter which I wish to acknowledge immediately. Before I endeavour to answer it, allow me—briefly if possible—to advert to the circumstances which occurred last autumn. Many years had occurred since I had seen any woman with whom there appeared to me a prospect of rational happiness. I now saw but one, to whom, however, I had no pretensions—or at least too slight for even the hope of success. It was, however, said that your heart was disengaged, and it was on that ground that Ly. Melbourne undertook to ascertain how far I might be permitted to cultivate your acquaintance, on the chance (a slender one I allow) of improving it into friendship and ultimately to a still kinder sentiment. In her zeal in my behalf—friendly and pardonable as it was—she in some degree exceeded my intentions when she made the more direct proposal, which yet I do not regret, except in so far as it appeared presumptuous on my part. That this is the truth you will allow, when I tell you that it was not till lately that I mentioned to her that I thought she had unwittingly committed me a little too far in the expectation that so abrupt an overture would be received. But I stated this casually in conversation, and without the least feeling of irritation towards her or pique against yourself. Such was the result of my first and nearest approach to that altar, to which, in the state of your feelings, I should only have led another victim. When I say the first, it may perhaps appear irreconcilable with some circumstances in my life, to which I conceive you allude in part of your letter. But such is the fact.

I was then too young to marry, tho' not to love; but this was the *first direct* or indirect approach ever made on my part to a permanent union with any woman, and in all probability it will be the last. Ly. M. was perfectly correct in her statement that I preferred you to all others; it was then the fact; it is so still. But it was no disappointment, because it is impossible to impart one drop more to a cup which already overflows with the waters of bitterness. We do not know ourselves; yet I do not think that my self-love was much wounded by the event. On the contrary, I feel a kind of pride even in *your rejection*— more I believe than I could derive from the attachment of another, for it reminds me that I once thought myself worthy of the affection of almost the only one of your sex I ever truly respected.

'To your letter—the first part surprises me—not that you should feel attachment, but that it should be "without hope". May you secure that hope with its object! To the part of your letter regarding myself I could say much; but I must be brief. If you hear of me, it is probably not untrue, though perhaps exaggerated. On any point on which you may honor me with an interest, I shall be glad to satisfy you—to confess the truth, or refute the calumny.

'I must be candid with you on the score of friendship. It is a feeling towards you with which I cannot trust myself. I doubt whether I could help loving you; but I trust I may appeal to my conduct since our *éclaircissement* for the proof that, whatever my feelings may be, they will exempt you from persecution; but I cannot yet profess indifference, and I fear that won't be the first step—at least in some points—from what I feel to that which you wish me to feel.

'You must pardon me and recollect that, if any thing displeases you in this letter, it is a difficult task for me to write to you at all. I have left many things unsaid, and have said others I did not mean to utter. My intended departure from this country is a little retarded by accounts of Plague, etc., etc., and I must bend my course to some more accessible region—

probably to Russia. I have only left myself space to sign
myself, Ever your obliged servant, Byron.'[1] Now, two days
before this letter—on August 23—here is what he wrote to
Lady Melbourne: 'My head is a little disturbed to-day. I have
to write—first, a soothing letter to C., a sentimental one to
X.Y.Z., a sincere one to T. Moore, and one, a mixture of all
three, to yourself, with as much of the ludicrous as you like to
find in it'.[2] From this we learn two things: first, that he had
received Annabella's letter when he wrote to Lady Melbourne
and therefore did not answer so immediately as he chose to
tell her; second, that if he respected her wish that Lady Melbourne should not know of the correspondence, he respected
it, as Ethel Colburn Mayne says, 'in his own manner', for with
the nickname of Princess of Parallelograms to help her, Lady
Melbourne was too shrewd not to guess that the 'sentimental
letter to X.Y.Z.' must be a *reply*. When I add that it was between the 23rd and 31st of August that Byron made the
avowal of incest to Lady Melbourne, we are left in no uncertainty as to the importance which his feelings for X.Y.Z.
could have for him at that moment, and recalling Byron's
epithet, we are once more taught that a *sentimental* letter is
not necessarily a letter in which sentiment is engaged. Though
this passage authorizes me, I shall not go so far as to say that
the letter was insincere, for in my view it *is* sincere in one
respect, the cardinal importance of which to the history of
this relation I have already indicated. The mere thought of
Miss Milbanke reacts upon Byron in the sense of esteem,
which in its turn causes him to write at his maximum of
seriousness—and causes him to do so quite spontaneously,
without the slightest effort, therefore without altering in any
way his own peculiar qualities. Like all the great morose
natures, as like all who from the disorders of their lives, when
they reflect on these and perhaps even more when they are led
so to reflect by some external solicitation, achieve that note of
the saddened which immediately invests the inner being with a

[1]*Letters and Journals*, iii. pp. 397-399.　　[2]*Corr.* i. p. 177.

singular dignity, Byron is every bit as *natural*, every bit as much himself, in the serious register as in the light one; and from this it results that while to Annabella he presents, even though involuntarily, all that is most propitious to the development of her love, he also conveys the illusion (to which a woman who loves is supremely susceptible) that to her alone he shows his true nature. From this to the deduction that no one else knows him, that she alone is in a position to have a really equitable judgment of him—that judgment so precious to its object, precisely because it helps him to become all that he is—there is but a step, which the woman who loves nearly always takes, can scarcely help taking if her vocation is moral, because then both love and duty towards another converge. Now at this time Annabella could, and even could not *but*, believe that Byron on his side knew her—knew her as she really was, knew what she asked of marriage, what she expected from it, what for her part she was ready to bring to it; and that his knowledge dated from the preceding October, and was derived from the most detailed of documents. For soon after her refusal of his offer, Lady Melbourne had asked her to define her views as to the kind of husband she did desire, and Annabella had at once, and with evident pleasure, done as she was asked to do, in the following two documents: 'Dear Aunt,—On the opposite side you will find what I promised—do not forget *your part*.[1] It is so difficult to speak of oneself exactly as one means, that I think you might mistake the account I gave of my defects of temper. As I do not wish you to think *worse* of me than I deserve, I will try to explain myself more correctly. I am never irritated except when others are so, and then I am too apt to imitate them. This makes good temper in my companions very necessary for my peace, and if I am not disturbed by others in this way I have not any disposition to disturb them. I am never sulky, but my spirits are easily depressed, particularly by seeing anybody unhappy. What I call *my Romance* is this—that if I had not acquired the

[1] Which was to communicate the document to Byron.

habit of reflecting before I act, I should sometimes have sacrificed considerations of prudence to the impulse of my feelings
—but I am not conscious of having *yielded* to the temptation
which assailed me. I can assure you *from experience* that I am
very thankfully submissive to correction, so tell me when I am
wrong. Yours affectly. A. I. Milbanke.' On the 'opposite
side' she wrote as follows: '*Husband*. He must have consistent
principles of Duty governing strong & *generous* feelings, and
reducing them under the command of Reason. Genius is not
in my opinion *necessary*, though desirable, *if united* with what
I have just mentioned. I require a freedom from suspicion, &
from *habitual* ill-humour—also an equal tenor of affection
towards me, not that violent attachment which is susceptible
of sudden encrease or diminution from trifles. I wish to be
considered by my husband as a *reasonable adviser*, not as a
guide on whom he could *implicitly* depend. So much for the
chief requisites of *mind*, and for the sake of these I could over-
look many imperfections in other respects. In regard to *external* qualifications I would have fortune enough to enable me
to continue without embarrassment in the kind of society to
which I have been accustomed. I have no inclination to ex-
travagance, and should be content to practise economy for the
attainment of this object. Rank is indifferent to me. *Good connections* I think an important advantage. I do not regard
beauty, but am influenced by the *manners of a gentleman*, without which I scarcely think that anyone could attract me. I
would not enter into a family where there was a strong tendency to Insanity.'[1] Assuredly it is but too easy to bring irony
to play on the systematic full-dress assumed by this avowal,
and we shall soon see that Byron did not deny himself that
pleasure. But if an ever-present sense of the ridiculous has its

[1]We now know that, in this respect emulating Byron, Lady Melbourne
had her own way of keeping a promise, and so she did not send Byron the
document of October, 1812, until the beginning of September, 1813, at the
same time enclosing (such contrasts always amused her) those detailed
instructions, inspired by the Marquise de Merteuil, on the art of seduction.
At this date, as Ethel Colburn Mayne remarks, she was doing her utmost
to put a stop to the incest (*Life of Lady Byron*, p. 65).

advantages, it sometimes carries with it a disadvantage which
more than counterbalances them—it makes blind. The de-
ficiencies of the form hide the nature of the content, the importance, the urgent necessity, of understanding it; the whole
is discounted, thrown to the winds, with the words (antici-
pated here from Byron's own) 'I don't understand it'—those
words which have so much to answer for in human relation-
ships. There are cases in which, if one is capable of understanding, the fact of *not* understanding constitutes nothing
less than a veritable crime. Having seen that document, and
being without the sole excuse which could here prevail, that
of love, the second proposal was, on Byron's part, a crime of
that sort. And the more inexcusable because of course Annabella took for granted that the document had been sent him;
so that when the second proposal reached her, it was impossible that she should not tell herself that at last they were in
accord, and that she might at last abandon herself to her feeling. But let us see how Byron acknowledged the List to Lady
Melbourne: 'September 5. I return you the plan of A(nnabella)'s spouse elect, of which I shall say nothing because I do
not understand it; though I daresay it is exactly what it ought
to be. . . . She seems to have been spoiled—not as children
usually are—but systematically Clarissa Harlowed into an
awkward kind of correctness, with a dependence upon her own
infallibility which will or may lead her into some egregious
blunder. I don't mean the usual error of young gentle-
women, but she will find exactly what she wants, and then
discover that it is much more dignified than entertaining.'[1]
Annabella was to commit (I adhere to the Byronic vocabulary) the most 'egregious blunder', that of believing in Byron;
and I have just pointed out the sense in which he himself was
the cause of this. Nevertheless, be it noted that, with a penetration which the course of events was to load with such cruel
significance, Byron was not wrong in perceiving that Annabella's belief in her own infallibility was the gravest of men-

[1]*Corr.* i. pp. 177-178.

aces to her future. Here, in fact, we touch the point on which irreproachable beings might be indicted. For there are two very different kinds of infallibility—that which is engendered by experience, and that which on the contrary anticipates it; and the tragedy of irreproachable beings, above all when their vocation is moral, is that, refusing to give play to the psychological sense, discounting, from a double care for generosity and justice, what intuition might do for them, they draw up in every situation, and that to the smallest detail, a synopsis of what *ought to be*, and would actually be if only those values intervened which, for themselves, alone exist.[1] An infallible synopsis in the world of Corneille; but (let me recall Lady Noel's remark about Annabella) 'not fit for common use', because in the world *as it is*, it is Racine who is, who always will be, right. It follows from this that prior to experience, precisely because the shock of reality has not yet been felt, because resistance has nowhere been encountered, the irreproachable being is perilously encouraged to trust in his own infallibility; and in that respect it should be said that, until the shock of the real encounter, Annabella never met Byron on his own ground. I may add—to finish once for all with this indictment of irreproachable beings—that the constant care for perfection tends to raise all things (not, of course, in the vision one has of them, but in the degree of execution to which it is desired to bring them) to a single rank, that which pertains to them all from the fact that each of them deserves to be fully accomplished; and thus the constant care for perfection creates an indefinable equality, even a uniformity of a quite special nature, by virtue of which it nearly always seems to the outside observer that in the eyes of the lover of perfection

[1] To Annabella's two documents Lady Melbourne had replied with the comment: 'The stilts on which you are mounted'. The solidity of Annabella banked the rebuke: she proceeded to examine minutely her own defects, sent the result to her aunt, and concluded her letter with: 'After so full an explanation you will perhaps take off my *stilts*, and allow that I am only *on tiptoe*'. But she added: 'I quite agree with what you say, and I am trying to show you that it agrees more nearly with what *I* said than you seem to suppose' (*In Whig Society*, pp. 138-140).

all things are equal, that he can no longer discern the diversities of planes, and so has lost the very sense of the values for which he claims to live. He has, of course, done nothing of the kind, but we are here in presence of an almost inevitable optical illusion, one which doubtless enters, unconsciously, into the prejudice against irreproachable people. These, in all circumstances, are *modellers*: no matter how humble the material, they disengage from it that *figurine* which legitimizes it, justifies it, endows it with the significance, sometimes infinitesimal, which is its own. But those who care nothing for perfection, or even hate it, wholly blind towards that sort of result, feel towards the persevering, indefinite labour of such modelling an irritable impatience which may become exasperation (let us remember that this is one of the very traits by which I have characterized the Byronic temperament) because, never having set themselves, much less solved, the problem of the whole, the true hierarchy, the invisible architecture, escape them; because they do not know that, once that vision has put everything in its place, there is never a detail but must be treated to the maximum—not independently of the whole, but on the contrary that it may keep, in its rigorously appointed place, its relation with the whole. They have to fall back on the only kind of hierarchy they *can* perceive, the apparent one; and so towards those who show themselves 'faithful in small things', they are prone to the usual misapprehension, which consists in holding that these perfectionists take the small things for the great ones. If it be further said that it is only in very rare instances—which postulate a still rarer species, one wholly *sui generis*, of saintliness—that a sense of humour and a moral vocation are combined, it is easy to see that, joined together, premature infallibility, a constant modelling of circumstance, and a deficiency in humour put into the hands of the enemies of irreproachable beings a massive weapon of attack—and that Byron's invariable esteem for Annabella constituted but a most precarious set-off against such an opportunity.

To Byron's first letter, Annabella replied in 'the panting answer', for her unusually brief, but in which, as Ethel Colburn Mayne remarks, 'How much more she said!' So much more that it must be given here: 'I will trouble you no more—only this to express—what I cannot withhold—my heartfelt thanks for your most kind, most indulgent answer. Nothing in your letter can displease me—the recollection of my own may. I ought more to have respected your sorrows, and I cannot forgive myself for having intruded on them from the impulse of an ill-judged kindness. That I may not encrease the error—farewell. I will not regret the friendship which you deem impossible, for the loss is *mine*, as the comfort would have been *mine*. God bless you'. He answered on August 31[1] in a letter, as always, consummate: I give only the postscript, which must have been the more gratifying because it opened the door to a continued correspondence: 'I perceive that I *begin* my letter with saying "I do not wish to draw you into a correspondence", and end by almost soliciting it. Admirably consistent! but it is human nature, and you will forgive it—if not you can punish.' Annabella replied in the letter of September 4 of which the *Life of Lady Byron* tells us that 'it was pathetically happy, for all its solemnity'. She welcomed him as a valuable friend 'at some future period, without a painful exertion on your part', and went on: 'I said the comfort would be *mine*, for the idea—is it a vain dream?—of alleviating the bitterness of your despondency, if only by the *will* to do so, would give me real comfort. It is my happiness to feel that in some degree I live for others' (*p. 65*). Byron answered as early as September 6[2] and made her this time an avowal which would have strangely enlightened her if, by all the evidence, her feeling had not already passed the stage at which enlightenment is possible. This avowal follows, it is true, on a passage which, contrariwise, must not only have encouraged,

[1]See *Life of Lady Byron*, pp. 60-62 for this letter.

[2]The beginning of this letter, given in the *Life of Lady Byron* (p. 66), had hitherto been unpublished. The remainder is in *Letters and Journals*, iii. pp. 397-401.

but reinforced Annabella: 'With all my presumed prejudice against your sex, or rather the perversion of manners and principle in many, which you admit in some circles, I think the worst woman that ever existed would have made a man of very passable reputation. They are all better than us, and their faults, such as they are, must originate with ourselves. Your sweeping sentence on "the circles where we have met" amuses me much when I recollect some of those who constituted that society. After all, bad as it is, it has its *agréments*'; and this last word giving him the transition, Byron goes on: 'The great object of life is sensation—to feel that we exist, even though in pain. It is this "craving void" which drives us to gaming—to battle—to travel—to intemperate, but keenly felt pursuits of any description, whose principal attraction is the agitation inseparable from their accomplishment. I am but an awkward dissembler; as my friend you will bear with my faults. I shall have the less constraint in what I say to you—firstly because I may derive some benefit from your observations—and next because I am very sure you can never be perverted by any paradoxes of mine'. Pervert her? No, indeed! But what a great deal she might have learnt from this! The more because the 'paradox', as we know, is here nothing less than the central Byronic fact. Sensation is everything for Byron, he lives but by it and for it; to few human beings of his rank does the Pascalian conception of *divertissement* apply with such absolute, such immutable literalness. With Annabella (as we shall see when they become engaged) sensation is, on the contrary, not the first thing, but the last: it is only when she has weighed all in the balance, when she feels assured of everything else, that she abandons herself to sensation; and, coming from her, such an abandonment seals an irreversible pledge. While for Byron, as for all those with whom sensation is the central fact, sensations must be renewed every minute, intensified, exacerbated, while with him the mere capacity for feeling is wholly subject to the rhythm of change,—with Annabella the very life of the sensation itself resides first in the singleness which alone ennobles it, and then in the duration which not only deepens but consecrates it, because in the heart of the present can be heard, recurrent and annunciative, the cadences of the past and of the future. Those who thus hear the low murmur of their identity are perhaps the only beings on earth who are immune from *divertissement*; but no two things are more irreconcilable, more incommensurable even, than are the primacy of sensation and that of reflection.

A great deal to learn—Annabella learnt it only in so far as she felt some discouragement, and apparently even that did little for her instruction. 'Unlike us', says Ethel Colburn Mayne, 'she did not relish her first really Byronic letter. . . . She took some days to answer, and Byron had left London for Aston Hall before her letter arrived. But he wrote to her from there, wondering why he had not heard[1]. . . . Back in town from another visit, he found a letter from her awaiting him: "I shall not be repelled by the irritable feelings of self-dissatisfaction which I imagine you sometimes indulge"; telling him (as she grew more genial) that he might be *gay* but had not convinced her that he was *content*, and giving her reason: "I do not think you good enough to possess the only real peace—that of reflection". But after this she was shrewd enough to administer the salve that suited Byron best of all—a reference to his Pride. "Do you not sometimes laugh when you feel, because you are too proud to accept of Sympathy?" . . . Then: "May I know your sentiments on Religion?" . . . Best regards from her father and mother. "You understand the wish that the knowledge of our correspondence should still be confined to them". Was there some second sight in that? For by this time every letter of hers was being sent to Lady Melbourne for reading'.[2] Byron did not answer until September 26, and his

[1] The letter is not given either in *Letters and Journals* or the *Life of Lady Byron*.

[2] *The Life of Lady Byron*, pp. 67-68.

letter began thus: 'My dear Friend—for such you will permit me to call you—On my return to town I find some consolation for having left a number of pleasant people in your letter —the more so as I began to doubt if I should ever receive another. You ask me some questions, and as they are about myself, you must pardon the egotism into which my answers must betray me. I am glad that you know any "good deed" that I am supposed ever to have blundered upon, simply because it proves that you have not heard me invariably ill-spoken of. . . . You don't like my "restless" doctrines—I should be very sorry if you did; but I can't stagnate nevertheless. If I must sail let it be on the ocean no matter how stormy —anything but a dull cruise on a land lake without ever losing sight of the same insipid shores by which it is surrounded. "Gay" but not "content"—very true. You say I never attempt to justify myself. You are right. At times I can't and occasionally I won't defend by explanation; life is not worth having on such terms. . . . You have detected a laughter "false to the heart"—allowed—yet I have been tolerably sincere with you and I fear sometimes troublesome. To the charge of pride I suspect I must plead guilty, because when a boy and a very young one it was the constant reproach of fellows and tutors. . . . I now come to a subject of your inquiry which you must have perceived I always hitherto avoided—an awful one— "Religion". I was bred in Scotland among Calvinists in the first part of my life which gave me a dislike to that persuasion. Since that period I have visited the most bigotted and credulous of countries—Spain, Greece, Turkey. As a spectacle the Catholic is more fascinating than the Greek or the Moslem; but the last is the only believer who practises the precepts of his Prophet to the last chapter of his creed. My opinions are quite undecided. I may say so sincerely, since, when given over at Patras in 1810, I rejected and ejected three Priest-loads of spiritual consolation by threatening to turn Mussulman if they did not leave me quiet. I was in great pain and looked upon death as in that respect a relief—without much regret for the past, and few speculations on the future. .... I believe doubtless in God, and should be happy to be convinced of much more. If I do not at present place implicit faith in tradition and revelation of any human creed, I hope it is not from want of reverence for the Creator but the created, and when I see a man publishing a pamphlet to prove that Mr. Pitt is risen from the dead (as was done a week ago), perfectly positive in the truth of his assertion, I must be permitted to doubt more miracles equally well attested; but the moral of Christianity is perfectly beautiful—and the very sublime of virtue—yet even there we find some of its finer precepts in the earlier axioms of the Greeks—particularly "do unto others as you would they should do unto you"—the forgiveness of injuries and more which I do not remember. .... You write remarkably well—which you won't like to hear, so I shall say no more about it. Ever yours most sincerely, Byron.'[1] Here again, though, I must not omit the other side, which we find in a letter of September 28 to Lady Melbourne: 'The epistles of your mathematician (A. would now be ambiguous) continue; and the last concludes with a repetition of a desire that none but papa and mamma should know it; why *you* should not, seems to me quite ludicrous, and is now past praying for; but observe, here is the strictest of St. Ursula's 11,000 what do you call 'ems? a wit, a moralist, and religionist, enters into a clandestine correspondence with a personage generally presumed a great *roué*, and drags her aged parents into this sacred treaty. It is, I believe, not usual for single ladies to risk such brilliant adventures; but this comes of infallibility; not that she ever says anything that might not be said by the town-crier, still it is imprudent, if I were rascal enough to take an unfair advantage. Alas! poor human nature, here is your niece writing, and doing a foolish thing, *I lecturing* Webster! and forgetting the tremendous "beam in my own eye!"[2] We know too well the nature, really terrible when Annabella is in question, of the Byronic 'other

[1] *Letters and Journals*, iii. pp. 401-403.   [2] *Corr*. i. p. 184.

sides'; I need not dwell upon them; and now we come to October, 1813, which we can guess to be an essential date for the definite fixation of Annabella's feeling. On her side, but only on hers, the correspondence with Byron was intensified; at Aston Hall, in October, he received another letter from her, 'restored to complacency by his appeal to go on with their correspondence. She was conscious, she told him, that her too great seriousness might fatigue him, and apologised for it; a valued woman friend was going abroad for medical advice, and she was anxious and sorrowful'. She went on: "By attributing my depression to this cause, I do not seek to invalidate what I once hinted of another impression. Subjected as it is to reason, I need not blush to own it. I *should* blush to be its slave". And all her guileless guile is in the immediately following words: "Once more of your Pride—it is perhaps so mingled with magnanimity that the vice might be mistaken for virtue. The distinction need not be *proved* to *you*". . . . From London at the end of October Byron wrote to Lady Melbourne: "My Seaham correspondence has ceased on both sides, and I shall not renew it". He had not answered Annabella's letter, with its recurrence to the "hopeless" attachment of her heart'.[1] Meanwhile, Lady Melbourne had also been hearing from her niece. In a letter of the beginning of October, Annabella wrote of the enlarged edition of *The Giaour* that she had been reading it, and admired the additions. 'The description of Love almost makes *me* in love. Certainly he excels in the language of Passion, whilst the power of delineating inanimate nature appears more copiously bestowed on other poets. Perhaps he has not displayed his excellence in that line only because it has not so much occupied his attention. In the *intellectual* he is truly sublime, yet I cannot believe that his Genius has yet attained its maturity. There is a progressive improvement in his writings. I shall be glad of his stay in England as I may hope to have some share of his agreeable society next year in London. . . .

[1] *Life of Lady Byron,* pp. 69-70.

I consider his acquaintance as so desirable that I would incur the risk of being called a Flirt for the sake of enjoying it, provided I may do so without detriment to himself—for you know that his welfare has been as much the object of my consideration as if it were connected with my own.'[1] I think there are reasons for giving an exceptional importance to this letter. On the one hand, it confirms the view that Annabella's feeling was originally an *amour de tête*, in which the poet was the attraction, and the man only in so far as he was the poet[2]— but here the transition from the one to the other was inevitable, since at that time the sole aim of Byron's poetry was to project a double, sombre, mysterious, and fatal, of himself. Annabella frequently interrogated him on this sombre, melancholy side of his nature, which she feared in a conjugal relation, but which none the less was the very thing that fascinated her. What she first loved in Byron was the Byronic hero; her little phrase: 'The description of Love almost makes *me* in love' is as revealing as can be—only the 'almost' is just one word too much. Correspondence, questions, inquiry were directed to the one purpose of trying to bring the two sides of Byron's nature into accordance, so that future happiness might thereby be ensured. On the other hand, the letter to Lady Melbourne shows that already the transition from poet to man had been made, that she desired nothing so much as to see him again, that she went to meet her destiny with a ready mind and heart. So for the moment the documents shall speak for themselves, with as little comment as may be. Annabella was evidently dissatisfied with Byron's answer concerning religion, and the more because he had not replied to her last letter. 'Her seriousness, then, *had* fatigued him— was this the end of their friendship? She bore the pangs until the end of November; then she could hold out no longer. Of all her letters to him this is the starchiest (as Byron said later

[1] *Corr*. ii. p. 308.

[2] I have already called attention to the indispensable corrective of this view.

of her style); the wounded feeling to be read between the lines is the only interest it possesses. Never did she use so many long words, tangled constructions, meaningless under-linings. It was all about Religion, Revelation, Reason—on Reason she got in a thrust: "I have not as high an opinion of your Reasoning as of your powers of Imagination. They are rarely united". On mathematics too she was crushing: "At your age [this science] is not to be commenced". But these touches of human nature are not enough to make the letter a readable one. "I am not exacting an answer. I only request to be informed when my communications become unacceptable, that I may discontinue them". On that resentful note she ended'.[1] It was on November 3rd that Annabella had written; the letter therefore reaches Byron on the day when, as we have seen, he himself writes to Lady Melbourne: 'For the last three days I have been quite shut up; my mind has been from *late* and *later* events in such a state of fermentation, that as usual I have been obliged to empty it in rhyme, and am in the very heart of another Eastern tale—something of the *Giaour* cast—but not so sombre, though rather more villain-ous. This is my usual resource; if it were not for some such occupation to dispel reflection during *inaction*, I verily believe I should very often go mad'.[2] However pale, on the printed page, *The Bride of Abydos*, we know from what inner furnace she proceeded, then red-hot with the amalgamation of Lady Frances and Augusta: if we add the possibility, at that moment looming, of a duel with Webster, we cannot deny that no time could well have been less propitious for the arrival of a 'starchy' letter from Annabella, and we must admit that it was rather meritorious that as early as November 10 Byron should sit down and begin an answer. It is true that, having begun, he not only left off, but for a week clean forgot that he had begun at all—but it is true also that that week is the very one that saw the opening of the prodigious *Journal*, destined, after *The Bride of Abydos*, to provide a new

[1]*Life of Lady Byron*, pp. 70-71.   [2]*Corr.* i. p. 214.

receptacle for the persisting 'state of fermentation'. With the circumstances now present to our mind, let us look, both in the *Life of Lady Byron* and in *Letters and Journals*, at the essential passages of a document that was to prove so important to Annabella: 'November 10th, 1813. A variety of circumstances and movements from place to place—none of which would be very amusing in detail, nor indeed pleasing to any one who (I may flatter myself) is my friend—have hitherto prevented me from answering your two last letters; but if my daily self-reproach for the omission can be of any atonement, I hope it may prove as satisfactory an apology to you as it has been a "compunctious visiting" to myself'.[1]— 'November 10th, 1813. Your opinion of my "reasoning powers" is so exactly my own, that you will not wonder if I avoid a controversy with so skilful a casuist,—particularly on a subject where I am certain to get the worst of it in this world, and perhaps incur a warmer confutation in the next. But I shall be most happy to hear your observations on the subject. If anybody could do me *good*, probably you might, as, by all accounts, you are a mistress of the practice as well as theory of that benevolent science (which I take to be even better than your *mathematics*). At all events it is my fault if I derive no benefit from your remarks. I agree with you quite upon mathematics too, and must be content to admire them at an incomprehensible distance, always adding them to the catalogue of my regrets. I know that two and two make four, and should be glad to prove it too, if I could—though, I must say, if by any sort of process I could convert 2 and 2 into 5, it would give me much greater pleasure. The only part I remember which gave me much delight were those theorems (is that the word), in which, after ringing the changes upon A B and C D, etc., I at last came to "which is absurd"— "which is impossible", and at this point I have always arrived and I fear always shall through life—very fortunate if I can continue to stop there".[2]—"When shall we meet in

[1] *Life of Lady Byron*, p. 71.   [2] *Letters and Journals*, iii. p. 404.

town? by the bye you won't take fright when we meet, will you? and imagine I am about to add to your thousand and one pretendants? I have taken exquisite care to prevent the possibility of that, tho' less likely than ever to become a Benedick. Indeed I have not seen (with one exception) for many years a Beatrice, and she will not be troubled to assume the part. I think we understand each other perfectly and may talk to each other occasionally without exciting speculation. The worst that can be said is that I *would* and you *won't*, and in this respect you can hardly be the sufferer and I am very sure I *shan't*. If I find my heart less philosophic on the subject than I at present believe it, I shall keep out of the way; but I now think it is well shielded—at least it has got a new suit of armour—and certainly it stood in need of it. I have heard a rumour of another added to your list of unacceptables, and I am sorry for him, as I know that he has talent, and his pedigree assures him wit and good humour. You make sad havoc among "us youth".'[1]—'*P.S.*—November 17th. The enclosed was written a week ago & has lain in my desk ever since. I have had forty thousand plagues to make me forget not *you* but *it*; and now I might as well burn it—but let it go, & pray forgive ye scrawl & the scribe. If you favour me with an answer, any letter addressed here will reach me wherever I may be. I have a little cousin Eliza Byron coming—no, going to school at Stockton. Will you notice her? It is the prettiest little black-eyed girl of Paradise, and but 7 years old.'[2]

How Byronic here the play of light and shade,—the both spontaneous and willed chiaroscuro: again it seems as if we witnessed the whole process, and it is indeed so Byronic that I am half-tempted to cancel my 'meritorious'. For it must have meant a relief to give in to playing with fire, and in this case (since the Annabella of that period could in no wise guess, or even conceive of, the truth) to discover an aspect of

---

[1]*Letters and Journals*, iii. pp. 407-408. This letter is wrongly dated November 29th, 1813, in *Letters and Journals*.

[2]*Life of Lady Byron*, p. 72.

the game that had the value of novelty and might be termed the platonic playing with fire. Two days earlier—the white rose, Lady Frances, beginning to droop—had not Byron resumed the correspondence with Augusta, had he not written to her: 'You do not know what mischief your being with me might have prevented': we can imagine the poisoned voluptuousness and also the terrible irony (an irony, in the circumstances, so secure against all detection) with which he penned the two sentences to Annabella: 'I have taken exquisite care to prevent the possibility of that. . . . I now think my heart is well shielded—at least it has got a new suit of armour—and certainly it stood in need of it'. But here the crowning irony (the greater because perhaps not intended as ironical by Byron himself: he remained long under the illusion that his capacity to respond to her seriousness constituted between them an understanding) is contained in the phrase: 'I think we understand each other perfectly'. Whenever met with, that phrase makes the onlooker shudder, but here it is poignant, for here, on Annabella's part, the misunderstanding was bound to be complete. So he was 'less likely than ever to become a Benedick', and yet there had been 'one exception' to his not meeting a Beatrice. 'And who was she—can *you* guess?' For two quite opposite reasons, lack of brain on the one side, lack of lightness on the other, neither Augusta nor Annabella was particularly gifted for reading between the lines: Augusta, Byron addressed point-blank; but between the lines written to Annabella even *she* could not help reading. Then that was what came of departing, were it but once, from the truth—it came to destroying with one's own hands the Beatrice that in fact one had been. Shakespeare's Beatrice? Well, yes, in so far as marriage was the goal; but a marriage which in itself is only a stepping-stone towards the marriage of souls . . . this is still Beatrice, but with a difference —the Beatrice of Dante. But whereas the Beatrice of Dante is justly entitled to charge her poet with his numerous sins of forgetfulness, her stranded young disciple finds herself in the predicament of being in her own eyes wholly responsible for the 'new suit of armour'. What can be done? As with all beings whose vocation is primarily moral, a predicament of this kind immediately engenders an irresistible need for action, which is no less immediately checked by the reflective faculty. Harm has been inflicted, but to attempt at once to redress it in the quarter where it has been inflicted would be to run the risk of only making things worse. No, Annabella cannot so soon write to Byron; yet, as Ethel Colburn Mayne well says, 'to someone she must speak out'. Hence the letter to M.G.: 'I do not always succeed when I wish to be *enjouée*. It is not quite my proper character. . . . Every one of my friends has a different influence on my humour. M.M. makes me romantic; you make me thoughtful; H.M. light-hearted (with a few exceptions); Joanna humble; By— religious; Miss Raine reasonable; Miss Doyle sanguine; Dr. Fenwick diffident, &c. &c. You will be surprised at the production of my piety; but surely the survey of Heaven-born genius without Heavenly grace must make a Christian clasp the blessing with greater reverence and love, mingled with a sorrow as Christian that it is not shared. Should it ever happen that he & I offer up a heartfelt worship together—I mean in a sacred spot—*my* worship will then be almost worthy of the spirit to whom it ascends. It will glow with all the devout and grateful joy which mortal breast can contain. It is a thought too dear to be indulged—not dear for *his* sake, but for the sake of *man*, my brother man, whoever he be—& for any poor, unknown tenant of this earth I believe I should feel the same. It is not the poet—it is the immortal soul lost or saved! Now I have written and thought till my tears flow— Could I have your sympathy at this moment, & could I feel it in the pressure of your hand on my heart, I should not experience this bursting feeling. Dearest Mary—receive these evaporations of a soul which does not melt quite in solitude if it flies to communicate its emotions to you'.[1] If I have

[1]*Life of Lady Byron*, p. 73.

called the misunderstanding poignant, it is because this text lays bare to us all its poignancy, which consists in the alliance of an admirable self-knowledge and an almost incredible self-ignorance: Annabella knows to perfection all the fundamentals, the ground-bass of her nature, but, even at this very juncture, she ignores (in the sense either of not being able or of refusing to take consciousness of its implications) the music that all the time love is playing on the instrument. 'By— makes me religious': here we get both the organ-tenor in which Annabella's feelings are keyed, and the utter hopelessness in the given case. What Annabella means, of course (though here again the self-ignorance hinders the fullness of the self-knowledge), is that her love for Byron brings out, develops, her religious strain: he does not make her believe— how could he!—but her love for him makes her belief *more so*,[1] with the unavoidable, noble, and fatal result that, of all things, she desires that the proposition should be inverted, that A. should make By— religious. 'Should it ever happen that he & I offer up a heartfelt worship together—I mean in a sacred spot—*my* worship will then be almost worthy of the spirit to whom it ascends',—ah! then pure bliss would be attained. That 'Heaven-born genius' should be without 'Heavenly grace': that is a fact which our contemporaries accept and applaud with a complacency equal to though antithetical of the Victorian one they so enjoy deriding, but there are still a few of us left who see in the fact nothing less and nothing more than the scandal of ingratitude (in the all too human, but human only, sense of the word), and these few

[1]With Annabella we are exactly in the inverted situation to that which we analysed apropos of Caroline's Good Friday letter. In Caroline, without her at all being conscious of them, all the religious possibilities are enlisted in the act of profane idolization, in the enthronement of Byron: nothing is left over. In Annabella, love for Byron makes her more religious in the most literal sense of the term—and with the perilous corollary that showing one's love to the beloved object no longer takes the form of idolizing him, but of hoping, and even trying, to convert him. Now, it would be difficult to gauge which Byron hated the more: being idolized, or being converted. To be amused, that is what he asked of woman: hence the triumphant privileges of Augusta.

are perhaps the best equipped to understand Annabella here. For, more almost than any other being—and, to the second degree, when he is a poet—the man of genius is the *receiver*: it is both his distinction and his responsibility; but, on the other hand, he is related to every one of us by the possession of 'the immortal soul', and if he is either too weak or too unconscious or both to ascend, as beseems a responsible agent, by dint of his distinction, he should at least be saved by his relatedness; and this, to my view, is the deepest and last meaning of Annabella's cry: 'It is not the poet—it is the immortal soul lost or saved!'—that cry, only recently revealed to us, but which those who sympathize with Annabella had always divined to be the leading motive of her whole conduct.

Truly, she had spoken out—and to the degree that when next day she feels equal to writing to Byron, she almost too much, to use Ethel Colburn Mayne's serviceable expression, 'summons all her familiar spirits—self-control, dignity, and the rest'. Yet Ethel Colburn Mayne is right; there are some touches that might have enabled Byron to read between the lines. 'Pray let me have your new composition—I have received more pleasure from your poetry than from all the Q.E.Ds in Euclid. Though I think mathematics eminently useful, they are by no means what I like and admire most, & I have not a friend more skilled in them than yourself. People of methodised feelings are to me very disagreeable, being myself so *un*demonstrative as to prefer, if not always to approve, those generous spirits "who are pleased they know not *why* & care not *wherefore*". I hope I have not appeared to assume either mathematical or any other superiority. Everyone has in some point what another wants, & thus the weakest may afford some aid to the strongest. On *that* principle I thought it not presumptuous to offer mine. . . . Perhaps I *have* occasionally forgotten the humility which should have regulated my opinions, and in giving advice I may have taken occasion to show my own wisdom at my neighbour's expense, but could you read my thoughts—and I hoped you could—you would know that my general feeling is very different. I never meant to engage you in religious controversy—you will remember that I owned myself not qualified for converting—I would only persuade you to take the means of convincing yourself. . . . I cannot now have the least fear of your entertaining a wish for more of my regard than you possess. By enabling you to form a closer estimate of my character, I was aware that the charm which Distance confers with persons of a warm Imagination would vanish, & that I must find my *just* level. But if I have thus permanently secured your peace (as far as I am concerned) and if I have spared you but a single regret . . . I resign my vanity, & wish the sacrifice could make me your equal in disinterestedness. I look forward to meeting you next spring in London as one of the most agreeable incidents which my residence there can produce. *I* shall not be distressed if the design to captivate should be imputed to *me* (which I think probable); but if my father & mother should be rendered uneasy . . . I shall try to avoid the occasions, & shall then frankly tell you why I do so, and what I wish—since you will not unkindly suppose that a doubt of your intentions can actuate me. . . . I was afraid you had experienced some vexations when Lady Melbourne wrote to me a short time ago that you were not looking well. You will never be allowed to remain at peace. Everyone (I must include myself) seems determined to interfere with your repose. After this reflection my conscience obliges me to conclude. *P.S.*—I shall like very much to be the playfellow of your little cousin if I can contrive it, for Stockton is 22 miles from hence, & we never go there except in our journeys to and from London. We will gladly send for her, if she may have leave to spend some holidays here. Whenever you are inclined to improve me by your criticisms, I will pay the poetical debt which I am to have the pleasure of incurring. Unfortunately Mathematics have sobered my Muse—not myself!'[1] Yes, most decidedly, he ought to have read between the lines, for, generally speaking, he had in that direction, if not an exceptional, at least a normal gift; but the curious thing—and one which adds another item to his misunderstanding of her whom he 'understands' so 'perfectly'—is that when it is a question of Annabella, even that normal gift seems to forsake him. As a matter of fact, between the lines he read exactly nothing, for in the Journal of September 30th he thus comments on the letter: 'A very pretty letter from Annabella which I answered. What an odd situation and friendship is ours!—without one spark of love on either side, and produced by circumstances which in general lead to coldness on one side and aversion on the other'.[2] Yes: incredible as it may appear, Byron no more believed at any time in Annabella's love than he had chosen to believe in Caroline's passion—so impossible, as I have already indicated, was it for him to believe in the fatality of others. So late as November, 1821, did he not say to Medwin: 'You ask if Lady Byron were ever in love with me. I have answered that question already—No! I was the fashion when she first came out: I had the character of being a great rake, and was a great dandy —both of which young ladies like. She married me from vanity, and the hope of reforming and fixing me. She was a spoiled child, and naturally of a jealous disposition'.[3]

Are we to see in this incredulity what Ethel Colburn Mayne suggests—that it was one of Byron's few naïvetés? I am much more inclined to think that it represents a ruse of the subconscious of a kind which more than once proved serviceable to him. When we are not in love, it is always more convenient to assume that the other one is not either, above all when that other is regarded solely in a matrimonial light, when one is an adept in the marriage of esteem and has decided beforehand that, in marriage, the intrusion of love can do nothing but spoil the whole scheme. Besides, in 1821, after the tragic

[1] *Life of Lady Byron*, pp. 73-75.   [2] *Letters and Journals*, ii. p. 357.
[3] Medwin, *Conversations*, p. 59 (2nd edition, 1824).

scenes which had led to the separation, Byron may well have felt the need of reasserting to himself that, after all, those scenes had been inflicted on an insensitive being.

But, if he had not read between the lines, he had answered immediately, answered even the day before that entry in the Journal. 'No one can *as*sume or *pre*sume less than you do, though very few with whom I am acquainted possess half your claims to that 'Superiority' which you are so fearful of affecting; nor can I recollect one expression since the commencement of our correspondence which has in any respect diminished my opinion of your talents, my respect for your virtues. My only reason for avoiding the discussion of *sacred* topics was the sense of my own ignorance & the fear of saying something that might displease; but I *have listened* & will listen to you with not merely patience but pleasure. When we meet—if we do meet—in Spring, you will find me ready to acquiesce in all your notions upon the point merely personal between ourselves. You will act according to circumstances. It would be premature in us both to anticipate reflections which may never be made—& if made at all, are certainly unfounded. You wrong yourself very much in supposing that 'the charm' has been broken by our nearer acquaintance. On ye contrary that very intercourse convinces me of the value of what I have lost—or rather never found; but I will not deny that circumstances have occurred to render it more supportable. You will think me very capricious. . . . It is true that I could not exist without some object of attachment, but I have shown that I am not quite a slave to impulse. But, however weak (or it may merit a harsher term) I may be in my disposition to attach myself (and as society is now much the same in this as in all other European countries it were difficult to avoid it), in my search for the 'ideal,'—the being to whom I would commit the whole happiness of my future life,—I have never yet seen but two approaching to the likeness. The first I was too young to have a prospect of obtaining, and subsequent events have proved that my expectations might not have been fulfilled, had I ever proposed to and received my idol. *The second*—the only woman to whom I ever seriously pretended as a wife—has disposed of her heart already, and I think it too late to look for a third. I shall take the world as I find it, and have seen it much the same in most climates. (More fiery in the East—a mixture of languid habits and stormy passions). But I have no confidence, and look for no constancy, in affections founded on caprice, and lucky conformity of disposition without any fixed principles. How far this may be my case at present, I know not, and have not had time to ascertain. I by no means rank poetry or poets high in the scale of intellect. This may look like affectation, but it is my real opinion. It is the lava of the imagination whose eruption prevents an earthquake. They say poets never or rarely go *mad*. Cowper and Collins are instances to the contrary (but Cowper was no poet). It is, however, to be remarked that they rarely do, but are generally so near it that I cannot help thinking rhyme is so far useful in anticipating and preventing the disorder. I prefer the talents of action—of war, or the senate, or even of science—to all the speculations of those mere dreamers of another existence (I don't mean religiously but fancifully) and spectators of this apathy. Disgust and perhaps incapacity have rendered me now a mere spectator; but I have occasionally mixed in the active and tumultuous departments of existence, and in these alone my recollection rests with any satisfaction, though not the best parts of it'.[1]

'Poetry is the lava of the imagination, whose eruption prevents an earthquake.' No one but Byron could have defined with such depth in the accuracy both his poetry and his very being; and on that day at any rate—a sign, and the most significant possible, of the esteem he bore her—he paid Annabella

[1]This letter I give partly from the *Life of Lady Byron* (pp. 75-76), partly from *Letters and Journals*, iii. (pp. 406-407, p. 405): as Ethel Colburn Mayne has shown, the editor of *Letters and Journals* has confused the letters of November 10 and November 29: all that is quoted above was written on November 29.

the tribute of a supreme sincerity. Such sincerity is peculiarly irresistible for its recipient; the intrinsic meaning of what is said, the warning, the message it may convey are not then the things that primarily matter; everything is fused in the gratitude felt for so unrestricted an avowal—and if it is love that receives the gift, it receives it as the most valuable of all treasures.

A treasure, yes; and for Annabella that letter was not without other treasures too, but at the same time all of them gave (in the sense in which one speaks of exquisite pain) an exquisite edge to her anguish. For now or never truth was to be retrieved: somehow or other, Byron was to be made aware that if 'she had already disposed of her heart', it was to him. Again M.G. was to become the recipient of the first outpouring: 'I feel very uneasy at the idea of keeping up a deception, & especially with one who has undoubtedly practised no deception with me. Had the circumstance not been mentioned, I should not have felt it necessary or conscientious to allude to it in any way, but now a continuation of silence is an acquiescence in untruth. If we have been so unfortunate as to forsake the path of Sincerity, it has always been my opinion that the sooner we return to it the better. . . . I shall be unhappy until I can regain *truth*.'[1] But truth never is as easily regained as abandoned; and in this particular case, the regaining of truth was to be a slow, a laborious process, indeed both so painful and (one must say things as they are) so tedious to witness that one cannot but pity Ethel Colburn Mayne for having had to play here the part of the exhaustive historian. As she has done so, we may consider the duty as discharged once for all, refer the reader for details to Chapter VII of the *Life of Lady Byron*, and confine ourselves to interpretation.

As a matter of fact, what happens here in spite, or rather

[1] *Life of Lady Byron*, pp. 78-79.

under the shelter, of the intensified correspondence, is a parting of the ways. Though utterly astray as regards Annabella's
feelings, Byron's entry in the Journal of November 30 is the
last kind word that he has to say of her until the second proposal ten months later. She, on the other side, not only multiplies her heavy-handed attempts at the retrieving of truth,
but in every other way crystallizes ever more and more. She
reads the *Corsair*, and on February 12, 1814, writes to Lady
Melbourne: 'I have just finished the *Corsair*—am in the
greatest admiration. In knowledge of the human heart & its
most secret workings surely he may without exaggeration be
compared to Shakespeare. He gives such wonderful life and
individuality to character that from *that* cause, as well as from
unjust prepossessions as to his *own* disposition, the idea that
he represents himself in his heroes may be partly accounted
for. It is difficult to believe that he could have known these
beings so thoroughly but from *introspection*.

> Who hath seen
> Man as himself—the secret spirit face?'

I am afraid the compliment to his poetry will not repay him
for the injury to his character.'[1] Here we see, amalgamated,
all the elements, originally dispersed, of Annabella's love: she
abandons herself to the poet's genius, she keeps for herself,
and as a treasure confided to her alone, the image of the still
better man in whom their correspondence has enabled her to
believe, and, without giving words to the conviction, she relies
on herself to produce, or at any rate obtain, the reconciling
synthesis. Filled with hope, she pursues her effort, and again
leads Byron to the subject which for her is central—religion.
In reply comes his letter of March 3, 1814: 'I thank you very
much for your suggestion on religion. But I must tell you, at
the hazard of losing whatever good opinion your gentleness
may have bestowed upon me, that it is a source from
which I never did, and I believe never can, derive comfort.
If I ever feel what is called devout, it is when I have

[1]*Corr*. ii. p. 309.

met with some good of which I did not conceive myself deserving, and then I am apt to thank anything but mankind. On the other hand, when I am ill or unlucky, I philosophize as well as I can, and wish it were over one way or the other—without any glimpses at the future. Why I came here, I know not. Where I shall go to, it is useless to inquire. In the midst of myriads of the living and the dead worlds—stars—systems —infinity—why should I be anxious about an atom? . . . P.S.—I was told to-day that you had refused me "a *second time*", so that you see I am supposed to be the most permanent of your plagues, & persevering of your suitors—a kind of successor to Wellesley Long Pole. If this multiplication-table of negatives don't embarrass you, I can assure you it don't disturb me. If it vexed me I could not, & if I thought it would do otherwise than amuse *you*—I certainly *should* not, have mentioned it.'[1] Here we must turn to Ethel Colburn Mayne: 'Her reply was of many pages; but she came to the point at last. "As for the report, it is absurd enough to excite a smile. In avoiding the possibility of being in a situation to refuse, I cannot consider myself as having refused". And though she tried by passages about Mme. de Staël and so on to cover up the hint that she was willing to be proposed to again, Byron read between the lines this time, for he remarked to his Diary: 'A letter from *Bella*, which I answered. I shall be in love with her again if I don't take care.'[2] The entry in the Journal is of March 15; from the answer written the same day, I extract this passage: 'You do not know how much I wish to see you—for there are so many things *said* in a moment, but tedious upon the tablets. Not that I should ever intrude upon your confidence anything (at least I hope not) you should not hear; yet there are several opinions of yours I want to request, & though I have two or three able & I believe very sincere *male* friends, there is something preferable to me in ye delicacy of a woman's perceptions. Of this at least I am sure—

[1] *Letters and Journals*, iii. p. 408, and *Life of Lady Byron*, p. 91.
[2] *Life of Lady Byron*, pp. 91-92.

that I am more liable to be convinced by their arguments. As for ye *report* I mentioned—*I* care not how often it is repeated. It would plague me much more to hear that I was *accepted* by anybody else than rejected by you'.[1] Entry and extract seem to contradict my statement above, but in the case of Byron it is always of utmost importance to keep chronology in sight: if, as I have written in the preceding chapter, at the end of this month of March, Byron, in accord with Augusta, begins to gravitate towards marriage, it is a very mild sort of gravitation, for we are in a period that lies between the poisonous *régime* of Mithridates (January) and the birth of Medora (April), which, because the child has so well escaped being 'an ape', is celebrated in the passionate verses to Augusta:

> And thine is that love which I would not forego
> Though that heart may be bought by Eternity's woe.

In the circumstances, we may safely assume that Byron had not much 'care' to 'take' for avoiding being 'in love with Bella again',—we may assume it all the more because any *again* postulates a *before*, and we have already expressed ourselves on the subject of the 'before'. Now, if we cast a glance at that faithful repository of Byron's sincerity in the nude, the Letters to Lady Melbourne, this is what on April 30 he writes to her ladyship: 'You—or rather *I*—have done *my A.* much injustice. The expression which you recollect as objectionable meant only "loving" in the *senseless* sense of that wide word, and it must be some selfish stupidity of mine in telling my own story, but really and truly—as I hope mercy and happiness for her—by that God who made me for my own misery, and not much for the good of others, *she* was not to blame, one thousandth part in comparison. She was not aware of her own peril till it was too late, and I can only account for her subsequent "*abandon*" by an observation which I think is not unjust, that women are much more *attached* than men if they are treated with anything like fairness or tenderness. As for *your* A., I don't know what to make of

[1] *Life of Lady Byron*, pp. 92-93.

her. I enclose her last but one, and *my* A.'s last but one, from which you may form your own conclusions on both. I think you will allow mine to be a very extraordinary person in point of *talent*, but I won't say more, only do not allow your good nature to lean to my side of this question; on all others I shall be glad to avail myself of your partiality. . . . You won't believe me, and won't care if you do, but I really believe that I have more true regard and affection for yourself than for any other existence. As for my A., my feelings towards her are a mixture of good and diabolical. I hardly know one passion which has not some share in them, but I won't run into the subject. Your niece has committed herself perhaps, but it can be of no consequence; if I pursued and succeeded in that quarter, of course I must give up all other pursuits, and the fact is that my wife, if she had common sense, would have more power over me than any other whatsoever, for my heart always alights on the nearest *perch*—if it is withdrawn it goes God knows where—but one must like something.'[1] A both sincere and cynical statement has at least the advantage of dispelling all ambiguities, but of the many valuable pieces of information that this one contains, that which concerns us is, 'your niece has committed herself perhaps'; and, for once more direct than even Byron himself, we must here erase the 'perhaps'. Yes, if at last she had retrieved the truth, Annabella had committed herself, and was to go on committing herself, of which the best proof is that in the late spring and summer of 1814, when Byron's replies were very dilatory, and sometimes never came at all, she wrote oftener and oftener. These two lines from a letter of hers on June 19 are enough to illuminate the situation: 'Pray write to me—for I have been rendered uneasy by your long silence, and you cannot wish to make me so'.[2] Now, it is here that, in comparison with the mere imprudence of October, 1812, Lady Melbourne's responsibility becomes terribly heavy. She herself had asked Annabella to define her views on marriage,

[1]*Corr.* i. pp. 254-255.   [2]*Life of Lady Byron*, p. 97.

and Annabella had drawn up articles that left no doubt at all as to what they were; moreover, Lady Melbourne was in the secret of the incest; and not only so, but she alone knew, from Byron's reiterated avowals, how deep the evil went and that its author held it to be well-nigh incurable. It is true that whenever the marriage question loomed up, Byron declared his intention (which was sincere) of putting an end to everything else; but on this point Lady Melbourne can be acquitted only if we deny her any psychological perception, an accusation which would be peculiarly unjustified. There are cases, and this is one of them, when morality itself is vitally concerned in its being the psychological rather than the moral sense which takes a part—an Annabella has the right to make a mistake because her vocation is moral; a pupil of the Marquise de Merteuil, whose vocation lies elsewhere, cannot plead, or benefit by, that excuse. The less because Byron, on his side, was very conscious of the serious alteration that the intrusion of incest had imposed upon the statement of his problem; hence, desirous that in any event he should have nothing to reproach himself with towards his unique confidante and friend, he wrote thus to Lady Melbourne so soon as April 18: 'Though I think *that chance* off the cards, and have no paramount inclination to try a fresh deal; yet, as what I may resolve to-day may be unresolved to-morrow, I should be not only unwilling, but unable to make the experiment without your acquiescence. Circumstances, which I need not recapitulate, may have changed *Aunt's* mind; I do not say that *Niece's* is changed, but I *should* laugh if their judgments had changed places, and were exactly reversed upon that point. In putting this question to you, my motive is all due to selfishness, as a word from you could and would put an end to that, or any similar possibility, without my being able to say anything but "thank you".'[1] This is as explicit as can be. If he

[1] *Corr.* i. p. 250. Lady Melbourne's responsibility is all the greater because she was here in the ideal position (almost unique in predicaments of this kind) of not having in any way to betray Byron's confidence: she had simply to say a No that was to be received with thanks.

marries, it will be only to escape from incest; he loves no one but Augusta, and in the event of marriage he does not now feel even for Annabella a preference more marked than for anybody else; if, therefore, Lady Melbourne considers this marriage, or any other, impossible, she has only to say a word, and Byron will have nothing to reply but 'Thank you'. Left to himself, he would continue the incestuous relation; if he is thinking of escape by the only way that remains to him— namely, marriage—it is chiefly, perhaps entirely, to please Lady Melbourne. Lady Melbourne did not say the 'one word', and the ensuing correspondence shows us that she continued to favour the idea of marriage. The truth must be faced—Lady Melbourne, knowing all about it, sacrificed her niece to the very slender possibility (which she could not but have known to be so) that Byron might get over his incestuous passion. Morality is, decidedly, a very dangerous weapon in the hands of those who are in no wise qualified to handle it.

Byron was thus in the position of having a permission in reserve which he was not in any hurry to make use of. But we must not forget that at this time there was, besides Lady Melbourne, Augusta—not yet the Augusta whom Annabella alone could awaken to the moral life, but already an Augusta who was in all good faith urging Byron to marry, an Augusta of whom, on October 4, soon after he had become engaged, Byron wrote to Lady Melbourne: 'She wished me much to marry, because it was the only chance of redemption for *two* persons'.[1] And by putting and keeping the emphasis on the necessity for marriage, Augusta was by a side-issue to hasten the course of events. By a side-issue, because for a time, as a mitigation of the future awaiting him, Byron hoped to receive his bride from her hands. On March 22, 1814, he wrote in his Journal: 'Let me see—what did I see? The only person who

[1]*Corr.* i. pp. 273-274.

much struck me was Lady S—d's [Stafford's] eldest daughter, Lady C. L. [Charlotte Leveson]. They say she is *not* pretty. I don't know—everything is pretty that pleases; but there is an air of *soul* about her—and her colour changes—and there is that shyness of the antelope (which I delight in) in her manner so much, that I observed her more than any other woman in the rooms, and only looked at anything else when I thought she might perceive and feel embarrassed by my scrutiny. After all, there may be something of association in this. She is a friend of Augusta's, and whatever she loves I can't help liking. Her mother, the Marchioness, talked to me a little; and I was twenty times on the point of asking her to introduce me to *sa fille*, but I stopped short. This comes of that affray with the Carlisles.'[1] Though on that evening he did not ask to be presented to Lady Charlotte, they were introduced to one another by Rogers at an evening party in June; and in a letter to Augusta of June 18 Byron describes the incoherent exchange of remarks to which they were reduced by mutual shyness. Nevertheless—probably because he had been able to make sure that Lady Charlotte's shyness was indeed of the kind that belongs to the beauty of the antelope—when he found that Augusta warmly approved this candidate, Byron authorized her to take soundings through a woman friend, but without letting it be known that he was aware of the proceeding. The friend managed so badly that not only did it lead to nothing, but gave rise to an obscure and futile misunderstanding which was not cleared up until the eve of Byron's formal engagement. As a result Byron, thinking that Augusta 'did not seem to be in luck', made up his mind to take charge of the matrimonial question himself; for as he was utterly indifferent, as his heart played no part in the transaction, why multiply vain alternatives? If the antelope did not dare

[1]*Letters and Journals*, ii. p. 406. Lady Charlotte, who afterwards became Countess of Surrey, was allied to the family of Lord Carlisle, Byron's guardian, with whom Byron had quarrelled; but he regretted the quarrel, and was seeking the means of reconciliation which such a marriage would doubtless have opened up.

(timidity has its moments of wisdom) to enter the cage of the higher species of human animal, was there not always she whom in the days of future calumny Mrs. Norton was so finely to denominate 'the sick and hunted deer of the herd', and who was awaiting, was indeed imploring, the second offensive? In her numerous letters of July and August, Annabella had been advancing, retreating, advancing again, and altogether (as Byron was to write to Lady Melbourne after the engagement) 'bewildering herself sadly'.[1] It behoved the new Alexander to cut the Gordian knot, and on September 9th, at Newstead, where Augusta was staying with him, he unsheathed. When he had finished his letter, he handed it to Augusta, 'who on reading it over observed: "Well, really this is a very pretty letter; it is a pity it should not go—I never read a prettier one". "Then it *shall* go," said Byron".[2] And so it went, and here it is: 'You were good enough in your last to say that I might write "soon"—but you did not add "*often*". I have therefore to apologise for again intruding on your time —to say nothing of your patience. There is something I wish to say; and as I may not see you for some time—I will endeavour to say it at once. A few weeks ago you asked me a question which I answered. I have now one to propose—to which, if improper, I need not add that your declining to reply to it will be sufficient reproof. It is this. Are the "objections" to which you alluded insuperable? or is there any line or change of conduct which could possibly remove them? I am well aware that all such changes are more easy in theory than practice; but at the same time there are few things I would not attempt to obtain your good opinion. At all events I would willingly know the worst. Still I neither wish you to promise or pledge yourself to anything; but merely to learn a

[1]*Corr.* i. p. 275.

[2]That is Moore's account, given 'so far as I could trust my recollection' from Byron's (destroyed) Memoirs.—Even if apocryphal, the anecdote should stand here on account of its symbolical value, for it consorts so admirably with that love of the wager, of the throw of the dice, in the most serious matters, which is so often present in those whom the need of fatality inhabits.

possibility which would not leave you the less a free agent. When I believed you attached, I had nothing to urge—indeed I have little now, except that having heard from yourself that your affections are not engaged, my importunities may appear not quite so selfish, however unsuccessful. It is not without a struggle that I address you once more on this subject; yet I am not very consistent—for it was to avoid troubling you upon it that I finally determined to remain an absent friend rather than become a tiresome guest. If I offend it is better at a distance. With the rest of my sentiments you are already acquainted. If I do not repeat them it is to avoid—or at least not increase—your displeasure.'[1] Not Alexander himself could have cut the knot more gracefully: the letter is far better than 'very pretty' (let us leave to Augusta her vocabulary): it is 'very beautiful', as forty-two years later Lady Byron was to say to Mrs. Beecher Stowe: 'At last he sent me a very beautiful letter, offering himself again. I thought it was sincere, and that I might now show him all I felt. I wrote just what was in my heart. Afterwards, I found in one of his Journals this notice of my letter: "a letter from Bell—it never rains but it pours".' 'There was through her habitual calm', says Mrs. Stowe, 'a shade of womanly indignation as she spoke these words. . . . I said "And did he not love you, then?" She answered, "No, my dear, he did not love me".'[2] Annabella's response to his 'offering' ran thus: 'I have your second letter— and am almost too agitated to write—but you will understand. It would be absurd to suppress anything—I am and have long been pledged to myself to make your happiness my first object in life. *If I can* make you happy, I have no other consideration. I will *trust* to you for all I should look up to—all I can love. The fear of not realizing your expectations is the only one I now feel. Convince me—it is all I wish—that my affection may supply what is wanting in my character to form your

[1] *Life of Lady Byron*, p. 111.

[2] Ethel Colburn Mayne, *Byron*, p. 205.—About Mrs. Beecher Stowe's publications all necessary details are given in Appendix I of the same book (pp. 445-447).

happiness. This is a moment of joy which I have too much despaired of ever experiencing—I *dared* not believe it possible, and I have painfully supported a determination founded in fact on the belief that you did not wish it removed—that its removal would not be for your good. There has in reality been scarcely a change in my sentiments. More of this I will defer. I wrote by last post—with what different feelings! Let me be grateful for those with which I now acknowledge myself. Most affectely yours'.[1] Annabella, sending her Yes to Newstead, by an excess of precaution sent a duplicate to London also; and doubtless there is something for smiles in such extreme minuteness—more even than there is in the *figurines* fashioned by irreproachable beings, because in this instance she was an interested party—but let us remember the situation. At last—and for the only time in her life—she could let her heart speak, could say all that was in it; that Byron was blind, chose to be blind to that, that on receiving her letter he wrote those words in his Journal, is possibly, in the sphere of feeling, the gravest crime which cynicism caused him to commit.

A crime in the sphere of feeling: yes, the entry in the Journal and, worse still, the using of the same expression to Augusta over the dinner-table at Newstead, are nothing less than that. And yet—such is the ever-recurring duality of what I have called the most formidable of all sincerities: the sincerity of moods—the other Byron, the Byron in whom the thought of Annabella can always awaken a true seriousness, robs me here of the right to say without qualification that he was then blind to her love. Indeed, for once seriousness takes fire, glows into a letter more 'beautiful' even than the preceding one: 'September 18, 1814.—Your letter has given me a new existence—it was unexpected—I need not say welcome—but *that* is a poor word to express my present

[1] *Life of Lady Byron*, pp. 111-112.

feelings—and yet equal to any other—for express them adequately I cannot. I have ever regarded you as one of the first of human beings—not merely from my own observation but that of others—as one whom it was as difficult *not* to love—as scarcely possible to deserve;—I know your worth—and revere your virtues as I love yourself and if every proof in my power of my full sense of what is due to you will contribute to *your* happiness—I shall have secured my own.—It *is* in your power to render me happy—you have made me so already.—I wish to answer your letter immediately—but am at present scarcely collected enough to do it rationally—I was upon the point of leaving England without hope, without fear—almost without feeling—but wished to make one effort to discover—not if I could pretend to your present affections—for to those I had given over all presumption—but whether time—and my most sincere endeavour to adopt any mode of conduct that might lead you to think well of me—might not eventually in securing your approbation awaken your regard.—These hopes are now dearer to me than ever; dear as they have ever been;—from the moment I became acquainted my attachment has been increasing & the very follies—give them a harsher name—with which I was beset and bewildered the conduct to which I had recourse for forgetfulness only made recollection more lively & bitter by the comparisons it forced on me in spite of Pride—and of Passions—which might have destroyed but never deceived me.—I am going to London on some business which once over—I hope to be permitted to visit Seaham; your father I will answer immediately & in the mean time beg you will present my best thanks and respects to him and Lady Milbanke. Will you write to me? & permit me to assure you how faithfully I shall ever be yr. most attached and obliged Sert.'[1]

But if the sincerity of moods takes fire, glows into feeling, the trouble with it is that it burns itself out in and by the very act of expression; and it is from this moment onwards that we

[1] *Life of Lady Byron*, pp. 112-113.

witness in Byron the radical severance, which moreover is part of his 'system', between the importance which rightly belongs to the state of marriage as such, and the indifference which no less rightly falls to the lot of the appointed bride. The Byron case represents the maximum of those wherein the respect paid to the wife has the result, and even perhaps subconsciously the aim, of authorizing, and as it were *setting no limits to*, the neglects towards the woman. Here one fact dominates the situation. Annabella's reply was accompanied by a letter from her father, inviting Byron to visit them at once in the country; and Byron allowed six weeks to elapse before going to Seaham. It is true that the delay is caused by arrangements in view of marriage—he has to see his lawyer, the elusive Hanson from whose dilatoriness Byron suffered throughout life; he has to put his financial affairs in order, not wishing to present himself to his future father-in-law until all has been settled as well as may be, and all advantageously for the future Lady Byron. It is also true that in letters to his friends Annabella receives the most laudatory certificates, and it is no less true that with a sincerity which at that date need not be questioned, his resolutions are at their best—he has done with all the scrapes of yesterday and is facing the future in a quite new frame of mind, as is proved by his many declarations to Lady Melbourne. But nothing in all this can for an instant prevail against the indifference—which we must not shrink from calling organic—that could, at such a time, keep him so long from Annabella's side. As a matter of course their correspondence was intensified; Byron's letters are, as usual, consummate; but a letter-writer, no matter how great, should not overdo 'sentimental' letters when no real sentiment exists, for then he runs the risk of verifying the adage:

L'ennui naquit un jour de l'uniformité.

I will say no more than that Annabella's letters, now that she was his betrothed, did at one point operate on the Byronic denseness; thanks to them he had made a surprising discovery—that 'Annabella was not so cold as he had thought'; but as this discovery had no effect in accelerating the rhythm of his departure, it not only emphasizes his indifference, but puts a keen edge to its cruelty. Lady Melbourne, so soon as the beginning of October, made no secret of her astonishment at his delay, going so far as to put the chief responsibility on the unfortunate Augusta, who had nothing to do with it. So, having exonerated Augusta in an earlier letter, Byron wrote to Lady Melbourne on October 7: 'You very much mistake me if you think I am lukewarm upon it; quite the reverse; and I have even the conceit to think that I shall suit her better than a better person might; because she is not so cold as I thought her; and if I think she likes me, I shall be exactly what she pleases; it is her fault if she don't govern me properly, for never was anybody so easily managed. *You ought* to like this match, for it is one of your making; and I hope not the worst of your performances in that way. You can't conceive how I long to call you Aunt. I hope then to see a great deal of you; and even of Brocket in the course of time.'[1] Whence it appears that Lady Melbourne had retrieved, though somewhat tardily, her psychological percipience, and that consequently she could not be more than half convinced by this Byronic *démenti*. When his affairs were nearing settlement, Byron did depart on October 30; he did not deny himself the inevitable halt at Newmarket, so as to see Augusta again; but on November 2 he arrived at Seaham.

Of his stay as fiancé we have the two versions.[2] I first give Byron's, as recorded in the three letters to Lady Melbourne which he wrote from Seaham: 'A[nnabella]'s meeting and mine made a kind of scene; though there was no acting, nor

[1]*Corr.* i. p. 277.

[2]Now, in Chapter IX of the *Life of Lady Byron*: 'The First Stay at Seaham: Letters', we possess a detailed and most interesting account of the whole episode, to which I can only refer the reader: I have found nothing in it to contradict my interpretation that follows.

even speaking, but the pantomime was very expressive. She seems to have more feeling than we imagined; but is the most *silent* woman I ever encountered; which perplexes me extremely. I like them to talk, because then they *think* less. Much cogitation will not be in my favour; besides, I can form my judgments better, since, unless the countenance is flexible, it is difficult to steer by mere looks. I am studying her, but can't boast at my progress in getting at her disposition; and if the conversation is to be all on one side I fear committing myself; and those who only listen, must have their thoughts so much about them as to seize any weak point at once. However the die is cast; neither party can recede; the lawyers are here—mine and all—and I presume, the parchment once scribbled, I shall become Lord Annabella. I can't yet tell whether we are to be happy or not. I have every disposition to do her all possible justice, but I fear she won't govern me; and if she don't it will not do at all; but perhaps she may mend of that fault. I have always thought—first, that she did not like me at all; and next, that her supposed afterliking was *imagination.* This last I conceive that my presence would—perhaps has removed—if so, I shall soon discover it, but mean to take it with great philosophy, and to behave attentively and . well, though I never could love but that which *loves;* and this I must say for myself, that my attachment always increases in due proportion to the return it meets with, and never changes in the presence of its object.'[1] 'Annabella and I go on extremely well. We have been much together, and if such details were not insipid to a third person, it would not be difficult to prove that we appear much attached, and I hope permanently so. She is, as you know, a perfectly good person; but I think, not only her feelings and affections, but her *passions* stronger than we supposed. Of these last I can't yet positively judge; my observations lead me to guess as much, however. She herself cannot be aware of this, nor could I, except from a habit of attending minutely in such cases to their

[1]*Corr.* i. pp. 287-288.

slightest indications, and, of course, I don't let her participate in the discovery, in which, after all, I may be mistaken.'[1]
'Do you know I have grave doubts if this will be a marriage
now? Her disposition is the very reverse of our imaginings.
She is overrun with fine feelings, scruples about herself and
her disposition (I suppose, in fact, she means mine), and to
crown all, is taken ill once every three days with I know not
what. But the day before, and the day after, she seems well;
looks and eats well, and is cheerful and confiding, and in short
like any other person in good health and spirits. A few days
ago she made one *scene*, not altogether out of C.'s style; it was
too long and too trifling, in fact, for me to transcribe, but it
did me no good. In the article of conversation, however, she
has improved with a vengeance, but I don't much admire
these same agitations upon slight occasions. I don't know, but
I think it by no means improbable, you will see me in town
soon. I can only interpret these things one way, and merely
wait to be certain, to make my obeisance and "exit singly". I
hear of nothing but "feeling" from morning till night, except
from Sir Ralph, with whom I go on to admiration. Ly M[il-
banke] too, is pretty well; but I am never sure of A. for a
moment. The least word, and you know I rattle on through
thick and thin (always, however, avoiding anything I think
can offend her favourite notions), if only to prevent me from
yawning. The least word, or alteration of tone, has some
inference drawn from it. Sometimes we are too much alike, and
then again too unlike. This comes of system, and squaring
her notions to the devil knows what. For my part, I have
lately had recourse to the eloquence of *action* (which Demos-
thenes calls the first part of oratory), and find it succeeds very
well, and makes her very quiet; which gives me some hope of
the efficacy of the "calming process", so renowned in "our
philosophy". In fact, and *entre nous*, it is really amusing; she
is like a child in that respect, and quite caressable into kindness, and good humour; though I don't think her temper *bad*

at any time, but very *self* tormenting and anxious, and romantic. In short, it is impossible to foresee how this will end *now*, any more than two years ago; if there is a break, it shall be her doing not mine.'[1] Let us now hear Annabella's version, given by her to Mrs. Beecher Stowe: 'The visit was to her full of disappointment. His appearance was so strange, moody and unaccountable, and his treatment of her so peculiar that she came to the conclusion that he did not love her, and sought an opportunity to converse with him alone. She told him that she saw from his manner that their engagement did not give him great pleasure; that she should never blame him if he wished to dissolve it . . . and if, on a nearer view of the situation, he shrank from it, she would release him and remain no less than ever his friend. "Upon this", she said, "he fainted entirely away". She stopped a moment, and then, as if speaking with great effort, added, "Then I was *sure* he must love me" '.[2] Such a diptych needs no commentary; but so many instructive things are to be gathered from it that one cannot easily tear one's-self away from the picture. Nothing can make up, during an engagement, for the defection of the heart: that failing, of all the other faculties there remains only, so to speak, the cranked-up machinery—they can still function, but they have lost their power to interpret, they have lost, in the deepest sense of the word, their use. Here as elsewhere, every observation made by Byron is exactitude itself—only he knows no longer what any of them means. With Annabella, he is in the situation of one who reads and even pronounces quite correctly all the words of a foreign language, but without understanding them. And so, refusing to begin with the essential fact—Annabella's love—and therefore unable to relate the beams to their real source, the truths of detail supplied by observation have no other result than to plunge him still deeper in error. 'I can only interpret these things one way, and merely want to be certain to make my obeisance and "exit singly".' This is the extreme of blindness.

[1]*Corr*. i. pp. 289-291.   [2]Ethel Colburn Mayne, *Byron*, p. 206.

Byron now could see nothing but the opposite of the truth, a state which will always be his who comes to a fiancée with the inward barometer at zero. Byron's apparatus in that kind consisted solely of a theoretical wish that his future wife should 'govern' him; he, the most ungovernable of creatures, always cherished the illusion that there existed somewhere the woman who would be able to rule him. In the letters to Lady Melbourne he incessantly toys with that illusion, going so far as to deploy for its benefit a little of the *myth-making* faculty which was so dear to him; what he seems above all to assign to the future Lady Byron is the part of lion-tamer—once inside the cage, it would be hers to keep watch on the wild animal's leaps and bounds. Now, in the document he had seen, Annabella had been careful to point out that she wanted to be 'considered by her husband as a *reasonable counsellor*, but not as a guide on whom he could implicitly rely'. How could it be otherwise with a young girl of two-and-twenty who, though assuredly ready to help him in any way she could, must of necessity want her husband to be himself the 'guide' in question? Besides—and forgetting, for the present, that in the Lady Frances period he had avoided the mistake of believing in the mythical 'cold woman'—Byron chose to amuse himself and his too-expert confidante by pretending to be surprised at Annabella's depth of feeling. And perhaps I, in my turn, may be wrong in saying 'pretend'; for one of the commonest chimeras (and assuredly the ugliest) created for themselves by those who have overdone experience is that of their very abuse of opportunity being the only way that leads to feeling certain sensations; whence it ensues that when they encounter such sensations in their spontaneous bloom, all guileless and 'within the law', flowers and fruits which repay the waiting-time with all its scruples and delays, there is nothing in that turbid overweighted experience of theirs which can interpret the innocence of such an abandonment. It at once surprises, amuses, and scandalizes them, and their reaction to it makes them in our eyes not a little absurd, and somewhat base; for when one has not an inkling of virtue, it is wiser not to form any image of it, since that image cannot but be irremediably wrecked on the reefs of a very special absurdity—that of unreality. It goes without saying that Annabella had instinctively drawn the right conclusion, namely, that Byron did not love her. It is a pity that insensibility of heart should not bring along with it inhibition of the nervous system, which, as things were, provided Byron with the too-convincing argument of a dead faint!

Profiting by this faint, Byron hastened back to London, where (as we learn from Hobhouse) he arrived on November 20. Though he made the most of the usual business complications that still further delayed the final preparations, the moment came when he had to put his head on the block; and on December 24 he left London with Hobhouse, who was to be his best man. As we might foresee, they parted next day for a Byronic visit of twenty-four hours to Augusta; and when they met again on the 26th, Hobhouse observes in his diary: 'Never was lover less in haste', emphasizing this the day after in a phrase made eloquent by its oddness: 'The bridegroom more and more *less impatient*'. When in 1816, at the time of the separation, Hobhouse was interrogated on this subject, he declared that 'Lord Byron frankly confessed that he was not in love with his intended bride; but at the same time he said that he felt for her that regard which was the surest guarantee of continued affection and matrimonial felicity'. They did not reach Seaham until December 30. This time the family had taken umbrage at the leisurely proceedings, and we learn that Annabella began by bursting into tears when she found herself alone with Byron. But she must have recovered quickly, for soon afterwards Hobhouse describes her as 'passionately in love' with his friend, and 'gazing with delight on his bold and animated countenance'. The marriage ceremony took place in the drawing-room at Seaham in the morning of

January 2, 1815, and the bridal pair left the same day for the drive to Halnaby, the country house in which they were to spend the honeymoon which Byron, with his usual cynicism, chose to call the 'treacle-moon'. Hobhouse's diary enables us to witness their departure: 'Lady Byron came down in her travelling-dress, a slate-coloured satin pelisse trimmed with white fur . . . Byron was calm and as usual. I felt as if I had buried a friend. . . . At a little before twelve, I handed Lady Byron downstairs, and into her carriage. When I wished her many years of happiness, she said: "If I am not happy it will be my own fault".'

*   *   *

Never were braver words more instantly belied. As in Racine's tragedies, where the preparations seem to be prolonged to the utmost for the sole purpose of making the crisis break upon us at its maximum, her crisis breaks upon her at once—in the carriage itself. Soon after the separation, here is what Annabella told Lady Anne Barnard, who had been her friend from childhood: 'We had not been an hour in the carriage when, breaking into a malignant sneer: "Oh, what a dupe you have been to your imagination! How is it possible a woman of your sense could form the wild hope of reforming *me*? It is enough for me that you are my wife for me to hate you. If you were the wife of any other man, I own you might have charms". . . . I who listened' (says Lady Anne) 'was astonished. "How could you go on after this, my dear?" I said, "why did you not return to your father's?" "Because I had not a conception he was in earnest. He laughed it over when he saw me appear hurt" '.

In Lady Byron's account to Mrs. Stowe, Byron's words are differently given: 'You *might* have saved me once, madam! You had all in your own power when I offered myself to you first. Then you might have made me what you pleased; but now you will find that you have married a devil'.[1] Not one of

[1] In the *Life of Lady Byron*, Chapter XI, there are further details of this drive 'in the gathering darkness'. To that chapter I can do no more than refer my readers.

these words but comes from the depths of Byron's nature. To the human wild beast everything is a cage; and Byron never rested until he had got himself into the super-cage which, for animals of his species, is represented—must necessarily be represented—by the matrimonial state. That done, he is gorged with the exasperation that has been accumulating, and goes on accumulating in the tête-à-tête of the carriage: on whom can he discharge it, if not on her who, by refusing to be a lion-tamer, has assigned to herself the part of victim? And he turns on Annabella with one of those hatreds which can never die because the mere existence of their object incessantly revives them. 'It is enough for you to be my wife for me to hate you': oh, how Byron's exclamation—which has at least the merit of straightforwardness—pierces to the region wherein, at the centre of certain organisms, the *animal* and the *demoniac* impulses assist one another. 'It is enough', indeed; left to himself, the animal might stop there—abandoning his prey, he might break the bars of his cage and rush towards a new prey; but the demoniac in him well knows that in this case there is something better to be done. Since this victim, guilty of having idealized him, of having trusted her imagination, of having—much worse—presumed to think of reforming him, had been so imprudent as to refuse to be caught at the first attempt, why not instil into her that torturing afterthought, generative perhaps of remorse, that 'everything was possible' *once*, that nothing is possible *now*, and that having declined at the propitious moment to evoke a hero, she must now put up with being married to a devil? Do not mistake me—I am not denying (for we know too well his tendency in that direction) that in that carriage, from the depths of his exasperation, the myth of a marriage-for-revenge may have been born in Byron, may even have been born in all sincerity, nor do I deny that in the days to come he adhered to it with the same passionate closeness as to all the other mythical fabrications of his mind. Not only do I not deny this, but I am convinced that it was so, since Annabella, whose psychological insight

248

was never for a moment at fault after the shock of the real encounter, wrote thus to Augusta on January 19, 1816, before there was any talk at all of the proceedings which led to the separation, and while she still had a faint hope that insanity might be accountable: 'Revenge, as you know, is a passion he is capable of feeling, and which has so long formed the *principle of conduct* towards me (as all my retrospections prove), that a change is impossible unless the whole mind was renovated or restored'. But what I do affirm is that Annabella's original refusal left Byron indifferent and even relieved, and that we cannot discern the smallest trace of a revengeful spirit in any of the events which—amid cross-currents arising much more from circumstances than from deliberate design —led to their marriage. No: the myth of a marriage for revenge never dawned on him, never played any part until, ready-made, it sprang into life at the precise moment when it abetted, when it served, the cruellest line of conduct.

'Her ladyship appeared always dismayed when she spoke of her residence at Halnaby.' This statement of Hobhouse's (who certainly cannot be suspected of any excessive sympathy for Annabella) throws light—if any were needed after such a prelude—upon the three ritual weeks of the 'treacle-moon'. The dismay was of two kinds—physical first, and how comprehensible that is when we remember that Byron's view of life was inseparable from the very weapons devised to destroy life, that on the merest drive he carried a pistol, and even in his bedroom could not be without one—the same kind of fancy as, at Newstead Abbey, made him offer his guests a skull to drink their wine from. The Fatal Being, even when authentic, does not always escape these deplorable stage-properties; and when his words too are perpetually explosive, it is natural enough for a girl of twenty-two to feel some apprehensions as to the acts which may follow them. But far more profoundly still, the dismay was moral; for from the first week Byron had seen to it that the idea of incest should be implanted in her brain. On July 11, 1816, Annabella wrote to Augusta in words underlined by herself: 'It is my comfort to remember that at the many times *from the first week of my marriage*, when *that* thought has nearly driven me to madness one unkind or inconsiderate feeling towards you has never actuated me'.[1] And later we learn from Annabella what had happened: 'The day after my marriage he had a letter from her—it affected him strangely, and excited a kind of fierce and exulting transport. He read to me the expression, "Dearest, first and best of human beings", and then said with suspicious inquisitiveness, "There—what do you think of that?"'[2] Here it is indeed necessary to remember what 'a fool' Augusta was, and how completely she always failed to understand Byron's character, if we are to forgive her for having, with that gushing insensibility of hers, written and dispatched those lines to arrive on the morning after his marriage! For it was inevitable that Byron should exult in them, that he should instantly brandish them, should give himself up to the favourite sport with which incest had provided him—that of playing with fire. To be on the brink of saying, and not to say; to challenge, so as to fly into a rage if the challenge should be in any way taken up— how resist that, if the only thing that can really thrill is what I have called the vein of voluptuously guilty reminiscence? Like those criminals of whom the police well know that they cannot help hovering on the edge of confession, to break with the incest *in fact* meant above all, with Byron, to light it up *in imagination*. While those who wish to be cured—in the sphere of imagination no less than in the sphere of action—begin by burying bygone secrets, so that later, much later, nothing but their purified essence may arise in the second and quasi-ideal life of memory, a Byron, on the contrary, wishing only to be poisoned, and who never poisons himself better than when he is poisoning others, incessantly opens, but never spills, the heady phial. Incest, when he cannot materialize it, more than ever becomes that forbidden scent—that 'outlaw' scent— which at any price must be breathed. Not only are such fumes

[1]*Astarte*, p. 230.　　　　[2]*Astarte*, p. 63.

his element *par excellence*, but he never savours to the full the sensation of being alive unless he is distilling their contagion into infecting the atmosphere around him. To this end, what could be more efficacious and more intoxicating than, before Annabella, to revert again and again to Augusta's letters, and speak of them with the same mysterious manner, the same wild transport of exultation? So intoxicating was the practice that he went so far as to offer Annabella as a gift—high token of *esteem!*—one of those inestimable letters, that of December 15, 1814: a production so inept, so puerile in its sentimentality, though innocence then reigned, that I have not the fortitude to transcribe it, and wherein Augusta, telling Byron that some visitors of hers knew his fiancée and 'praised her to the skies', added (to complete the grace of Byron's gift): 'They say her health has been hurt by *studying*, etc.' But in Byron's first transport of exultation, in the opening words of Augusta's letter, in Byron's question: 'What do you think of that?' Annabella at first discerns nothing more than one of those sombre clouds that unexpectedly detach themselves from a background which, left to herself, she would always forbid herself to explore; besides, had she not, in the carriage, had to withstand the assault of words quite differently agonizing? It was not until next day, or the day after that, that there occurred the significant incident thus related by Lord Lovelace: 'At Halnaby, two or three days after the marriage, Lady Byron—who had been reading Dryden's tragedy of *Don Sebastian*—thoughtlessly alluded to the subject: an incestuous union of brother and sister through ignorance of their parentage. He probably supposed the allusion designed, and made a strange and violent scene which first gave her an indefinite but most painful suspicion. Her first idea was that he might have had some connection with some girl whom he afterwards discovered to be a natural sister. This was rendered more probable by his father's libertine character. After this scene she carefully avoided the subject, though he made it difficult by continual allusions to it as if for the purpose of ascertaining whether she had any suspicion or not. She was in constant fear of being supposed to be trying to find out his secrets, but knew not what subjects to avoid.'[1] With these two episodes—that of Augusta's letter and the reading of Dryden—we have, in this domain, the entire Byronic process. Now he takes the first step, now he seizes on the opportunity afforded him; in the former case he prompts, stimulates his companion—in the current phrase, here tragically appropriate, 'gives her to think'; in the latter, he flies into a rage, so as the more surely to drive her into her last entrenchments, and if she beats a retreat, abandons the position, resolves to avoid any such discussion in future, he at once returns to the charge, will never tire of returning to it. For what he seeks is—by no means what one might be inclined to think, namely, to ascertain once for all that no suspicion exists; but on the contrary to be able to dwell, to *stay* on the only subject that interests him. This in the first place; and then, and above all, to make certain that, thanks to the repeated instillations, suspicion *is* there, is defining itself, feeling its way, that, as they say in hide-and-seek, it is *getting warm*. To know that the other knows, scarcely dares to know, will never dare to formulate, and yet knows . . . to have in that way with her (and in spite of her) a complicity—is not this the situation and the state from which indeed Byron draws his intensest vital glow!

The expressions used by Annabella in the letter to Augusta of July 11, 1816, leave no doubt whatever that from the first week of marriage Augusta's person was associated with 'the thought that has nearly driven me to madness'; and I should be inclined to believe that the hypothesis of involuntary incest with a natural sister was of later growth, represents one of those mere defensive reactions which Annabella's moral organism felt to be so imperatively needful. Very probably, in my view, the scene about *Don Sebastian*, recalling the letter-episode, drove her to seek some interpretation of it. However, this does not greatly matter; suspicion is in the citadel, it is

[1] *Astarte*, p. 54.

suffered, but no terms are made with it: to the last the garrison will fight to dislodge it; will surrender only at that extremity when not to surrender would mean for an Annabella sinning against truth. 'Lady Byron's whole effort was to resist the light, or rather the darkness that *would* flow into her mind';[1] Lord Lovelace's phrase sums up, with arresting fitness, the whole of that poignant, high-souled debate of which we must now sound the depths.

'She felt as though her thoughts would never again be pure'. Such is the reflection forced, in the most grievous hour of her life, upon Edith Wharton's heroine, Anna Leath, in *The Reef*—Anna, likewise irreproachable, from whose whole personality emanated a charm which I do not claim for Annabella, but who (happily for her) encountered the masculine *insoluble* in a species more normal than the Byronic;—and that reflection, better than any other, helps us to reach the very centre of the problem. As a young girl, an Annabella both by her nature and the conditions in which destiny has placed her —because she does not even conceive that physical purity comes into question, because in her eyes the object of marriage is to consecrate that in her much rather than to despoil it . . . such a girl, while still inexperienced, possesses a treasure of which she does not yet know the name, but which fills her with gladness—I mean, purity of mind. The soul of a young girl is as a spacious sunny room with large glass-doors that are always wide open and that lead out into the world; it is all receptive hospitality. She only asks to welcome; every questioning is trustful, sure that every answer can but give her fresh cause for delight. Her face does not necessarily reveal the inward glow of life; Annabella's 'placid countenance', quite as much as Caroline's eagerness, treasures an immense, as yet inviolated hopefulness; quite as much, perhaps more, if on the threshold of life reflection develops (in the photo-

[1] *Astarte*, p. 135.

graphic sense of the word) gladness itself. When, as the result of some external intervention—and nearly always the first offensive fails, nearly always there must be repeated assaults —her purity of mind is sullied by the action of miasmic elements, when scales begin to form upon it, then with a feeling which, much more than a reproach addressèd to things outside herself, is a sense of humiliation that immediately turns into self-accusation, it seems to the girl as if her very soul was soiled and, as it were, dishonoured, and she sees it in the aspect—so commonplace yet so queerly degrading—of the room which has not been 'done'.

Let me here remind you of what I said on a previous page about psychologists against the grain: 'Their only hope is that they may have been mistaken, but fear mingles with that hope, for in the possibility of such error they at once perceive the sign of an imagination monstrous, impure, radically depraved—and now we are in presence of the very picture of what was one day to be Annabella's state, fighting as she was against her indwelling suspicions'. There indeed is the central point not only of her debate, but of her grief itself—a grief so *pure* that it at once classes her who feels it, disclasses all with whom she is at odds—and that is why Lord Lovelace's phrase is of such arresting fitness. For to one created for the light, one who has believed herself to be vowed to it, there could be no keener torment, nor one more plainly stamped as the ordeal, than to have to acknowledge that here the darkness is the abode of light—the light of truth. If she responds to that light, it is to her as though she were blaspheming against the primal splendour, the uncreated light; if on the other hand she refuses to respond, then, disloyal to truth, she is disloyal both to her conscience and to Him who gave it her, and thus offends against the uncreated light by the very act which would fain respect it. 'And the light shineth in darkness'—but what if the light be, sadly, no more than that of a very human and very atrocious truth? Annabella's special ordeal was that she had to live out to the letter that profane version of the Bible-text; but the harder the ordeal, the more the other 'light' shines forth, and Annabella had 'received' it.

The three weeks of tête-à-tête at Halnaby were, as Ethel Colburn Mayne says, 'her initiation', in every sense of the word; and for the reason I have indicated above, perhaps these three weeks were the cruellest of all for Annabella. Purity of mind was lost, and she could not be sure that it was not by her own fault—which for her meant that she had never been pure-minded, had only imagined that she was. Suspicion is here the key-note, but as a matter of course Byron's conduct was in unison. Her maid Mrs. Minns, who had known her from childhood, long afterwards gave an account of this period to the *Newcastle Chronicle*[1]: 'The irregularities of Lord Byron occasioned [Lady Byron] the greatest distress, and she even contemplated returning to her father. Mrs. Minns was throughout her constant companion, and she does not believe that her ladyship concealed a thought from her'. But the lady's-maid absolutely refused to disclose the particulars of Byron's conduct: 'she had given Lady Byron a solemn promise not to do so'.[2] We have those particulars now, and can divine that the euphemism of 'irregularities' used by Mrs. Minns meant, among other things, the physical danger possibly threatening Lady Byron, especially when we remember

[1] In 1869, at the time of Mrs. Stowe's revelations.

[2] On the other hand, the few letters written by Byron from Halnaby convey an impression of easy indifference; but I do not give them here, nor shall I henceforth give any of his letters, for the following reason. Both from prudence and a sense of fitness, Byron never lifted the veil of conjugal intimacy. Until the outbursts from his exile, all that is revealed—but this in a crescendo uninterrupted though discreetly kept in bounds—is the comically complete reversal (justified in the circumstances, but unfortunately coming too late) of the values in marriage. Before marriage, his 'system' maintained that the state itself was delightful, no matter what the wife might be like; afterwards it was the state that was insupportable, though the wife were perfect. The *afterwards* point of view is summed up in a phrase from Hobhouse's diary: 'Byron advises me not to marry, though he has the best of wives'.

that in the days after the wedding, condemned to the tête-à-tête, his exasperation must have been at its height. These dangers were to be still more menacing at the close of the year, on the eve of her confinement—when, on the testimony of witnesses not to be suspected of partiality for Augusta, the sister's presence in Lady Byron's house was her sole protection. It is easy to understand that the Halnaby terrors nearly drove her to tell all to her parents, and still easier to understand why on reflection she kept silence. She was, as I have said, of a solidity that was proof against anything, and she feared suffering far less than the idea of wronging anyone whatever. Had she not suspected, perhaps she would have confided her distress to her parents; but it was precisely the suspicion which laid a seal upon her lips, for fear (or rather, in hope) that she might be mistaken.

At all events, she must, even with her secret, have felt the atmosphere of Seaham a refreshment. They went there after Halnaby, for six weeks; and Byron, conventional in this as in so much else, was bored to death, that being the proper thing in his people-in-law's house. On March 9 they left for Six Mile Bottom on a visit to Augusta, and stayed there until the 28th, when they went to London. Of this visit also we now have the detailed account in the *Life of Lady Byron*; I will not dwell upon its anguish for the bride. But there is a letter from her to Augusta of July 30, 1816, and thus belonging to the period immediately before Augusta's confession, when, after the few months' coolness following on the separation, their intimacy was about to be resumed on the basis of 'mutual confidence'. Augusta had consulted Annabella as to the line of conduct to be observed in her (Augusta's) correspondence with Byron, who had left England three months previously—how she might best hope to exercise some salutary influence upon him; and Annabella in this letter told her why she thought it impossible that such influence could now be the sister's: 'Associations most prejudicial to a good influence from you, have subsisted too deeply & too habitually in *his* mind—What has passed *on his part* since my marriage, in my presence, as well as in my absence, must on reconsideration, convince you they were in no degree done away—*Our* visit to SMB—even the first night will make you sensible of this—He then made me most sensible of what engrossed his thoughts & actuated his conduct—*His* visit to you afterwards, when his resentment was excited by the blameless principle of your opposition, in short, many more facts I shall not recall, lead to the same conclusion—His feelings towards you have varied —& they were seldom suppressed with me—Sometimes he has spoken of you with compassion—sometimes with bitter scorn—& sometimes with dispositions still more reprehensible—The only time when I believe he was really on the very brink of Suicide, was on an occasion relating to his remorse about you'.[1] To this text we must add these lines from an earlier letter of Annabella's to Augusta, of July 17, 1816: 'Perhaps with you he has not given way to the frantic agonies of Remorse—alas! far from repentance, which I have seen awakened by anything in connection with that fatal remembrance'.[2] To which Augusta replied on July 23: 'I never witnessed anything like what you have, alas! and describe to have been *his* agonies—and whatever I have suffered I have always carefully concealed from him, although could I have hoped for any good effect it might have been greater kindness not to have done so'.[3] And in the long interviews which took place between the two women at the time of the full confession in the beginning of September, 1816, Augusta told Annabella that 'she had never seen remorse for his guilt towards her in him but once—the night before they last parted, previous to his going abroad'.[4]

These texts—and principally perhaps the two contradictory versions concerning remorse—enable us to get a little

[1] *Astarte*, p. 247.   [2] *Astarte*, p. 236.   [3] *Astarte*, pp. 242-243.
[4] *Astarte*, p. 65 (from Lady Byron's statements G and K).

further in our understanding of Byron's nature. We must not forget that till he arrived at Six Mile Bottom Byron had not, since his marriage, seen Augusta again. The situation of June, 1813, was reproduced, and formidably aggravated; but the aggravation made it all the more intoxicating to him who lived but for sensation. For the second time in his life Augusta was a novelty—a novelty made the newer by his own new married state. On the evening of their re-union not only did he realise that the pact of rupture had never been signed and sealed by *him*, but he discovered that circumstances had supplied the very conditions in which passion could attain its maximum. Lord Lovelace tells us that it was in the first half of 1815 that Byron's 'inclination for Augusta was most violent'; we may be sure that that first half began on the evening of his arrival. And Annabella's presence, very far from restraining, stimulated it, was now even indispensable; for, thanks to that, the welcome sensation of revived passion was doubled by another joy, which made its first appearance on that evening and was to make so many others during the months to come—the joy of *confronting*, of being able to confront, the two women. When the three were together Byron, while giving free play to demonstrations of love for Augusta, could have the added satisfaction of telling himself that every one of them wrought upon Annabella's troubled mind, and that when husband and wife should again be alone together, the atmosphere would be all the better prepared for a renewed playing with fire. Now that the two women had been confronted, he was in a position to carry the game a stage further by introducing a factor which for the Fatal Being is invaluable, because it is inherent in his organism itself—the factor of remorse; and nothing could be at once more logical and, psychologically speaking, more easily explained than the contradiction between Augusta's and Annabella's testimonies on this point. With Augusta, Byron's attitude was the normal one of the man who, so that he may satisfy his passion, has definitely resolved to abandon himself to it, to follow it out to the end. It is clear, since we have it from Augusta, whose interest it evidently was to be able to tell Annabella the contrary, that with her he never felt or manifested any remorse.[1] Since Byron was of those who feel nothing that they do not manifest, this testimony must be accepted as decisive; and it may be added that from the point we have now reached, Byron's whole endeavour being to persuade Augusta to resume their intercourse, remorse was of all factors the least indicated. With Annabella, on the other hand, to be able to deploy this factor was an unhoped-for resource. Numerous are the men for whom the wife can import sensations only by the canal of the scenes they make her, and who, often unwittingly, multiply those scenes for that very reason; we have seen Byron resorting from the earliest moment to this classic method; but when it comes to playing on people, a woman of 'solid' character is not, for the amateur of sensations, the most propitious instrument. Her strings do not quiver so much as is needed, she responds but slightly under the bow, she may even inflict upon the performer the humiliation of not responding at all—I daresay it sometimes was so with Annabella. Since she did not know how to do her part, it was for Byron to do all—the letting loose of remorse had the advantage that a mediocre co-performer would at once be transformed into a tragically interested spectator. Here again, do not mistake me. Nothing is further from my thoughts than to deny the sincerity of the 'frantic agonies' of Byron's remorse. Byron, as we know, was never more sincere than when he was frantic, nor than when he was playing a part; and when, as here, frenzy and acting were combined . . . why! the acme of his own peculiar sin-

[1]Except, of course, that of which she did speak, on the last evening they spent together, and which, breaking forth then, must have been as sincere as can be. In every way, indeed, we can imagine that evening to have been unique in Byron's whole experience—the last tête-à-tête with the only woman he had loved, the recapitulation of the so recent, so overwhelming past, the contemplation of the ruins, still smoking, of three lives (his own included), the foreboding that on the only plane that mattered to him he had now no future; finally, the armour of pride itself for once shed, while the tears gathered and fell.

cerity was reached. Let me recall Lord Lovelace's penetrating words, which I have set as a sign above this study: 'He was in turn dominated by frenzy and master of his frenzy, able to direct it to a purpose. . . . He would play at being mad, and gradually get more and more serious, as if he believed himself destined to wreck his own life and that of everyone near him'. The factor of remorse at last, in Byron's eyes, gave Annabella her rôle. Her feelings, her situation, everything was designed to make her the listener to that chamber-music, at once so strident and so yearning, which the fatal being incessantly plays for himself, but which he himself listens to all the better if he is not alone to hear it. When a prey to frenzy, did Byron go so far as to make confession of the incest to Annabella—I mean, of its perpetration? Evidently not; we have a proof of that in the fluctuations of opinion to which until February, 1816, she was subject, and which such a confession would have once for all eliminated. That even in his frenzies Byron should have abstained from the avowal sufficiently shows how right Lord Lovelace is in saying that 'he was master of his frenzy'. Lord Lovelace adds, 'able to direct it to a purpose'; and in Annabella's presence the 'purpose' was the outburst of remorse—a remorse which consisted in letting it appear that he had cherished guilty desire for Augusta, that he was obsessed by the memory of it, that Augusta knew nothing about it and never should, but that because of it there was a curse on his very existence, and he was condemned to inflict suffering on all around him. Thanks to which, keeping dark the precise nature of his secret, Byron figured to himself as invested with all the prestige of the fatal being, while he retained the privileges due to him who struggles against his thoughts, and who in any case deserves the pity, perhaps even the sympathy, of his audience. We can imagine all that, in such conditions, outbursts of remorse could do for the Byronic sub-consciousness.

'Remorse, alas! very far from repentance'—so we have seen that Annabella wrote of it; and her words admirably define the remorse of the Fatal Being. Remorse without repentance is equivalent to a clinical symptom which by itself is enough to indicate the 'need of fatality'; and with Byron such remorse is as closely as can be united with pride—pride of which at this very time he wrote in *The Siege of Corinth* about a character which as usual is no other than himself:

> But his heart was swollen, and turned aside,
> By deep interminable pride.

But what did Augusta think of the Six Mile Bottom incidents? In a letter to Hodgson, after having duly expatiated on the happiness of the bridal pair, though adding that Byron's 'nerves and spirits were very far from what she wished them' (but attributing this to the uncomfortable state of his affairs), Augusta went on to say that in Annabella he had found a phoenix. 'I think I never saw or heard or read of a more perfect being in mortal mould than she appears to be.' Here I do not think we need question her sincerity, and that because she had been, I am persuaded, sincere in wishing—for herself at least as much as for him—that Byron should marry; hence she would be all the readier to abound for Annabella in that affectionateness with which she was so indiscriminately lavish; besides, she was always deferentially admiring of talents and virtues which had not been bestowed on herself. On her side, the pact of rupture *had* been signed and sealed, and, to do her justice, she was for her part to keep it to the end. She considered that marriage had closed the past; but just because she did, and had what one might call a genius for oblivion, the past with her was apt to be confused with the inexistent. This genius for oblivion was in her allied with the other genius which we have analysed, but which now appeared in a new but not less dangerous form—that for passivity; and these are the two responsible factors which make it comprehensible that if, as I am convinced, Augusta was telling the truth when she incessantly said that she had never had the smallest intention of injuring Annabella, she nevertheless became for her the cause of so much suffering.

For, beyond the fact—in the circumstances, it is true, a cardinal one—that she never again yielded to the *act* of incest,[1] Augusta was always absolutely passive in face of Byron's demonstrations, after marriage no less than before it—which for the looker-on has the inevitable disadvantage that such an attitude seems susceptible of but one interpretation, namely, that the woman who unprotestingly submits to such treatment cannot but be the mistress of him who subjects her to it. For months Annabella struggled with that thought. It is probable that in this particular case Augusta's passivity was reinforced by those innumerable habitual familiarities which develop between people who have been lovers, which sometimes survive a rupture, and sometimes are actually intensified because all the rest has been abolished, and of which, feeling safe in that abolishment, the two then become so unconscious that they cannot in the least measure the effect on themselves or others. Of this last point, Augusta herself is about to give us a verification which shows her, mentally speaking, as passive as in other things.

For the Byrons, on leaving Six Mile Bottom at the end of March, had invited Augusta to come to them in London for an indefinite stay, and she had accepted. (We cannot but surmise that, just then, Annabella was heroically trying to repel her encroaching suspicions, since she yielded to Byron's desire for this visit). In Augusta's letter of July 3, 1816, referring to her acceptance of the invitation, she says to Annabella: 'Had I even entertained the slightest suspicions of any *"doubts"* of yours—I never could or would have entered your house—perhaps I did wrong as it was to do so, but I was

[1]Was Augusta telling the truth when, in the hour of confession, she declared to Annabella that incest had never taken place after Byron's marriage? Annabella always believed, or at any rate *wished* to believe, that she had not lied. This is a case in which there is certainly no necessity for being more royalist than the queen, and so—and the more because I am not otherwise very indulgent towards her—I shall here give Augusta the benefit of the doubt.

under delusion'. In my view, here again we are bound to re-
cognise her sincerity; but here the recognition only sheds a
clearer light on what was ineradicable, incurable, in Augusta's
outlook, and puts the final seal to the authenticity of Annabella's phrase of 'a kind of moral idiocy from birth'. At bottom, she never quite renounced the view that there was not
much harm provided the other did not know, was not made
unhappy; she never was capable of apprehending that conscience and the moral life itself have not begun to be until the
directly opposite question is put: 'Would I do this if she did
know?' and until, that question answered, every step is regulated as if the other did know, and the more because she does
not.

The Byrons arrived at Piccadilly Terrace at the end of
March; Hobhouse had rented the house for them from the
Duchess of Devonshire, and for ten months it was to be an
atrociously exclusive torture-chamber. Augusta installed herself there in early April; Annabella had been pregnant for
some little time.

Augusta's first stay lasted until the end of June, and this
period is very definitely that of the intensive culture of every
one of the elements we have just seen to be present. An intensive culture favoured by the fact that the three were alone together, and that, in consequence of serious money-troubles
and (if we are to believe a letter from Byron to Moore of June
12) Annabella's state of health, they were very much confined
to their forcing-house. Byron, of course, asked nothing better
than never to leave it. That from the very beginning this
régime was fruitful in results for him is proved by a later letter
of Annabella's, which is in every respect an important one. I
mean that of May 6, 1816, to the Hon. Mrs. Villiers, Augusta's most intimate friend, to whom, after the separation,
Annabella had been led to confide the truth—on the one
hand that Mrs. Villiers might understand her reasons for
seeing less of Augusta; on the other, that she might assist in

Augusta's moral rescue. In the April of the year before (1815) Lady Byron had had to leave London for some days, on a sudden call to Kirkby Mallory, where her uncle Lord Wentworth was lying mortally ill; and Mrs. Villiers now showed surprise that knowing what she knew, she had then not only left Byron and Augusta alone together, but had expressed satisfaction in her husband's having his sister's company. In her reply Annabella thus states the case: 'There are parts of my conduct I wish to explain to you—particularly how I came to express satisfaction in her remaining in London during my first visit here[1]—though before I left it I had strongly advised her removal for her own sake. I had even told her what Dr. Baillie said, upon the presumption of Insanity, that *he* ought not to be left with ANY young woman after my departure. My anxiety to prevent her continuing in the house was such, that I thought it my duty to confide to Mrs. Byron[2] *only*, the horrible desires he had entertained, and gave her permission to communicate them to A— if absolutely necessary to save her from imprudence about him. I afterwards wrote to Mrs. B— from hence, saying that my apprehensions were relieved by Capt. B—'s residence in the house—A—'s letters to me here also weakened these impressions of *existing* danger, which I was always struggling to repel. Still it was only when my enfeebled & distracted state of mind was worked upon by the representations of hazard to Lord B— if left alone, that I uttered those expressions, which almost all her letters were calculated to *extort*—& before I left this place, I decidedly expressed to her my conviction that those fears which were the *alledged* causes of her stay were groundless.'[3] From this we learn a great deal. First, it is clear that Augusta's arrival in London was quickly followed by such a state of affairs that the hypothesis of Byron's insanity (which was again, and more insistently, to be resorted to just before the separation) was

[1]Annabella writes from Kirkby which, since the death of Lord Wentworth, had become her mother's property.
[2]Mrs. Sophia Byron, 'Aunt Sophy.'　　　　[3]*Astarte*, pp. 200-201.

forced upon his wife. As both women feared an outburst of
fury if they ventured even to suggest his seeing a doctor, Dr.
Baillie did not visit Byron either at this time or later (when
another doctor had to be called in); hence Baillie—who *had*
seen Byron in his childhood, having been consulted about his
lameness—could only conjecture that there was some mental
disturbance. But from a distance he proved himself to be a
shrewd diagnostician, even if perhaps unwittingly, for his
prescription seems to imply that he was thinking of the not
infrequent form of insanity which may be traced to eroticism.
We also learn that Annabella still believed not only in Augusta's innocence, but in her ignorance, so much so that she
took measures for her protection. And this was the moment
chosen by Augusta to be for once something other than passive. Here she does incur very strong suspicion, to such an
extent that it almost annuls the 'clean sheet' I had been ready,
as concerns Lady Byron, to accord her; and as might be expected—for nothing is so disastrous to a purely passive nature
as a sudden attack of activity—her move is highly unfortunate. True, she succeeds in 'extorting' the desired sanction;
but after it has been sent, Annabella's clear-sightedness anew
prevails; on the question of insanity, and perhaps on many
others too, she trusts Dr. Baillie's judgment more than
Augusta's; in fairness she warns the sister of her 'mistake', but
it is probable that there too the reaction does its work in making Annabella ask herself whether it *was* a 'mistake', whether
it was not merely a pretext, the 'alledged cause' of Augusta's
wish to remain at Piccadilly. I am inclined to think that she
comes back to London in a very different frame of mind from
that in which she left it. Absence is sometimes the best way of
getting a clear vision, and, on the return, presence puts the
finishing-touches to the vision itself—all the more that, meanwhile, absence has encouraged, emboldened those left
behind; so that, back at Piccadilly Terrace, Annabella was
to encounter the Byronic manifestations most apt to crystal-
lise suspicions. We must not forget that on the one hand the

period from April to the end of June, 1815, represents the climax of his passion for Augusta, and on the other that circumstances then favoured his abandoning himself to the utmost to what I have called the glee in *confronting*. That glee was deeply rooted in Byron's nature, and it bears a certain close relation to the fundamentally turbid character of his favourite 'cogitations'. Hardly any sensation yielded him so much as that of thus keeping a sort of secret harem inhabited by all the women who had had with him—to adopt Racine's charming euphemism—*les derniers engagements*. To this the tale he so enjoyed telling Medwin is testimony sufficient: 'It so happened that three married women were on a wedding-visit to my wife (and in the same room at the same time) whom I had known to be all birds of the same nest'. As with many other things told to Medwin, the actual facts were otherwise; but here this serves but to emphasise Byron's propensity in that direction, since the incident is so typical of what he liked that he invented it, and perhaps even succeeded in persuading himself that it was true.

For this period I cannot do better than conclude with the following passage from *Astarte*: 'The impressions of Mrs. Leigh's guilt had been forced into Lady Byron's mind chiefly by incidents and conversations which occurred while they were all under one roof. Lord Byron never then long abstained from allusions that could not be otherwise interpreted, and Mrs. Leigh was unaccountably passive under his hardly-veiled hints. But as soon as Mrs. Leigh was out of the way, and there was sensible relief from the frenzy excited in Lord Byron by her presence, Lady Byron began to reproach herself for her involuntary suspicions, and resolved to quell and repudiate them. These suspicions flowed and ebbed with the feelings that burst from Lord Byron and Mrs. Leigh's manner. It was in the earlier half of 1815 that his inclination towards her was most violent, and there were moments when Lady Byron felt nearly certain of the past and had even a strong apprehension of a renewal. At that time Mrs. Leigh comfortably ignored all the strange appearances called forth by her presence in Piccadilly. She was preternaturally cool and collected, seemingly unaware that she could be an object of suspicion or anxiety. She slipped out of explanation and shifted the point with an obtuseness hardly natural, though it seemed unaffected at the time. She almost overdid it; but only on reflection would the thought occur: '*Très polie! mais pas moyen de s'expliquer avec elle!*' She could not and would not comprehend; answered what had not been said with something else that was perfectly trivial. This went on with all sorts of vicissitudes till the close of her first visit to Piccadilly a little before the end of June, 1815. Lady Byron was then really anxious to get rid of her, made her fix a time to go, and held her to it.'[1]

Suspicion had gained its first victory over Annabella, but for that very reason it immediately suffered the defeat by which, with her, every such victory was followed. Frenzied in Augusta's presence, when absence succeeded to it—and by no means a definitive absence, but one which he could shorten at will—Byron spontaneously relapsed into that indifferent torpor in which, as in a hammock, the amateur of sensations willingly lets things slide; and it is at what might be called an *entr'acte* that we look on until the end of August —an *entr'acte* which Annabella's heroism again makes use of to 'quell and repudiate' her suspicions, and so efficaciously that in August she writes to Augusta to say that Byron had spoken 'very lovingly' of her, and had made a will in her and her children's favour, and she goes so far as to add: 'I am as apt to fancy that the sort of things which please me are to be traced more or less to you, as that those which pain me come from another quarter—and I always feel as if I had more *reason* to love you than I can exactly know'.[2] A document which sufficiently testifies to the extent of the fresh defeat she had inflicted on the recently victorious suspicion, and which

[1] *Astarte*, p. 163.

[2] Jeaffreson, *The Real Lord Byron* (1883), App. p. 475.

is explained by the need, invincible with Annabella, of repairing to the utmost the least semblance of injustice—thus
leading her even to exaggerate, she who never exaggerates.

But sometimes nothing is more deceptive than an *entr'acte*
of this kind, when under the shelter of indifferent torpor the
mind is at ease to nurture vast ambitions, and takes advantage
of silence the better to ensure their achievement. It seems
that this was the case with Byron, that the interval was very
useful to him for preparing the ground, since a little before
the end of August he departs, alone, to spend a week with
Augusta. He arrives at her house with the most definitive of
intentions. The three months at Piccadilly Terrace had been
precious—yes, no doubt they had; but after all, despite many
an upbraiding, he had not had his way with her. Now he is
alone with her, and now he calls upon her to resume their
relations. Augusta refuses, and (the only·time in her life when
decision plays a part)[1] very decidedly refuses—the proof of
which is that from this moment until the eve of the separation, Byron turns from her, and speaks of her in the vein of
'bitter scorn' to which Annabella alludes in the letter we have
read.

No defeat could have hit Byron so hard as this one, and
though he consigned Augusta to 'bitter scorn', it is only too
evident that he turned against Annabella with the feeling

[1]Here comes in 'a singular circumstance', mentioned by Annabella in
a letter to Mrs. Villiers of May 23, 1816: 'After his visit of a week to
S. M. B. (August 31), she wrote to me more than once saying she had
things that might be very material to communicate to me—but would not
trust them on paper. When she came, and I asked what they were—having
been most anxious to see her for that reason as well as others, she made
an embarrassed excuse, and had nothing to communicate' (*Astarte*, p.
209). Are we to see in this contradictory behaviour Augusta's wish to confess to Annabella at that date, and make the confession easier by appealing
to her refusal of Byron's urgencies—a wish that either her innate weakness or her dread of reprisals from Byron caused to waver when she was
back at Piccadilly Terrace? It may be so, for the Augusta of the second
visit did, as we shall see, differ in more than one way from her of the
first. But to this day there is no explanation of that 'singular circumstance'.

which, towards her, was never-failing—hatred. If there is one thing that a wife is always sure of reaping from a ruptured love-affair of her husband's, it is his exasperation, and the Byronic genius in that line made the reaction terrible. A man of far higher inward rank than Byron, and who amid many weaknesses always contrived to keep alive in himself his respect for human beings and their sufferings—Benjamin Constant, the master of infallible introspection, wrote one day of himself: 'Frustration drives me mad'. But the sort of madness it induced in Byron was nothing less than maniacal fury; and now we have come to the phase which is under the sign of *utter lawlessness*. Such lawlessness is, in essence, a quite internal phenomenon which according to the person concerned—and sometimes in the same person—may present the most widely contradictory aspects. In Byron, both extremes are present—the *vehement* and the *morose*; he passes from one to the other, alternately 'taciturn' and frantic. We know him in the morose aspect: with Annabella he was capable of 'maintaining an insulting and exasperating taciturnity for days together', and an episode of this period belongs, so to speak, to the border-line between the two states. 'One day she entered his study, and found him standing before the fire, musing on his troubles. "Byron, am I in your way?" she asked. "Damnably", he answered.' . . . A reply typical of the morose being who will say no word until a question, and perhaps the mere sound of the human voice, obliges him to come out of his moroseness. On the other hand, here is a specimen of the vehement aspect: 'One day in a fit of wrath, he threw a favourite watch on the hearth, and smashed it to pieces with the poker'. We remember the china saucer out of which, as a tiny child, he had bitten a large piece, and about which he afterwards wrote: 'One of my silent rages'. This episode testifies that he could savour noisy rages too: there is hardly any species of rage which Byron did not know and practise.

There were two external aids to his moroseness—laudanum (to which he then became addicted) and liver-troubles;

for some time he had been threatened with an attack of jaundice. But there was a third factor which acted on the other pole, that of frenzy: this was the brandy of his friend Douglas Kinnaird, as valiant a drunkard as Scrope Davies himself, and, it would seem, the lowest type of libertine. Just then, as it happened, Byron had been for some months on the Drury Lane Committee of Management, of which Kinnaird was chairman; and Augusta, during her first visit, had written to Hobhouse about this: 'At first it struck me as a good thing, employment being desirable, but as in other good things, one may discover objections'. The objection was above all the brandy, at the dinners for which the Committee formed a pretext, to which Byron went more and more frequently as a means of escaping from his home, and from which he would return to Piccadilly Terrace in a state of intoxication peculiarly propitious to his most violent scenes. If, intrinsically, we need not attach much weight to his relations with the Drury Lane actresses—the existence of which, moreover, is not strictly speaking proved, and to which, in any case, Byron would assuredly have given nothing of himself—we must on the contrary attach a very great deal to the dual use which, at this particular moment, Byron could make of such relations by keeping them in the foreground, parading them; for not only did this afford him a new implement of torture for Annabella, but it might indirectly serve to bring Augusta back to Piccadilly Terrace—a proposal to which Byron feigns, and for some time goes on feigning, to be indifferent, though his sub-conscious is not of the same mind. And that was what was to come to pass.

Annabella was getting near her time. Her confinement was expected at the beginning of December; and in the early days of November, Byron had taken the precaution of telling her that while she was laid-up, he intended to instal a mistress in the house. This put her in a poignant dilemma of which afterwards she very lucidly told Mrs. Villiers in a letter of May 12, 1816. Mrs. Villiers had felt that in Annabella's line of conduct, which she was sure must have been in every respect irreproachable, there was one point that perplexed her —the circumstances being what they were, why had the wife insisted on Augusta's coming back to stay for her confinement? Here is Annabella's reply: 'It must be remembered that my *Conviction* was progressively formed, and not till lately fixed—and though my suspicion had been awakened very early, it was not at the period you allude to, sufficiently corroborated to have been made a principle of conduct without risking a cruel injury to one who professed herself most affectionately & disinterestedly devoted to my welfare. There was no medium—I must either have treated her as guilty or innocent—My *Instinct* too strongly dictated the former, but the *evidence then* rested chiefly on his words & manners, & her *otherwise* unaccountable assent & submission to both. If you regret that I did not attach more weight to my own wretched doubts, you will not dislike the feeling which rejected them as long as possible. Besides, at the time of her return to Piccadilly, I conceived there was no danger to her from him, as his inclinations were most averse from her, & absorbed in another direction—and believing that the residence of any human being in the house would be the means of saving myself and my child, I had but her to look to, and was almost compelled to banish the ideas that would have deprived me of this last resource. Nevertheless before I allowed her to come, for she had many times offered it, I seriously urged her to reflect on the consequences that might ensue to herself. During her last visit my suspicions as to *previous* circumstances were most strongly corroborated— above all by *her* confessions & admissions when in a state of despair & distraction. They were of the most unequivocal nature possible, unless she had expressly named the subject of her remorse and horror. I have answered them in as pointed a manner—and have urged to her that *everything* was expiable by repentance, when she repeatedly said she had forfeited all hope of salvation—I must have had a heart of iron could I then have cast her off—No—she was only dearer to me, and I felt more bound to be the support of one whom I thought broken-hearted'.[1] And in her next letter to Mrs. Villiers, that of May 23, she still more definitely emphasised her dilemma: 'He had threatened to bring a mistress into the house during my confinement—and to this moment I believe he would, had she not been there—So that between his actual cruelty—and her seeming kindness I can scarcely say I had an option'.[2] A dilemma so utterly atrocious that it needs no commentary, and a striking example of that lucid sorrow—sorrow and lucidity sharpening each other—which was Annabella's burden, ceaseless, overwhelming, yet so nobly borne. Enough to note here that though Augusta's general attitude during her first visit was just what Lord Lovelace describes, she nevertheless did, when alone with Annabella in hours of 'despair and distraction', come very near to a confession; beyond all doubt, it was remembrance of those hours which helped her to wrest from herself the definite refusal which Byron had to take at the end of August; and it was because the two women had lived through those hours together that Annabella on her side—she whose heart had all the impulse, all the generosity, which on principle are denied to reflective natures—conceived for her the affection which prevailed over all. ' I have sometimes thought that a tacit understanding existed between her and me—particularly when she believed *him* acquitted by Insanity, and seemed herself sinking under the most dreadful remorse. . . . It is scarcely possible she could on various occasions have supposed me unconscious, unless that tenderness towards her which encreased my grief & compassion, rendered her blind to impressions that anyone, situated as I was, must have received'.[3] But supremely conscious as she was, Annabella here no longer reckons with that 'genius for oblivion' which always enabled Augusta to throw overboard what she had possibly for a moment perceived, but preferred not to

[1]*Astarte*, p. 203.   [2]*Astarte*, p. 209.   [3]*Astarte*, p. 199.

have seen at all. It was not until after the full confession in September 1816 that, to Byron's fury, and until the time of his death, there was an explicit understanding between the two women.

At the period we are now considering, Byron had in his own way established this understanding beforehand. He had just inaugurated a new method of confronting by associating the two women together in the feelings that he bore them. In a letter to Augusta towards the end of 1815, Annabella wrote: 'B. speaks to me only to upbraid me with having married him when he wished not, and says he is therefore acquitted of all principle towards me, and I must consider myself only to be answerable for the vicious courses to which his despair is driving or will drive him. . . . Oh, Augusta, will it ever change for me? . . . It seemed impossible to tell whether his feelings towards you or me were most completely reversed; for, as I have told you, he loves or hates us together'.[1] A phrase which admirably depicts the Byronic attitude; but, at this period, hatred alone was at work. Augusta arrives at Piccadilly Terrace on November 15. Byron at first treats her with all the indifference she deserves for her refusal in the previous summer; but as he more and more perceives her sincere good-will for Annabella, the affection and care with which she surrounds her, the evident wish to protect her against his outbursts, indifference itself transmutes itself into a daily exacerbated craving for revenge which includes both women equally. To this end, when the three are together, he boasts of his relations with the actresses, addressing himself by preference to Augusta, so as to indicate clearly that she in especial is supposed to resent it. Such was the atmosphere in which, on December 10, 1815, the infant Augusta Ada entered the world. Despite indifference, 'bitter scorn', craving for revenge, Byron of course would never have allowed his daughter to forego the only Christian name which

[1]*Byron*, Ethel Colburn Mayne, pp. 238-239.

meant anything to him; and he took some pleasure in announcing to Moore that the second name of Ada was 'a very antique family name, I believe not used since the reign of King John'. But this was the only pleasure he took in his daughter's birth, for when he saw her for the first time in her cradle, he exclaimed, 'Oh, what an implement of torture have I received in thee!'[1] Towards his wife he had already acquitted himself, since his first remark to her after her delivery was an inquiry whether the child had not been stillborn. It would seem that even Byron could not have gone much further, but it is unwise to defy him in that respect, for in fact a few weeks before there had already taken place the incident which, this time, could not be surpassed. Here it is, as related by Annabella in 1816 to Lady Anne Barnard. One night when he came in drunk from a Kinnaird dinner, calling himself a monster he threw himself at his wife's feet, prey to an agony of remorse more moving, doubtless, even than usual; for Annabella goes on: 'Astonished at the return of virtue, my tears, I believe, flowed over my face, and I said, "Byron, all is forgotten; never, never shall you hear of it more". He started up, and folding his arms while he looked at me, burst into laughter. "What do you mean?" said I. "Only a philosophical experiment; that's all", said he. "I wished to ascertain the value of your resolutions".'[2] Not only could this not be surpassed, but at that particular moment Byron surpassed himself if, as I think, in his whole life there is nothing else of such finished abomination.

From that moment—and apart even from the explosions of hatred—Annabella was no more than the object of his insur-

[1] We already know of Byron's respect for Herod's drastic proceedings with children. Here is an anecdote told by James Wedderburn Webster. His eldest son had been christened Byron Wedderburn. The child died young, and when the father gave Byron this news, he (who was godfather) 'chuckled with joy or irony, and said: "Well, I cautioned you, and told you that my name would damn almost any thing or creature" ' (*Letters and Journals*, ii. p. 259).

[2] Ethel Colburn Mayne, *Byron*, pp. 249-250.

mountable aversion. 'About three weeks after her confinement, the aversion he had already from time to time displayed
for her struck everyone in the house as more alarming than
ever. Augusta, his cousin George Byron, and Mrs. Clermont,
who were all under his roof, were distressed beyond measure
by his behaviour and his incredible speeches. Towards Lady
Byron he assumed an attitude daily more threatening',[1] and
we can understand why it was more necessary than ever to
adopt the hypothesis of insanity. As we have seen, Augusta
was especially anxious to believe in it, sinking as she was
under the burden of her own remorse, saving by her presence
the very life of Annabella,[2] and at the same time saved by the
wife from the extremes of her 'despair and distraction'.
Between these two women so strangely, so pathetically allied
in escaping from the assaults of that force of nature doubled
by a demoniac force which was Byron let loose, what sufferings — overwhelming, contradictory, informulable — must
have quivered through the atmosphere! Assuredly Ethel
Colburn Mayne is right in saying: 'We look on one of the
great problems of human relationship as we look on the three
at Piccadilly Terrace in December 1815';[3] and Lord Lovelace
was still more right when he chose for motto to one of the
chapters in *Astarte* Stevenson's words in *Weir of Hermiston*:

[1] *Astarte*, p. 39.

[2] Mrs. Clermont, Annabella's one-time governess, who was then at
Piccadilly Terrace and whom nothing predisposed in Augusta's favour,
but very much the contrary, wrote on March 9, 1816, to Lady Byron's
mother: 'I can never forget the kindness A. (Annabella) experienced from
her the latter part of the time she was at Piccadilly. Even for her life I
believe we can thank Mrs. Leigh' (*Astarte*, p. 324). And at this time and
during the separation-proceedings, Mrs. Clermont showed both devotion
and perfect moderation—which procured her the honour of being calumniated in verse by Byron in the piece entitled *A Sketch*, to which she replied in a short and very dignified letter.

[3] It was in December 1815 that Augusta, in one of the moments when
she was on the point of saying all, exclaimed to Annabella: 'Ah—you don't
know *what* a fool I have been about him!' (*Astarte*, p. 63—Lady Byron's
Narrative G). One of the rare sayings which gives us some idea of her
feelings—and here the more moving because Annabella did know, and
Augusta was not yet aware that she did.

' "Perhaps not a pleasant spectacle", said Glenalmond. "And yet, do you know, I think somehow a great one".' When the unpleasant attains such greatness, it changes its name: it is called the tragic.

On January 3, 1816, Byron went to Annabella's room for the purpose of making her a scene about the actresses, and an extremely violent one. Three days elapsed without his seeing wife or child, and on January 6, Annabella received the following note from him: 'When you are disposed to leave London, it would be convenient that a day should be fixed—and (if possible) not a very remote one for that purpose. Of my opinion upon that subject you are sufficiently in possession, & of the circumstances which have led to it—as also to my plans—or rather—intentions—for the future—When in the country I will write to you more fully—as Lady Noel has asked you to Kirkby—there you can be for the present—unless you prefer Seaham—As the dismissal of the present establishment[1] is of importance to me—the sooner you can fix on the day the better—though of course your convenience & inclination shall be first consulted—The Child will of course accompany you—there is a more easy & safer carriage than the chariot (unless you prefer it) which I mentioned before—on that you can do as you please—'. Annabella replied in these words on the following day: 'I shall obey your wishes and fix the earliest day that circumstances will admit for leaving London'. She left London for her parents' home, now at Kirkby Mallory, on January 15. It is useless to

---

[1]It was quite true that Byron was then in serious financial difficulties. Annabella had always been looked upon as Lord Wentworth's heiress; but her uncle had finally decided to leave his fortune to her mother, from whom she would in time inherit. But when Lord Wentworth died in April 1815, Byron's creditors behaved as though the inheritance were at once to fall to them, with the result that from April to January bailiffs were frequently in the house. But this fact, far from excusing Byron's conduct, and still less the sending of the note and its contents, makes them rather worse, if it is true that money-troubles tend to draw husband and wife nearer together when both are worthy of those names.

examine here the varying interpretations to which this departure and the subsequent events gave rise, since in 1830—
and, as she had promised herself, without touching on the
incest—Annabella stated the facts exactly as they had been,
in a document familiar to all readers of the Byron bio-
graphies.[1] She did this in answer to the inaccurate, and even
perhaps deliberately inaccurate, allegations of Moore with
regard to the part played by her parents in the proceedings
which led to the separation.

This statement of hers bears the hall-mark of truth, of that
finality which I have already claimed for her, and which I
defined as 'the finality belonging to those who take each
human being into consideration, esteem him in advance,
open the most extensive credit to him, pronounce upon him
only when every alternative is exhausted—and then say the
last word'. Now the Byronic proceedings as a whole culmi-
nated in that note of January 6, 1816, and their result was
literally to create that 'finality' in Annabella; so that we have
now reached the hour for the last word. Only one hypothesis
could arrest it—that of his insanity; if that had been con-
firmed, we can imagine what treasures of active devotion
Annabella would have lavished on caring for Byron's health,
alleviating his malady, possibly curing it—she would have
thought herself repaid for all the rest, for she would then have
found the vocation which her heart had always sought, and
which in this world was always denied it. But Dr. Le Mann,
who was treating Byron for his liver-trouble, now could not
only see him but study his case, and at the end of January
he gives a decisive verdict which rules out altogether the
question of madness. Thenceforth—to use the words which
Annabella was later to use—'If I were to consider Lord
Byron's past conduct as that of a person of sound mind,
nothing could induce me to return to him'; and there are
three texts from her, dating from the time when she made up

[1]These Remarks (as she entitled them) were bound up with the second
volume of Moore's *Life of Byron*, and are also given in *Letters and
Journals*, iii. pp. 287-290.

her mind to leave him, which throw an irrefutable light on the reasons rendering her return impossible. The first is in a letter to Augusta of February 3, 1816: 'I will only recall to Lord Byron's mind his avowed and insurmountable aversion to the married state, and the desire and determination he has expressed ever since its commencement to free himself from that bondage, as finding it quite insupportable, though candidly acknowledging that no effort of duty or affection has been wanting on my part. He has too painfully convinced me that all those attempts to contribute to his happiness were wholly useless, and most unwelcome to him'.[1] The other two I quote from her replies to two letters from Byron. She wrote to him on February 7: 'After seriously and dispassionately reviewing the misery that I have experienced almost without an interval from the day of my marriage, I have finally determined on the measure of separation. . . . It is unhappily your disposition to consider what you *have* as worthless—what you have *lost* as invaluable. But remember that you believed yourself most miserable when I was yours'.[2] And on the 13th, after having alluded to the hypothesis of insanity which had for a time been considered, she goes on: 'If for these reasons (to which others were perhaps added) I did not remonstrate at the time of leaving your house, you cannot forget that I had before warned you, earnestly and affectionately, of the unhappy and irreparable consequences which must ensue from your conduct, both to yourself and me—that to these representations you had replied by a determination to be wicked, though it should break my heart. What then had I to expect? I cannot attribute your "state of mind" to any cause so much as that *total* dereliction of principle which, *since* our marriage, you have professed and gloried in. Your acknowledgments have not been accompanied by any intentions of amendment. I have *consistently* fulfilled my duty as your wife. It was too dear to be abandoned till it became hopeless. Now

[1] *Letters and Journals*, iii. p. 302.
[2] Ethel Colburn Mayne, *Byron*, p. 224.

my resolution cannot be changed'.[1] Of set purpose, and in
conformity with motives stated by her to her advisers,[2] she
made no allusion to the incest—exercising then, and until
Augusta's and her own daughter's deaths, what Fanny
Kemble was afterwards to call 'Lady Byron's beautiful power
of silence'. And moreover, apart from that, there were such
elements in the situation that I do not imagine the woman
has ever existed who, having at last escaped from Byron,
would have, of her own free will, again put herself in his
power. But here I am wrong: such a woman did exist, and she
was Annabella herself. A document written by her forty
years afterwards definitely establishes the fact that, had it not
been for the incest, she would have consented to reconstruct
that hell: 'And now, after the lapse of forty years, I look back
on the past as a calm spectator, and *at last* can speak of it. I
see what was, what *might* have been, had there been one
person less amongst the living when I married. Then I might
have had duties, however steeped in sorrow, more congenial
with my nature than those I was compelled to adopt. Then
my life would not have been the concealment of a Truth,
whilst my conduct was in harmony with it'.[3] Lord Lovelace
tells us that this is part of a sketch for the preface to an un-
finished narrative composed by Lady Byron about 1854. The
concluding sentence—luminous for those who know the details underlying the Byron story, but for others elliptical to a
degree—refers to the central contradiction on which, from the
time of the separation, Lady Byron's life was based. She
knew the truth, from September 1816 she had Augusta's own
confession; but that was precisely why she was 'compelled' to
adopt the most painful, the most unnatural of duties. She was
obliged to conceal the truth from everyone, and at the same
time to watch unremittingly over the person from whom
everything would seem to have separated her—because thus

[1] *Letters and Journals*, iii. p. 310.
[2] See Ethel Colburn Mayne's *Byron*, pp. 229-231.
[3] *Astarte*, p. 140.

she might at last bring Augusta to see that Byron's appeals must be resisted, that his sister must not join him abroad, a step which in Annabella's eyes would complete the destruction of both; and by destruction she meant the loss of two souls in whom she did not admit that her right to be interested could ever be disputed. And here, while taking into consideration Lord Lovelace's family feeling, his natural vexation at the wrong done to his grandmother's memory for nearly a century, I cannot, any more than Ethel Colburn Mayne, agree with him in regretting that Lady Byron did not let Augusta go to Byron abroad. Doubtless he is right in saying that if Augusta had fled, 'the victory remained with Lady Byron, solid and single'; but I can only repeat, with Ethel Colburn Mayne, 'I imagine that most of us applaud her for rejecting such a victory'. Here we come upon the inevitable, and perhaps unalterable, point of departure between unbelievers and believers. The former put the accent on the liberty that any human being preserves of destroying himself; the latter, on the duty which transcends all others, that of trying to save at any cost; and on that point even more than on all the rest, Lady Byron's faith was of 'a solidity that was proof against anything'.

Yes—had it not been for Augusta, and no matter what the Byronic inferno might have contained of diversified tortures, Annabella would have had duties more congenial to her nature, because they would have been those dictated by her heart. For, in spite of all, she never ceased to love Byron; and now that we, in our turn, must separate from her, I can do no better, as far as she is concerned—and as far as is concerned the inexhaustible capacity for feeling in those who are reputed 'cold'—than conclude with what the woman of twenty-four, with her life in ruins about her, wrote to Lady Anne Barnard in 1816: 'It is not necessary to think ill of his heart in general—it is sufficient that to me it was hard and impenetrable, that my own must have been broken before his could have been touched. . . . As long as I live, my chief difficulty will probably be not to remember him too kindly'.[1]

*   *   *

The finality of Annabella's decision prostrated Byron, but it is important to understand why. Doubtless she had been, when *present*, no more than an object of aversion; once *lost*, she was instantly invested with the value which, for Byron, absence alone (except in Augusta's case) could confer. But though she was thus instantly invested, his mythic faculty did not begin to work until later on; and at the moment itself, other causes—by no means of the mythical, but of the very conventionally social, order—intervened and influenced him. Annabella diagnosed them with unerring perspicacity in a letter to Augusta of February 14, 1816; we have not Augusta's letter, but from this answer it is clear that the sister had dwelt upon the question of happiness, and above all upon the consequences, the sensation that society would make out of the separation. To all this Annabella replied: '*Happiness* no longer enters into my views, it can never be restored, and the greater or less degree of misery I must endure will depend on the *principles* of my conduct, not on its *consequences*. Now, independent of any advice whatever, I deem it *my duty to God* to act as I am acting, and I am resigned to the misfor-

---

[1]Of the relations between Annabella and Augusta, enough to say here that they were at their most intimate in the summer and autumn of 1816, the period when the resumption of correspondence opened the way to Augusta's full confession in September. The intimacy lasted until 1829, though in 1819 there was some dissension between them, arising from the question of what Augusta's attitude should be if Byron returned to England, as he thought of doing. But Annabella had prevailed in what to her was the essential, in that Augusta did not go to him abroad. From 1829 until Augusta's death at the end of 1851, they were completely alienated; in 1851 there was an interview between them, but its result was painful, and this time it seems that the misunderstanding was on Annabella's side. But with her, the heart was sure to have the last word; and a week before Augusta's death, she wrote to Emily Leigh, a daughter and her godchild, and asked her to whisper to her mother 'two words of affection long disused: *Dearest Augusta*, to which the dying woman could just articulate in reply: 'My greatest consolation.' The question of their relations is treated in full in the *Life of Lady Byron*, and should be read there.

tunes that may flow from that source, since by any other conduct I should forfeit my peace of conscience, the only good that remains to me. No temporal advantages or privations will have the least weight. In regard to him, it is my decided opinion that there will be no fatal event, and I think it a great error to regard "worldly disgrace" as a serious evil compared to some that must ensue, with his character, from worldly prosperity. If Pride be not expiated on earth, but indulged, who may dare to look beyond? The lessons of adversity may be most beneficial when they are most bitter. Not that I would voluntarily be the means of chastisement, but I seem to have been made so, and am doomed to participate in the suffering. His grief and despair, which I do not doubt, are of the same too worldly nature. The loss of character by the anticipation of a measure which he had long intended, only with advantages of which he is deprived in this case, touches him most sensibly. It is not for *me*, but for the *accompanying circumstances*, that he feels so deeply. All this it is in his disposition to revenge on the object, if *in his power*. When his revenge avowedly began as soon as I became so by marriage, and seems to have increased in force rather than diminished, what would it be *now*? Those who consider his welfare ought not to desire my return, there is nothing of which *I* am more certain'.[1] 'The accompanying circumstances' —in them lies the key to Byron's collapse; for, apart from any mythical scheme, he had another reason, and only one, for wanting Annabella. So long as she was his wife and Augusta's friend, her presence covered the sister's, ensured it to him, kept up for society a façade which might be precarious, even threatened, but which society had no justification for bringing to the ground until Annabella struck the first blow at it. Now she had struck that blow, and events followed fast on one another; in two months and a half Byron was to lose both Augusta, the only creature whom he loved, and his place in English society, the only circumstance that mattered to him.

[1]*Letters and Journals*, iii. pp. 310-311.

For though in mind and heart Byron was so much the outlaw, socially speaking he was, on the contrary, the conformer; and it was in spite of himself that, socially speaking, he was to remain the outlaw unto the end.

Augusta having remained at Piccadilly Terrace until March 15, and when at last she brought herself to leave the house, having stayed, instead of returning to Newmarket, in her rooms at St. James' Palace, the scandal broke out in London and grew more resounding with every day. In one of those attacks of cant to which English society has from all time been subject, and which Macaulay in his essay on Byron justly denounced, Byron and Augusta were chosen to be the scapegoats; and when they both appeared at a party given in April by Lady Jersey, one of the only women-friends of Byron's who then remained faithful to him, and who hoped by this means to rehabilitate him, the brother and sister met with such a reception as removed all doubt. Augusta was cut by many people, and Byron by many more.[1] By this circumstance not only was Augusta's social position, but her reputation itself, destroyed so long as Byron remained in England, while Byron's pride was by no means of a nature to put up with such indignities. On April 21 he signed the deed of separation; he left Piccadilly Terrace on April 23, spent two nights at Dover, and on April 25 sailed for Ostend, foreseeing that his absence would be a long one, but not foreseeing that he was never to behold England again.

*　　*　　*

[1]Mrs. George Lamb was among those who cut Augusta. She was probably indignant at Augusta's braving of public opinion, and therefore withdrew the sentiments of pity which, in a letter to Annabella at the end of the preceding month, she had expressed: 'As to the other person, I do not wish to reveal her faults, for I could almost pity her, when I think how unhappy she must be, and I look upon her more as his victim than as his accomplice'. To which Annabella replied on April 1: 'I am glad that you think of *her* with the feelings of pity which prevail in my mind, and surely if in *mine* there must be some cause for them. I never was, nor ever can be so *mercilessly* virtuous, as to admit *no* excuse for even the worst of errors'. *Astarte*, p. 50.

On January 26, 1816, Annabella's friend, Miss Selina Doyle, wrote to her: 'As a real wife you were contemned, but when you become again the *beau idéal* of his imagination, between the possession of which and him there is an insuperable barrier, you will be a second Theresa (Thyrza), perhaps supplant her totally. These are prophecies and may appear irrelevant, but as I think them now, I like to say them, they may possibly save you a pang hereafter when you hear of his love and misery at being deprived of you, which nothing can replace. No, nothing indeed, for were you to return, the excitement produced by desire of you would cease, I am convinced'. Miss Doyle gives proof of remarkable penetration into Byron's nature; and perhaps Annabella was recalling her words when on February 7 she wrote to Byron himself, defining him so completely: 'It is unhappily your disposition to consider what you *have* as worthless—what you have *lost* as invaluable'. It was because Byron had *lost* everything (and lost it by his own fault: that duplication, that aggravation are in his case indispensable, essential) that he now *had*—in the most secret, but not the least real, sense of the verb *to have*—all that henceforth he needed; and the day on which he sailed leaving everything behind him, he took with him a full cargo for the sub-conscious side of his genius—his hold was filled with those turgid, composite, and massive treasures which, ceaselessly stirred-up, ceaselessly brewed in the sombre nightwatches of imagination, were to form almost the sole material —but how prestigious it was!—for the works that exploded throughout the eight years of his maturity. Because the 'great reverse' had set on the incest the seal of catastrophe, nothing was now lacking to his need of fatality; and because insurmountable was now the barrier which separated him from Augusta, the only creature whom he loved, and from those others whom, without loving, he required as thralls to his destiny, there was henceforth nothing lacking to his *mythical* activity. Here again Goethe said the last word: 'Lord Byron's separation from his wife was so poetical in its circumstances, and the mystery which envelops it, that if Byron had invented it, he could hardly have had a subject more propitious for his genius'. From the moment that, by the outcome of the 'great reverse', the myth of Annabella is joined to that of Augusta, the cup is full; the era of facts is closed, that of the works and myths begins. There is a time to live, and a time to produce: for four years—from March 10, 1812, to April 25, 1816— Byron has lived, and with what frenzied intensity; until his death he will render—and in the only works of his which truly count—the deposit of those four years.[1]

For on that 25th of April, 1816, Byron's life—in the order of events—was over; nothing more was to *happen* to him, unless we reckon among events the achievement through the death in Greece. The Venetian debauches represent no more than the instrument—and the classic instrument—of that 'love of self-destruction' which has already been pointed out; and the liaison with the Countess Guiccioli represents

[1]If these chapters had been conceived from the *aesthetic* and not from the *zoological* point of view, if I had been dealing with the works rather than with the human animal of the higher species, I should here have to make a point of the radical disjunction between *Don Juan* and all the rest. My Byron, the Byron to whom fatality was a need, and whom I persist in regarding as the most *Byronic* of all, expresses himself to the maximum in *Manfred*; but it is a matter of course that in the order of verse (where I also persist in considering even the Byron of *Don Juan* as inferior to him of the Journals and Letters), it is not *Manfred* but *Don Juan* which is the masterpiece. But *Don Juan* represents, in Byron, the quite contrary need of what might be called *anti-fatality*—being the panorama of the *natural* man, the man who is nothing *but* natural, presented (without the least trace of declamation) *au naturel*, so that the poem institutes a kind of its own: *objective satire*; while as regards form, Byron's triumph consists in having solved, and with genius, the problem set by that line from Horace which in certain editions of *Don Juan* appears as motto: '*Difficile est proprie communia dicere*'. The Byron of *Don Juan* represents the complementary pole of the Byron to whom I have chosen to restrict myself here. To compensate for my silence on that aspect of him, let me transcribe the fine passage from Swinburne which was inspired by *Juan*: 'Across the stanzas we swim forward as over the "broad backs of the sea": they break and glitter, hiss and laugh, murmur, and move like waves that sound or that subside. There is about them a wide wholesome air, full of vivid light and constant wind, which is only felt at sea. Life undulates and death palpitates in the splendid verse. This gift of life and variety is the supreme quality of Byron's chief poem.'

perhaps even less—the satiety with debauch, the 'impossibility of existing without some object of attachment', the combined disarray and exasperation at Augusta's persistent refusal to come to him abroad, despite the passionate appeals he made to her; perhaps also—ironic retribution !—an involuntary avengement of poor Caroline Lamb. 'This ignominious fan-carrying bondage', he wrote one day to Augusta, and again to her: 'In short she was a kind of Italian Caroline Lamb—but very pretty and gentle, at least to me; for I never knew so docile a creature as far as we lived together'. Towards her, and to the last, he scrupulously performed those rites of the heart which we know that he was readiest to pay when his feelings were least involved; but Byron was not to finish in an atmosphere of gentleness and docility, and there is no undercurrent of regret in our salutation of the awakening of him whose resemblance to Achilles lay not only in the heel or even in the anger, who set sail to join the Achillean shade, and who, at the propitious moment, woke up to the benefit of the Greek awakening.

*   *   *

On Easter-Sunday, April 18, 1824, at Missolonghi, at five o'clock in the afternoon Byron's delirium left him, and by his desire Fletcher was called to his side—Fletcher, the valet who had been with him for so many years, who knew all about his life and that of those nearest to him. 'It is now nearly over', he panted, 'I must tell you all without losing a moment'. I then said, "Shall I go, my Lord, and fetch pen, ink and paper?"—"Oh, my God! no, you will lose too much time, and I have it not to spare, for my time is now short", said his Lordship; and immediately after, "Now, pay attention!" His Lordship commenced by saying, "You will be provided for". I begged him, however, to proceed with things of more consequence. He then continued, "Oh, my poor dear child! My dear Ada! My God! could I but have seen her! Give her my blessing, and my dear sister Augusta and her children—and you will go to Lady Byron, and say—tell her everything—you are friends with her". His Lordship appeared to be greatly affected at this moment. Here my master's voice failed him, so that I could only catch a word at intervals; but he kept muttering something very seriously for some time, and would often raise his voice and say, "Fletcher, now if you do not execute every order which I have given you, I will torment you hereafter if possible". Here I told His Lordship, in a state of the greatest perplexity, that I had not understood a word of what he said; to which he replied, "Oh, my God! then all is lost, for it is now too late! Can it be possible you have not understood me?"—"No, my Lord", said I; "but I pray you to try and inform me once more". "How can I?" rejoined my master; "it is now too late, and all is over!" I said, "Not our will, but God's be done!" and he answered, "Yes, not mine be done—but I will try—" His Lordship did indeed make several efforts to speak, but could only repeat two or three words at a time—such as "My wife! my child! my sister!—you know all—you must say all— you know my wishes!" The rest was quite unintelligible.'[1]

Faithful in all things, Fletcher, after having brought his master's body back to England, went to Lady Byron with the unintelligible last message, and we are told that 'she walked about the room, her whole frame shaken by her sobs, imploring the servant to "remember" the words he had never heard'.[2]

That on his death-bed, desiring above all to send a message to Annabella, to open to her at last the heart that she had had to abandon all hope of ever reaching, Byron should have found the message beyond his power to articulate; that, on the verge of access, Annabella should have seen reft from her the promised land of memory to which the messenger would so fain have led her in—ah! it is on that diptych that these two must be left, in the hour when, though words forsook them, for this once the intentions had met.

[1]Harold Nicolson's *Byron*, pp. 265-266.
[2]Ethel Colburn Mayne, *Byron*, p. 244.

'Poetry is the lava of the imagination, whose eruption prevents an earthquake'. An active volcano, and one of the grandest of which human history presents the spectacle—such, in the last issue, seems to me the essential Byron.